WINNING AT INTRAPRENEURSHIP

12 LABORS
to Overcome Corporate Culture and Achieve Startup Success

Guillaume Hervé

G3point0 CONSULTING

Winning at Intrapreneurship

12 Labors to Overcome Corporate Culture
and Achieve Startup Success

First Edition – April 2015

Published by G3point0 Consulting
Beaconsfield, Quebec, Canada
www.g3point0consulting.com

CIP data available.
ISBN 978-0-9938693-0-3

Edited by Jane Pavanel, Knockout Communications

Proofread by May Antaki

Designed by Sara Morley and Kate McDonnell, Design Postimage

Cover art: Hercules doodt de draak Ladon, by Jan Luyken (1649–1712)
Rijksmuseum, Amsterdam

Printed by CreateSpace.
Available from Amazon.com and other retail outlets.

For my family,
Carol-Lynn, Nicolas, and Alexandre

CONTENTS

It is not the new business backed by the strongest corporation that succeeds, nor the one with the most compelling business model. Rather, it is the corporate startup led by a qualified and engaged intrapreneur who is able to effectively leverage the corporate parent, fend off its immune system, learn from the marketplace, adapt and modify as necessary, and execute flawlessly.

– Guillaume Hervé

Preface

I wrote this book to share critical insights into what it takes to successfully launch a new business within an existing company. I am what some might call a serial intrapreneur. I have led or played an executive role in launching more than a dozen new businesses and joint ventures within the corporate environment. In the process, I undertook the 12 labors described in the following chapters, and while working through them I increased my knowledge exponentially. I wholeheartedly believe that my intrapreneurial efforts would have been significantly less onerous, and certainly less risky, if I had had access to the information found here.

If you are to play a leadership or supporting role in your company's drive to launch a corporate startup and grow it into a profitable and sustainable business, reading *Winning at Intrapreneurship* will help you achieve a deeper understanding of the unique challenges faced by companies seeking to grow via corporate entrepreneurship. You will also be equipped to recognize the constraints your organization will impose and the obstacles it will set in motion, often unknowingly. But recognizing constraints and obstacles is not enough. As an astute leader, you know that seeing a problem, and even outlining a strategy to deal with it, is only half the battle. The other half is taking correct action.

The good news is that you can overcome internal challenges and ensure your success by using the strategies and tools in this book. They will guide you in establishing the winning conditions that will put you and your corporate startup in a position to thrive, and they will facilitate your journey along the way. It gives me great satisfaction to think I will have played a small part in helping you succeed at the exciting and fulfilling business of intrapreneurship.

Introduction: The Business of Intrapreneurship

Imagine the following scenario: A corporate executive decides on a strategy that will position his company for growth. Following a careful review of the organization's capabilities, he concludes it has valuable assets and core competencies that can be leveraged to enter new markets or penetrate new segments within its existing market. After discussing this with his executive team, he finds out there is a leader in the corporation who has previous experience working with corporate startups. He schedules a meeting. The corporate executive begins by explaining the strategy to the enterprising leader, and then asks him to draw on his experience to tell him what would be required to succeed. The enterprising leader replies:

"You must start with a small team that will play by its own rules without any corporate interference. The team will likely launch a preliminary product that will be less than perfect. Its goal will be to seek customer feedback so it can validate and refine the offering over several iterations. You must accept that the team will learn as it goes and modify its strategy in real time according to the requirements of its new customers and market. It won't always have all the answers and will make some mistakes.

"Your role is to be the startup's sponsor and you must enlist a senior executive to act as gatekeeper. The gatekeeper's task is to protect the startup from interference or resistance that comes from the corporation, which will have a strong desire to interfere or resist when existing business practices prove to be incompatible with the startup's needs, for example, in sales, operations, human resources, IT, marketing, communications, and contracting.

"You will become very uncomfortable when you realize that while the new business remains in startup mode, you won't track its success using existing corporate performance measures like revenues, sales, EBIT, EBITDA, return on capital employed (ROCE), or return on net assets (RONA). Progress will be tracked according to the startup's particular needs until its business model is stable, the value proposition is successful with early adopters, and it is securely anchored for growth. You should also know that it will burn lots of cash in the first couple of years and this will make many members of your executive team anxious.

"Oh, and there's one last thing. Your investment will be hugely disproportional to the short-term benefits the new business will generate because it won't become financially viable or material to our core business for three to five years. You will have to combat the urge to accelerate its growth via opportunistic acquisitions until the intrapreneur informs you that the startup is ready.

"Speaking of the leader who will make all this happen, are you aware of the unique knowledge, skills, and abilities required of a successful intrapreneur?"

How did you react to the enterprising leader's response? I am sure several thoughts came to mind that challenged some of your deeply held leadership, management, and business beliefs developed over years of successfully managing businesses in established companies. If you were the corporate executive in this scenario, your leadership instincts probably would have told you to take a second look at whether or not your organization is ready to embark on this strategy. In addition, your management experience might have pointed to the need to achieve a much better understanding of what you and your team could do to be prepared. You may also have realized that you underestimated the selection process for identifying the right leader for this intrapreneurial venture.

If the corporate executive decides to go ahead, what references will he have at his disposal to help? Chances are, he will find very little information to draw on. Throughout my career of successfully launching new business initiatives or joint ventures within existing corporations, there were moments when I needed to educate myself on how to effectively manage the complex process of intrapreneurship. I looked for help in books about entrepreneurship and discovered that most focus on independent entrepreneurs and startups. There was no significant body of knowledge on intrapreneurship I could turn to when I was trying to work through the phases of the business cycle, learning as I went and inevitably making some mistakes.

The few publications I found that tackled corporate entrepreneurship tended to focus on four main themes:

1. Establishing and managing an effective innovation process to generate winning ideas
2. Assessing the corporation's internal strengths and the external market environment to best match core competencies to the customer segment or subsegment most likely to benefit from corporate innovations
3. Launching new products or services into new or existing markets
4. Learning from the world of independent entrepreneurs and implementing entrepreneurial practices within an existing corporation

In fact, these are four of the five gears that drive the engine of successful intrapreneurship. They cover critical concepts and provide invaluable information that can help leaders transform great ideas into thriving corporate startups.

The Fifth Gear

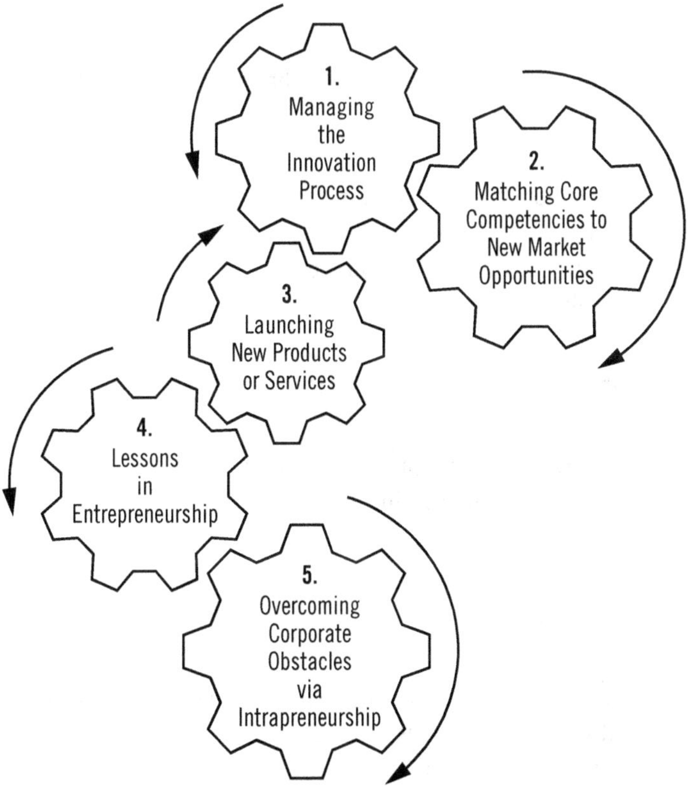

But these four gears are not the whole story. The books I read failed to treat intrapreneurship as a separate discipline that identifies the internal obstacles a corporation creates that must be addressed if the new business is to be effectively launched. This is an essential fifth gear called intrapreneurship and it involves identifying and overcoming the many obstacles that have their origins in the corporation itself. Anyone wanting to reap the rewards of successfully transitioning from idea generation and innovation to launching a winning new business must grasp the intricacies of this fifth gear. Reading this book will not only familiarize you with the difficulties your parent company will present, it will show you how to overcome them. The insights and tools I provide are for anyone who is leading or supporting the launch of a new business within an existing organization and wishes to unlock the full force of their organization's intrapreneurial potential.

You will want to read this book if you are:

- The CEO of an enterprise, a senior executive responsible for a division, or the leader of a business segment about to initiate a growth strategy founded on intrapreneurship and the launch of a new business
- A COO or head of operations who has been mandated to ensure that your organization is ready to support your company's growth strategy
- The sponsor of a new business or an HR leader who must understand the knowledge, skills, and abilities required of the intrapreneur who will lead your corporate startup, and the hurdles you will face
- An intrapreneur who has been charged with, or might be charged with, executing a business strategy that will turn an innovation into a profitable new business
- An independent entrepreneur whose company was recently acquired and you now find yourself leading within a larger corporation
- A manager wanting to know how you can be a better corporate partner when it comes to supporting your company's new business ventures
- Struggling to figure out why your company's new business venture has not been as successful as it should have been given favorable market conditions

Intrapreneurship is an extremely rewarding and fulfilling business opportunity. As a journey and destination, it offers a ride like no other. Being an intrapreneur will challenge your management and leadership thinking, make you tap into the deepest aspects of your emotional intelligence, test your ability to influence organizations and the people around you to adapt to novel business environments, and force you to embrace unique paradigms. When the ride is over you will experience the immense satisfaction of having created something new and positioned your organization for growth.

If you are a CEO or executive who has decided to embark on this kind of growth strategy, know that you are in excellent company, as you will see in the following paragraphs. If you are a business leader making the shift towards intrapreneurship, you have demonstrated the courage to take a road less traveled, which will stand you in good stead on your journey. If you have been assigned the responsibility of leading a business launch within your corporation, you are one of a very few who has the opportunity to meet this challenge. It is an extraordinary honor and a compliment to your leadership, adaptability, creativity, and tenacity. It is a testament to your track record.

Banking on Intrapreneurship

In today's rapidly evolving and highly competitive global business environment, companies that want to remain relevant to their customer base and attractive to investors must grow. Some companies follow an incremental growth strategy that focuses on improving existing market offerings or optimizing certain features of products or services to keep them fresh, while at the same time squeezing efficiencies out of operations for better margins. But incremental improvements can only take a company so far, and a corporation cannot squeeze its way to growth.

Companies wishing to experience significant long-term growth must look to launching sustainable new businesses. This type of growth can be achieved via acquisitions or organically. In the growth-by-acquisitions model, a company targets a market or market segment and selectively, or opportunistically, acquires established companies. This is considered to be a more expensive approach due to the premiums paid for buying businesses that are already operational, on top of which are subsequent integration costs.

Growth by acquisition has a high failure rate that can be associated with a variety of factors: culture clash, improperly conducted due diligence that leads to surprises, inferior integration strategies and follow-through, the premature departure of key leaders from the acquired company, and poor strategic fit. On the other hand, growth by acquisition can provide rapid access to markets, an instant customer base, and newly available technology and resources, in addition to having an immediate impact on the top and bottom lines and the company's earnings per share.

In the organic-growth model, a company chooses to grow from within by leveraging its business infrastructure, assets, and strengths to expand in its existing market or to enter new ones. Organic growth is often viewed as cheaper to execute and having a higher chance of success because a great deal can be learned as a new business is incubated and launched, and there is greater control too. A company can establish objective assessment criteria to gauge if a business initiative is showing enough promise to continue to receive funding or should be terminated because the risks far outweigh the potential rewards. Businesses launched organically often take some years to achieve a given financial target because incubating, launching, and growing a new business is a time-consuming endeavor.

This is not to say that organic growth and growth via acquisition are mutually exclusive. Quite the contrary. In my experience the right balance of risk and reward is achieved through acquiring companies to augment a business strategy that began with the organic launch of an innovation. After learning the challenges and intricacies of a new business model, a new market, and a new set of customers, a management team is much better equipped to evaluate potential acquisitions, conduct buy-versus-build-versus-borrow assessments, understand the targets' strategic fit, properly price their value, and conduct due diligence that is insightful and meaningful.

Many companies have been hugely successful following an organic growth strategy. Well-documented examples of some of the world's most recognizable brands include IBM, Virgin, Boeing, Cisco Systems, Google, Apple, 3M, the Walt Disney Company, Procter & Gamble, Audi, Whirlpool, Toyota Motor, and AirAsia, to name a few. Companies that have done this consistently have mastered the concept of intrapreneurship – launching new companies or lines of business from within – and developed a culture that supports and nurtures the intrapreneurial spirit.

Intrapreneurship remains top of mind for today's CEOs. In its 17th Annual Global CEO Survey, published in 2014, PwC interviewed 1,344 CEOs in 68 countries and reported that, "a third of CEOs are pinning their hopes on new products or services, primarily to fuel organic growth in existing markets." The article also reveals "44% of CEOs say their organization is focusing on developing an innovation ecosystem which supports growth, as a priority over the next three years."

According to the 2014 report from the Boston Consulting Group (BCG) on the world's most innovative companies, innovation is among the top three priorities of executives worldwide, but only a small percentage feel confident that their organization can successfully deliver on their innovations. BCG states, "Strong innovators put a high value on innovation... They demonstrate a consistent commitment, even – or especially – in the face of failure. They encourage collaboration, they reward ideas, and they seek to capitalize on good ideas both quickly and with an appropriate level of support."

Richard Branson, founder of Virgin Group, says the following about intrapreneurship in a 2011 article in *Entrepreneur Magazine*: "Many millions of people proudly claim the title 'entrepreneur.' On the other hand, a title that hasn't gotten nearly the amount of attention it deserves is entrepreneur's little brother, 'intrapreneur.'" Branson offers this definition: "An employee who is given freedom and financial support to create new products, services and systems, who does not have to follow the company's usual routines or protocols." He goes on to say, "Virgin could never have grown into the group of more than 200 companies it is now, were it not for a steady stream of intrapreneurs who looked for and developed opportunities, often leading efforts that went against the grain."

What about Steve Jobs, was he an entrepreneur or intrapreneur? The answer is both. He started out as an entrepreneur in the purest sense. As Apple grew, the company became increasingly entrenched in rigid business practices and established ways of conducting innovation, and as we all know, it underwent several transformations and faced many ups and downs. Do you recall the early 1980s, when Jobs and Apple were struggling to make the Apple III and Macintosh succeed in the home PC market? How about the late 1990s, when Jobs returned to Apple to begin the drive towards the iMac? In both these periods Apple was a large corporation with deep-rooted corporate business practices, systems, and processes that Jobs had to confront. He was no longer starting from a clean slate but had to work within a more confined corporate environment that was very different from the wide-open startup environment that existed when he launched Apple in the mid-1970s.

Branson, Jobs, and other innovative business leaders understood the need to make intrapreneurship a top priority for achieving sustainable growth. These leaders repeatedly launched new lines of business by encouraging innovation and developing a culture of intrapreneurship. In doing so, they grew and reinforced their brands while increasing shareholder value.

Distinguishing Intrapreneurship from Innovation

Intrapreneurship should not be confused with ongoing innovations aimed at optimizing a company's existing business by differentiating its brand or improving its products, services, and internal performance. The process of ongoing innovations, which often includes a pipeline to encourage the flow of ideas, is necessary for maintaining a competitive advantage and keeping customers happy, and ultimately it drives sales levels and profit margins. But none of this can be equated with intrapreneurial activities.

While innovation is key for corporations to survive and grow in today's fast-changing business environment, intrapreneurship involves a much higher level of risk-taking and transformation and results in the successful creation of a new business within the corporate home. Many organizations have active research and development groups that regularly come up with novel ideas and impressive innovations, but if the resulting visions and inventions sit on a shelf instead of leading to significant new business ventures, then the organization does not have an intrapreneurial culture.

Confusing innovation and intrapreneurship can lead to major business failure. The literature is full of studies that demonstrate how most companies fail at innovation because they underestimate the effort required to execute the strategy developed to bring their innovation to the marketplace. The word to focus on in the previous sentence is "execute." In other words, intrapreneurship is the ability to execute a strategy that turns an innovation into a profitable and sustainable business that operates inside the corporate environment. Intrapreneurship will secure new revenue streams that are projected by the parent company (CoreCo) to be substantial enough to warrant creating a new business (NewCo) in the form of a new profit and loss (P&L) or income statement.

The terms CoreCo and NewCo were coined by Vijay Govindarajan and Chris Trimble, co-authors of the excellent book *10 Rules for Strategic Innovators: From Idea to Execution.* NewCo refers to a new line of business that springs from CoreCo that is likely quite different from CoreCo's other lines, perhaps so much so that it requires a new division. Or perhaps it will be set up within an existing division. Regardless of its position, NewCo will generate original sources of revenues and profits. In *10 Rules for Strategic Innovators* the authors also tell us that what drives companies to innovate successfully is a combination of creativity and execution. I could not agree more. In my experience the capacity of a company to execute is directly related to its ability to succeed at intrapreneurship.

What Does Hercules Have to Do with Intrapreneurship?

If you have read this far, I have at least piqued your interest. At best I have motivated you to try to understand the complexities of intrapreneurship. Your next question might be about the 12 labors in the book's subtitle. I draw a parallel between the 12 intrapreneurial labors outlined in these pages and the 12 labors of Hercules because the experience of the intrapreneur who launches a startup within a corporation is in many ways like the long, arduous journey undertaken by Hercules. There is the obvious parallel of the Herculean effort that is required to set any new business in motion. They also share relentless drive, unshakeable confidence, inventiveness, and the ability to attract supporters. As you read on, you will identify other similarities, but the point is, Hercules had to meet and vanquish 12 formidable challenges, and so will the intrapreneur.

A Short History of Hercules

According to Greek mythology Hercules killed his beloved wife and two sons after being driven mad by the goddess Hera, who was the spiteful wife of his father, Zeus. When his sanity returned he was consumed by anguish and sought a way to atone for his sins. The oracle at Delphi promised that Hercules would be purified if he performed 10 heroic labors for the hated King Eurystheus, who later added two new labors. With his immense strength and ingenuity Hercules conquered each of the 12 labors and became the greatest hero the world had ever known.

The challenges faced by the intrapreneur, while not humanly impossible like the ones undertaken by Hercules, are still daunting. The intrapreneur is asked to enter a new market, place the startup in a winning position, and at the same time meet the demanding expectations of the corporation's top executives. Along the way he will confront unexpected business realities for which few or no provisions were made. Although the corporation's leadership team will have given NewCo and the intrapreneur their endorsement and promised to provide full support, they will have misunderstood what NewCo requires of them in terms of its evolving needs, the suitability of CoreCo's existing practices for NewCo's business model, and how quickly the customers being targeted will adopt NewCo's new offering.

When it comes to the labors themselves, many parallels can be drawn. Hercules achieved his goal of exoneration by completing each of the labors demanded of him. Similarly, the intrapreneur will be able to successfully launch NewCo only if he tackles all of the 12 labors identified in this book. When he began, Hercules knew nothing about the tasks that lay before him, but he was highly motivated and passionate about getting them done, like a successful intrapreneur must be. Furthermore, Hercules' initial 10 labors became 12 when King Eurystheus discovered that Hercules had not strictly adhered to the rules he had set. Similarly, just when the intrapreneur believes that everything is in place to succeed, new challenges will suddenly surface.

Then there is the question of supporters and naysayers. The fact is, Hercules did not complete all 12 labors on his own. From time to time he received assistance from various supporters, sometimes human, sometimes celestial. So it will be for the intrapreneur, who cannot achieve his goals alone. From the outset, allies within the corporation will need to offer assistance if many of the labors are to be successfully completed. But not everyone will be an ally. Hercules had gods and goddesses on his side, but others were against him, not unlike the intrapreneur, who will face resistance from some of the organization's executives. Without a doubt the intrapreneur will come across many unforeseen obstacles, as Hercules did before him, but NewCo's obstacles will spring from CoreCo's stakeholders and the powerful corporate immune system. I describe the corporate immune system in labor 11, but for now think of it as the corporate controls, leadership behaviors, and organizational resistance that are triggered, like antibodies in the human body, when an activity inside the corporation is perceived as threatening, different, or leading to undesired change.

Many people benefited when Hercules slayed a vicious lion or a multi-headed beast, and after completing his twelfth and final labor he realized he had gained countless new supporters during his epic journey. He became a hero, was granted immortality, and went on to experience a long string of amazing adventures. The same will hold true for the successful intrapreneur, who will grow with NewCo and will have many opportunities in the future to conquer new corporate challenges.

The 12 intrapreneurial labors identified in the diagram on page 21 represent the most difficult internal challenges associated with launching a new business within a corporate environment. Some might appear innocuous at first glance, but do not underestimate their impact. My many years of experience have taught me that to ignore even a few of these challenges would be tantamount to corporate startup suicide.

The 12 Labors

Labors 1, 2, and 3 are about becoming aware of the important differences between intrapreneurship and entrepreneurship. They also look at the criteria that must be considered when selecting the intrapreneur who will lead the initiative and the people who will surround him with support. Labors 4, 5, 6, and 7 outline ways to ensure that CoreCo and NewCo are well prepared for the journey ahead. They include verifying that expectations are properly set, preparing CoreCo for the changes to come, and setting controls suitable for an intrapreneurial business. In labors 8, 9, and 10, we discuss how to accelerate NewCo's success by leveraging CoreCo effectively. Insights are provided regarding the careful selection of resources from CoreCo, timing NewCo's launch, and positioning the new business within the corporation so as to increase its prospects for success. The last two labors, 11 and 12, are the most difficult. They tackle the corporate immune system and how to prevent NewCo's descent into failure.

The book's final chapter introduces a process that has been honed in the real world and proven to be effective when launching and managing new businesses. It includes a methodology that will help the startup clarify its strategic direction, develop a map, compass, and ruler that will reliably guide its journey, and establish a culture of transparency, which is so crucial to success.

In each chapter I recommend practical leadership and management techniques for identifying and dealing with various pitfalls. If you are the intrapreneur, I hope you will take a proactive approach rather than a reactive one. The more proactive you are, the better your chance of mitigating the impact of what will largely be internally driven obstacles. This risk-mitigation approach will give you more time to work with and learn from your new external environment and customers. By validating your business model early and frequently, you will put your startup on a solid footing.

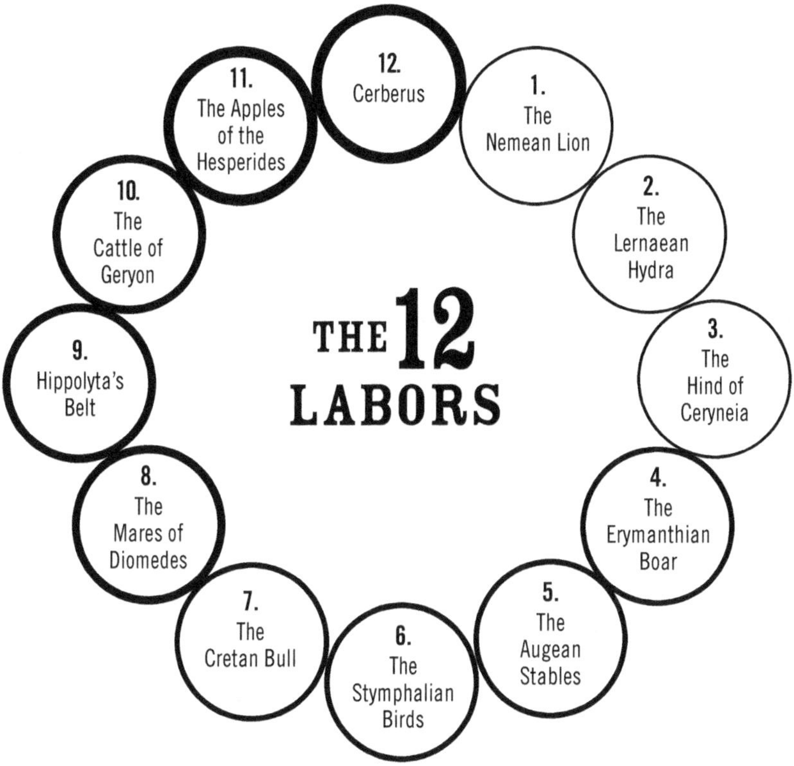

1. Battling the Myth of Entrepreneurship
2. The Dangers of the Quick Fix
3. The Sponsor, the Gatekeeper, and the Allies Needed to Survive
4. Creating and Mastering Expectations
5. The Long-Term Benefits of Skillful Change Management
6. Avoiding the Materiality Minefield
7. The Compounding Cushion and the Forecasting Trap
8. Preparing the Startup for Corporate Exposure
9. Rules for Designing and Positioning the New Business
10. Leveraging the Parent Company for Strategic Advantage
11. The Threat of the Corporate Immune System
12. How to Prevent a Controlled Descent into Failure

The Nemean Lion

For his first labor Hercules was told to kill the Nemean lion and bring its hide to King Eurystheus. The lion was legendary in size and ferociousness, but the real challenge lay in its golden fur, which was impervious to weapons. When Hercules realized his arrows were useless, he strategized that his best chance was to corner the beast and knock it unconscious with his club. He then used his brute strength to strangle it. When he tried to skin the lion he discovered that even in death the fur was invincible. Fortunately, Hercules had a friend in the goddess Athena, who told him to remove the hide using the lion's own claws. When the job was done he carried the pelt to King Eurystheus and waited to learn what his next labor would be.

LABOR 1

Battling the Myth of Entrepreneurship

When it comes to launching a new business within a corporation, the first labor is to fight the myths that typically surround a project of this type. These myths are based on the fallacy that starting a new business from within the borders of CoreCo exactly mimics the experience of an independent entrepreneur who sets a startup in motion from a clean slate. Similar to Hercules, who underestimated the power of the Nemean lion's golden fur, NewCo's leader might underestimate the extent to which people in CoreCo believe in these myths, which take the form of strongly held assumptions about entrepreneurship.

If you are NewCo's intrapreneur you will need a strategy, as Hercules did, to deal with their assumptions. This is not as simple as it sounds. Most people have never heard the term intrapreneur, and your own understanding may be limited. So your first job is to educate yourself and others. If you neglect this job or do it poorly, you will miss the opportunity to properly set the stage and obstacles will surface that will cause you much hardship on your journey.

I came upon the term intrapreneurship in 2005. I was researching the topic of innovation as part of a major corporate initiative I had been asked to co-lead, whose aim was to reinvent how the corporation went about innovating. Our first step was to put together a small team of individuals from across the organization who had proven to be innovators in their own right. We were given the choice to select anyone, from anywhere. Among the 10 people we recruited, some were business innovators, some were technology innovators, and some were process innovators.

We had four months to identify ways to capitalize on the corporation's technical and innovative capabilities, with the goal of diversifying into new markets by leveraging our CoreCo's capabilities and know-how.

Our tasks included reviewing documented best practices in the business world and learning from other companies with a track record of successful innovations. We divided our group into two teams. One analyzed best practices that had been written up in literature and the other interviewed companies recognized for their innovation, such as P&G, 3M, Virgin Atlantic, Johnson & Johnson, and Whirlpool, and at the same time identified their best practices. The group also conducted an internal assessment via questionnaires and interviews, wanting to determine what was working well in the corporation's innovation activities and what was not.

This was an incredible learning period for me. I accumulated a volume of knowledge that is only possible when carrying out an intense mandate in a collegial atmosphere marked by open communication, lively meetings, and teamwork. As part of our research I read *10 Rules for Strategic Innovators: From Idea to Execution*, in which authors Vijay Govindarajan and Chris Trimble briefly touch on the work of Gifford Pinchot, one of the first to define intrapreneurship as an activity that is separate and distinct from entrepreneurship. In Pinchot's words an intrapreneur is "a person within a large corporation who takes direct responsibility for turning [an] idea into a profitable finished product through risk-taking and innovation [intra(corporate) + (entre)preneur]."

When I read this definition, I exclaimed, "That's it! That's what I do!" And then I thought to myself, "And that's exactly what our company struggles with." I was not the only one in our group to experience a eureka moment. One of my colleagues had come across an article by Pinchot on the same topic, and we discussed it with the other members of the team, who all had identical reactions. We realized we needed to develop a better awareness of how intrapreneurship and entrepreneurship were different.

We went on to read various works on entrepreneurship, which were plentiful, and the few texts we could find on intrapreneurship. They helped us make sense of the challenges our company would face when taking innovative ideas to market. Remember, all of the team members were innovators, but not all were intrapreneurs. They could, however, relate to what we were hearing from companies regarding the difficulties inherent in bringing innovations to the marketplace.

The result of our comprehensive investigation was a briefing to the CEO and executive leadership team, who accepted the majority of our recommendations. We had made the challenges of intrapreneurship a centerpiece of our briefing because understanding them was key to understanding the level of commitment required from CoreCo for future

NewCos to succeed. Our recommendations were implemented across the corporation, and soon two NewCos were launched, whose purpose was to bring the company's core simulation expertise and simulation-based learning methodologies to new markets.

As it turned out we had underestimated one of the challenges: the need to ensure clarity around the terms intrapreneur and intrapreneurship. We did this despite our collective epiphany after reading Pinchot's definition. As I discovered later, terminology matters a great deal when launching an innovation within a corporation. This is because "entrepreneur" is associated with particular management styles that many in your organization probably incorrectly assume the intrapreneur will also use. Some may associate the term with the lone wolf who will go to any lengths to achieve his or her goals. Others may think of the bull in the china shop – someone who is so driven that he creates havoc along the way. The term entrepreneur also implies freedom of movement, which is never available to the intrapreneur to the same degree.

Many go even further and presume that intrapreneurship is easier than entrepreneurship because it comes with access to resources and some sort of safety net. I can tell you, there is no safety net. Leading the launch of a new business venture from within a corporation comes with significant risk to the intrapreneur and very narrow margins for error. Furthermore, CoreCo has scant patience with the intrapreneur's learning curve and can easily feel uncomfortable pivoting a strategy that was sold to an executive leadership team, a board, and maybe even investors. In truth, chances are that patience and time are in much shorter supply within a corporation than on the playing field where the independent entrepreneur operates.

Compounding the problem is the fact that in many corporations, compensation and benefits systems are geared towards encouraging corporate behaviors that follow the bigger-is-better mentality. Larger corporations tend to reward projects with the most impressive budgets, more material P&Ls, and the largest number of employees. This makes it very difficult to attract people to NewCo, people who may be reluctant to leave behind the so-called "bigger" – and often safer – jobs. In practice, once an employee vacates a job within CoreCo, it quickly gets backfilled and is no longer available as a safety net.

The assumptions people have about the entrepreneur's reality do not apply to the intrapreneur's experiences. Many successful independent entrepreneurs would likely fail at launching a new business within a large corporation, and I have met several who did not last more than a few months after a corporation acquired their company. The reason is simple. Entrepreneurs and intrapreneurs are not the same, though similarities do exist. Having a solid grasp of their fundamental differences forms the foundational basis for successfully running an intrapreneurial business.

Let's begin with some existing definitions. The key ideas in each are **bolded.**

1. The *Collins English Dictionary* provides the following definition of intrapreneur: "A person who while remaining within a larger organization uses entrepreneurial skills to **develop a new product or line of business** as a subsidiary of the organization."
2. The online *Financial Times Lexicon* has this to say: "Intrapreneurship involves creating or discovering new ideas or opportunities for the purpose of creating value, where this activity involves **creating a new and self-financing organization** within or under the auspices of an existing company. An intrapreneur is a person who practices intrapreneurship."
3. As we previously covered, Gifford Pinchot wrote: "An intrapreneur is a person within a large corporation who **takes direct responsibility** for turning [an] idea into a profitable finished product through risk-taking and innovation."
4. BusinessDictionary.com says: "Intrapreneurship **applies the 'start up' style of management** (characterized by flexibility, innovation, and risk-taking) to a secure and stable firm. The objective is to fast track product development (by circumventing the bureaucracy) to take advantage of a new opportunity or to assess feasibility of a new process or design."

1. Develop a new product or line of business

This captures the concept that intrapreneurship goes beyond innovation. A finished and profitable product means you have done the research and validated that someone is willing to buy your innovation. It also means that the innovation has been assessed as having enough financial potential to support the decision to establish it under a NewCo.

2. Create a new and self-financing organization

It cannot be overstated that the end goal of innovation activities is to turn great ideas into profit-generating products or services. Intrapreneurship is action-oriented, and its actions are necessary for the new business to achieve enough financial success to ensure that it will eventually become financially autonomous.

3. Take direct responsibility

This means more than leadership. It demands ownership, which is key to the intrapreneur's ability to succeed within the corporation. Only by assuming full responsibility will the intrapreneur have the mindset required to undertake the 12 labors. This is not to say that intrapreneurs do not need the help and support of other people in CoreCo, they do, but they must take real ownership of NewCo's vision and the strategies needed to ensure its success. At the same time CoreCo's leaders must accept the intrapreneur's sense of ownership.

4. Apply a startup style of management

The intrapreneur, who is *not* an entrepreneur, nonetheless makes use of several entrepreneurial skills when developing a new product or service into a line of business as a subsidiary of the corporation or as a business segment within an existing unit. This new business is, however, inextricably linked to CoreCo and, as such, does not have carte blanche to behave like an independent startup.

The Corporate Entrepreneur

You may have heard the term corporate entrepreneur and assumed you know what it means. Because it seems self-explanatory, it is often used to describe someone who acts like an entrepreneur but from inside a corporation. But that person is an **intrapreneur**. Corporate entrepreneur does a disservice because it does not create a clear distinction between the very different worlds of entrepreneurship and intrapreneurship. One day that difference may be readily understood and people will use corporate entrepreneur and intrapreneur interchangeably, but until that day comes we will stick to intrapreneur for the sake of clarity and as a building block to success.

2 Definitions

To fully appreciate the essence of the intrapreneurial challenge it helps to have a clear definition of intrapreneurship, which encompasses an area of unique expertise, and intrapreneur, the person who possesses that expertise.

INTRAPRENEURSHIP	INTRAPRENEUR
Monetizing an innovation and turning it into a profitable and sustainable business within a corporate environment.	An employee of a corporation who uses entrepreneurial skills and concepts, coupled with corporate leadership and change management skills and a keen understanding of how to leverage the corporation, to position innovations in the marketplace as viable businesses that drive new sources of profit.

Distinguishing Intrapreneurs from Entrepreneurs

I have worked with many entrepreneurs in my career, predominantly through growing new businesses or acquiring them as part of a corporation. I have had countless conversations and meetings with entrepreneurs looking for partnerships or wanting to exchange business ideas and insights, and with others who were interested in selling their company. In recent years I have enjoyed being a mentor to young entrepreneurs.

I should also point out that entrepreneurship runs in my family. My father, Henri, was a businessman who created two international freight-forwarding businesses, and my two brothers and I seem to have inherited his entrepreneurial spirit. My older brother, Xavier-Henri, co-founded a flight simulation company that grew from a startup into a global provider of full-flight simulators and related training devices for the aviation industry. After Textron Inc. acquired the company in 2013, he turned his attention to the bright young minds at Montreal's Concordia University and founded the District 3 Innovation Center, a technology and business incubator that Xavier-Henri refers to as "a hatchery for new entrepreneurs."

My younger brother, Hugues, is a PhD and internationally recognized expert in high-risk assessments in forensic psychology and victimization. He co-founded an education and consulting business called the Forensic Alliance that caters to the demand for high-quality, evidence-based best practices that help people working in the fields of applied forensic psychology and related behavioral sciences make more confident and better-informed decisions.

All three of us are passionate about inspiring teams of motivated individuals to deliver solutions to unmet needs. We are equally devoted to creating unique value propositions and ensuring that the voice of the customer is heard loud and clear within our respective organizations.

Despite my professional and family exposure, I decided it would be a good idea before writing this book to see what other experts in entrepreneurship had to say about how intrapreneurs and entrepreneurs compare. There are key areas of similarity and vital differences. To understand them, one must look at the similarities and differences in the broad business activities they must manage. These are represented in Figure 1.1.

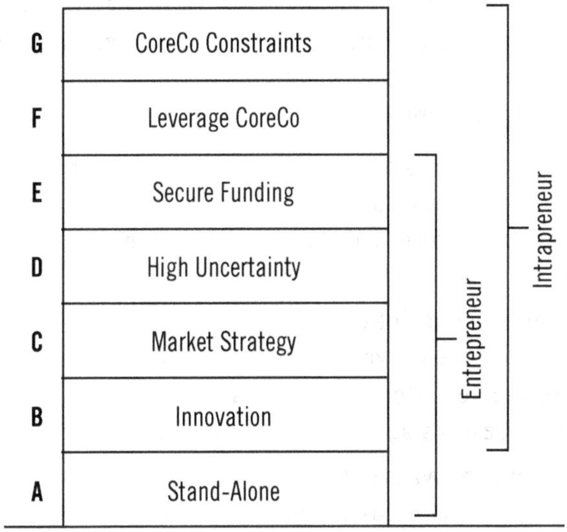

Figure 1.1 Similarities and Differences

A. The entrepreneur must build a business from scratch on a stand-alone basis.

B. Both the independent entrepreneur and the corporate-based intrapreneur need an innovation.

C. Both must establish a strategy that will successfully take their innovation to market, where it will generate profits.

D. Whether you are an intrapreneur or an entrepreneur, you will experience a high level of uncertainty in bringing your innovation to market.

E. Securing funding is a top priority for both the intrapreneur and entrepreneur, though the intrapreneur can usually count on the parent company for funding or to access external sources of funding, while the entrepreneur must use her own money or find angel investors, venture capitalists, or other funding sources.
F. The intrapreneur is able to leverage CoreCo's assets and know-how to achieve NewCo's goals.
G. A major challenge for the intrapreneur is to overcome obstacles created by CoreCo, which will want to dictate how aspects of the startup are handled.

The areas of overlap show that the intrapreneur must possess various entrepreneurial attributes to successfully launch and grow a startup within a corporation. I have concluded that there are 12 attributes that are critical to the entrepreneur, though in some cases these are shared among two or more co-founders whose enterprise benefits from their complementary personalities, talents, attitudes, and experience.

1. **Risk-taker.** Risk does not frighten entrepreneurs when it comes to achieving business success. They are ready and willing to take personal, professional, and financial risks, and even risk their reputation and relationships, if necessary.
2. **Customer-focused.** Entrepreneurs know that success comes from understanding the market and their customers' needs. They wisely pay attention to customer feedback and act as the voice of the customer at every stage of their company's growth.
3. **Creative and innovative.** Typical entrepreneurs find novel solutions to unmet needs and then find innovative ways to bring them to market. Interestingly, I have observed that their creativity is not always in the solution itself, but in their ability to make the link between an unmet need and an already existing solution.
4. **Passionate.** All successful entrepreneurs are passionate about what they do. In my experience their original venture was often far less about making money and far more about bringing something new and better to the world.
5. **Energetic.** True entrepreneurs have lots of energy. They can burn the candle at both ends day in and day out, and can work through hunger and exhaustion.

6. **Emotionally resilient.** Entrepreneurs bounce back from failure and learn from it, not just once but repeatedly. They epitomize what Thomas Edison once said: "I have not failed. I've just found 10,000 ways that won't work."
7. **Persevering.** Few people are as tenacious as entrepreneurs. In *The Lean Startup*, Eric Ries refers to the entrepreneur's ability to shift direction as they get a better read of the market and see opportunities that present themselves in unexpected ways. They persevere. My father, who besides being an entrepreneur is also an avid sailor and proud Breton, named his boat *Kendal'ch* and wears a silver bracelet inscribed with the same word. *Kendal'ch* means perseverance.
8. **Self-disciplined, self-motivated, self-starter.** Entrepreneurs have a strong work ethic and need no help getting going or staying excited or focused. They drive a demanding agenda and expect others around them to do the same.
9. **Self-assured.** No one beats entrepreneurs for self-confidence in their domain. Other subjects may bore them, but broach a topic that is in or even on the periphery of their business area and they will speak about it with a high level of authority. It is their self-assurance that makes them believe they will achieve their vision despite difficulties.
10. **Adept negotiator.** Winning entrepreneurs have strong negotiating skills and instincts. They inevitably create attractive scenarios for their customers, suppliers, and partners.
11. **Decisive.** Success demands making choices quickly and decisively. Entrepreneurs realize that the buck stops with them, and any day of the week they will choose action and getting results over bureaucracy and procrastination.
12. **Inspiring.** Entrepreneurs know how to bring other people into their vision. This is not the same as having good people or communication skills (I have met many entrepreneurs who display neither). Rather, they have an indefinable way of motivating others around their innovation and strategies.

This list could certainly be the topic of several hot debates. No doubt you know entrepreneurs who have other characteristics and skills than the ones enumerated here. I agree that one size does not fit all. But these 12 attributes have been at the core of every successful entrepreneur I have ever seen in action, and it is hard to imagine an innovation that is successfully launched without them.

Now let's look at the intrapreneur, keeping in mind the definition I presented on page 28. It does not describe innovators who come up with neat new ideas or prototypes, nor are we discussing employees who discover fresh ways of improving an existing business or operational process, or how to drive better productivity internally. The intrapreneur is someone who is tasked to take a new product or service to market within an existing corporation and turn it into a profitable business. To be successful, he needs to have the 12 attributes of the entrepreneur, plus seven more.

1. **Change agent.** Turning a new product or service into a thriving startup and ensuring sustainable growth and profitability requires challenging some of CoreCo's established ways of doing things. The intrapreneur must convince CoreCo to replace certain aspects of its own successful business model with new systems and processes that will support NewCo. Corporate transformation and managing change are covered in more detail in labor 5.
2. **Corporate leader.** The successful intrapreneur needs to be able to lead in a large matrix organization. CoreCo managers will want to see strong leadership skills prior to being persuaded to expend their limited resources on NewCo. There will be many instances where success will depend on the intrapreneur's skill at obtaining the support of the people at CoreCo who control access to resources.
3. **Corporate leverager.** It is expected that the intrapreneur will skillfully take advantage of CoreCo's resources, and in fact proficiency at leveraging CoreCo is key to intrapreneurial success. This book introduces the term corporate force multiplier (CFM), which is outlined in labor 10. In the meantime, know that CFMs will help NewCo move faster and appear larger and more material to the external world and its new customers.
4. **Protective.** One of the intrapreneur's most demanding tasks is to shield NewCo from a) people who want to get involved but are not needed, and b) CoreCo's natural tendency to want to take or regain control of NewCo's activities. Improperly managed, protecting NewCo from CoreCo can consume an exorbitant amount of the intrapreneur's time. This characteristic is so

important to the success of NewCo that I cover it extensively in labor 3.

5. **Expectations manager.** The challenge of managing unrealistic corporate expectations about progress and growth is always present, and it starts on day one (entrepreneurs involved with venture capitalists or funding organizations also must manage expectations, but not usually so early in the game). While the intrapreneur's passion and vision are essential to NewCo's startup, the consequence of engaging CoreCo's executives is that they will want to see results, and when the first sales figures come in they will want things to move faster. Further pressure is exerted if NewCo is located in a publicly traded company, where quarterly results and market expectations rule the day. In this environment expectations can change every three months. More on this in labor 4.
6. **Emotionally intelligent.** Intrapreneurs require a high degree of emotional intelligence, which is the ability to read the reactions of CoreCo colleagues and to sense unease and resistance as soon as they show up. More emotional intelligence is needed as more leveraging is required of CoreCo's resources and business processes. Keep in mind that not everyone will be behind NewCo. As with anything that is new, there will be a small group of early supporters, a large group of neutral managers who will wait and see, and some early resistors. Identifying who falls into which category is key to determining how to garner internal support.
7. **Team player.** Because a major part of the intrapreneur's success will come from working well with people at CoreCo, it is paramount to be a strong team player. This includes fostering effective team dynamics and giving others a chance to share in the limelight and accolades, as well as ensuring that the sponsor receives the exposure he or she seeks.

I can already hear the entrepreneurs among you saying, "Hey, Guillaume, we need to display these traits too, you know." It is true that some entrepreneurs will at one point or another require some of the intrapreneurial skills and characteristics listed here, most likely when their startup begins to gain steam. The entrepreneur who takes an enterprise from newborn to large, established business will certainly have to demonstrate a number of them along the way. Rarely, however, will she require all seven at the beginning of the new venture. In fact, some will never require them at all. But the intrapreneur will rely on them every step of the way, from the moment the discussions around NewCo's launch stop and the intrapreneur is given a budget, a timeline, expectations, and the go-ahead.

You are now aware of the many challenges that lie in wait as the intrapreneur completes the first labor of making sure CoreCo clearly understands and accepts his or her role and mandate. Like Hercules, who was stumped when it came to removing the hide from the Nemean lion, the intrapreneur needs tools to help cut through CoreCo's existing perceptions and biases regarding intrapreneurship, which have their source in entrepreneurial myths.

3 Helpful Tools

Tool 1: Selecting the intrapreneur

NewCo's success will largely be a factor of the intrapreneur's ability to effectively lead and manage the startup's launch and growth. Taking the time to properly assess potential leaders for this major initiative will pay off in the long run and be of great value when it comes time to tackle labor 2. Table 1.1 is divided into the entrepreneurial and intrapreneurial attributes previously described. Finding an individual who possesses each and every attribute will be difficult, so the key will be to identify those criteria that are most relevant to the particular challenges your NewCo is facing.

Table 1.1 Intrapreneur Selection Criteria

ENTREPRENEURIAL CHARACTERISTICS AND SKILLS	INTRAPRENEURIAL CHARACTERISTICS AND SKILLS
1. Risk-taker	1. Change agent
2. Customer-focused	2. Corporate leader
3. Creative and innovative	3. Corporate leverager
4. Passionate	4. Protective
5. Energetic	5. Expectations manager
6. Emotionally resilient	6. Emotionally intelligent
7. Persevering	7. Team player
8. Self-disciplined, self-motivated, self-starter	
9. Self-assured	
10. Adept negotiator	
11. Decisive	
12. Inspiring	

Each CoreCo experiences unique challenges when launching their NewCo, and they face these challenges with varying levels of intrapreneurial experience, expected corporate resistance, and intimacy with the new market. For these reasons CoreCo must rank the attributes in table 1.1 in order of importance according to the needs of its startup. The sponsor, who is deeply involved with choosing the intrapreneur, must be uncompromising when measuring candidates against them.

It is crucial to surround the intrapreneur with key individuals who can compensate for and over time help strengthen any personal weaknesses. Self-awareness is another important intrapreneurial quality, as the intrapreneur must be able to identify his areas of deficit so people with complementary skills and characteristics can be recruited to the team.

Tool 2: The elevator speech

The second tool is something I have used many times: a well-articulated elevator speech. It is a simple concept that pays long-term dividends. The elevator speech is often used in change management, sales, and re-engineering contexts as an easy, effective method of getting a message across and engaging an audience in a cause. The trick is to keep it short and to always recount it the same way. Consistency ensures clarity and increases buy-in, so that over time the various people in an organization whose support is needed will share the intrapreneur's understanding of his role. The elevator speech is also a useful tool to achieve organizational alignment, which is discussed in great detail in the book's final chapter.

The intrapreneurial elevator speech must be no longer than two minutes and is usually composed of two parts. The first explains, in one long sentence or two or three shorter ones, what NewCo is all about. The focus at this point is to deliver the key and most compelling aspects of NewCo's mission, strategic intent, and goals (also covered in the final chapter). This part of the elevator speech must resonate with the CoreCo audience and get them thinking, "Yes, this makes good sense." It is a call to action to the people whose cooperation and support NewCo will rely on.

The purpose of the second part is to clarify the role of the intrapreneur in a manner that addresses preconceptions and calms the automatic defensive response of CoreCo's immune system. This part should also be no more than three or four sentences.

In both parts of the elevator speech it is necessary to include words and statements that answer the WIIFM reaction (What's in it for me?) of the people you are speaking to. After all, they are being asked to adopt change. The goal is not only to educate these people but to engage them, and the intrapreneur should deliver this speech at every possible occasion. Another person who is ideally positioned to deliver the speech, and just as frequently, is the startup's sponsor. As we will see in labor 3, the sponsor is the senior executive within CoreCo who probably decided on the need for NewCo in the first place. She plays a pivotal role in ensuring corporate buy-in and that the intrapreneur receives the support that is necessary to succeed.

The following is an example of what the two parts of the elevator speech look like. It is based on a fictitious robotics company that decided to create a new business to supply robotics solutions directly to the automotive industry.

> Our goal at We-R-Robotics is to create a new subsidiary in the self-driven automobile market with a revenue target of $20 million in year 5, growing to $75 million in year 10, and contributing $10 million to our corporate bottom line. To do this we will launch a startup called SelfDrive that will draw on our core expertise in robotics and control systems and on our existing relationships with suppliers to the automotive industry, which is seeing a surge in the demand for safe and reliable robotics and control systems technology. We have validated that our expertise in these domains can be effectively leveraged to address this growing need.
>
> John Intrepid is the intrapreneur assigned to lead this venture. Unlike independent entrepreneurs who run their startups pretty much how they want, John will have to make sure SelfDrive grows into a successful business and will be expected to achieve this within numerous internal corporate constraints. However, he will be able to take advantage of some of We-R-Robotics's existing resources, and I am counting on you to help him make the best use of them to grow SelfDrive. At the same time it is essential to acknowledge that SelfDrive is entering a new market that will likely require us to modify some of our business practices so it can be effective in that market.

The intrapreneur needs to have the elevator speech down pat, as does the sponsor. Even CoreCo's key executives should know it by heart, and so should the members of NewCo's team. Everyone involved must be able to recount it convincingly. For this to happen it must be written very early on, towards the end of the innovation phase. It is not unusual for the intrapreneur and sponsor to write it together, focusing on the telling details of the intrapreneurial challenge.

When word gets out that CoreCo has launched NewCo, people will want to hear about this exciting new business from their respective leaders as well as from the intrapreneur. But CoreCo's middle managers will have already made their first assumptions based on their preconceived beliefs about what launching the startup will entail. They will have heard that an intrapreneur was assigned, but they probably mentally superimposed the word entrepreneur (without realizing it) and are already caught up in the myths we reviewed earlier. This means they see the positives of the role without appreciating the constraints, and they imagine how lucky the new leader is. Or they peg the person as someone who will challenge the status quo and create work for them, and are already thinking WIIFM.

When the elevator speech is ready the sponsor will set up a meeting between the intrapreneur and CoreCo's CEO and executive team, during which the intrapreneur will deliver the speech. It is critical that it resonates, as I already mentioned. Buy-in at this point would be optimal, but if the executives do not buy in, the intrapreneur will know it from their questions and comments, and even their body language.

If you are the intrapreneur, stay open to their feedback. This is where your intrapreneurial skills will spring into action, because entrepreneurs do not have to convince superiors of the merits of their startup. There have been many times when I have watched an entrepreneur acquired into a corporation lose patience with company executives because, referring to the newly purchased business, he thinks, "They don't get my vision" or "They just don't understand our customer base and needs."

CoreCo's executives are NewCo's internal stakeholders, and their feedback is neither good nor bad. Rather, it is necessary and valuable because it provides insights regarding the degree to which CoreCo's executives comprehend NewCo's mandate and whether or not they are aligned in supporting it. Their comments or objections following the elevator speech most likely reflect legitimate concerns, ordinary fear, or simply a lack of clarity, and these must be understood so they can be answered and alleviated.

Keep in mind that CoreCo's executives are banking on you to make NewCo a success for the company. In fact, NewCo's success may be reflected in their own business objectives, key performance indicators, and management bonuses. Gathering their feedback and ensuring it is aligned with NewCo's goals is imperative. Once alignment is achieved the elevator speech must be adjusted so it continues to resonate with the executives and secures their support. It should never be modified on an ad hoc basis, dumbed down for a particular audience, or rendered generic in an effort to please everybody. All of the above requires you to demonstrate corporate leadership early on.

Senior leaders in the rung below the executive office must also be targeted. Always keep in mind that how colleagues talk about NewCo when you are not around – while on coffee breaks or standing around the water cooler or during lunch – will have a significant impact on when and how they begin to support it. If two colleagues compare notes on NewCo and you role as NewCo's leader, and it turns out they have different perceptions, someone has created a misalignment that can plague your fledgling business for a long time.

The last thing you want is the following scenario: During a regularly scheduled management meeting a vice president hears a manager paraphrase your elevator speech. When the manager is done the VP explains to him that you, as the project's leader, got it all wrong. Or in a similar scenario the VP says that what he has just heard is not what he understood the mandate to be. Either way, this constitutes a major blow to your efforts to complete the first labor. There is confusion in the company that could torpedo NewCo. But you are not doomed if the VP or someone who was in the room informs you of the exchange, giving you the opportunity to reset the message, which will require significant work. If you never hear about the misunderstanding, the VP and related departments may continually question your role or harden their resistance to your mandate. Both scenarios are tough to overcome.

Tool 3: The 3Fs

The third tool is a memory jogger to be used by the intrapreneur. I call it the 3Fs of the elevator speech: **Fresh, Frequent**, and **For everyone**. The success of NewCo depends on the intrapreneur's role and mandate being clearly understood, and the 3Fs will go a long way to making sure this happens.

Fresh

The elevator speech must always be updated to reflect NewCo's reality, for example, if NewCo has adjusted its strategic plan to take into account discoveries that were made about the market. Because NewCo will evolve as it grows, the elevator speech will likely go through several iterations.

Frequent

The elevator speech must be delivered at every opportunity to the people at CoreCo in leadership and management positions who will play an important role in supporting NewCo.

For everyone

Everyone involved with NewCo owns the elevator speech, not just the intrapreneur. This includes the sponsor, CoreCo's key executives, and NewCo's team. They must memorize it and be as engaging and convincing as the intrapreneur when they deliver it to their co-workers.

Labor 1 cannot be completed in one fell swoop. During its infancy and toddler years the corporate startup requires intensive nurturing. The intrapreneur's compelling elevator speech is invaluable throughout this period for distinguishing intrapreneurship from entrepreneurship and ensuring that CoreCo remains aligned with NewCo. With alignment, CoreCo will be more than willing to provide its startup business with any necessary help.

Revisit labor 1 regularly, keeping in mind that if NewCo has to modify its strategy in response to new market or customer information, sudden opportunities, or emerging constraints, the elevator speech will need to be revised accordingly. The intrapreneur can customize the second half of the speech as necessary to meet the needs of various stakeholders, which will be useful when engaging them in NewCo's strategy for leveraging CoreCo's resources. Labor 1 will be successfully completed only when NewCo has become self-reliant.

Leading Up to NewCo's Formal Launch

Launching a NewCo is not a one-time, isolated event. In fact, the formal launch is the culmination of a series of steps that were taken to prepare NewCo, the intrapreneur, and CoreCo for what was to come. Being familiar with the sequencing of these steps and keeping it in mind when reading later chapters will help you grasp why the steps must be completed, and certain tools used, in the order presented.

Every situation is different, but in general terms the intrapreneurship phase, which includes the creation and growth of NewCo, is preceded by an idea generation phase and then by an innovation process phase as shown in Figure 1.2. Eventually the intrapreneurship phase ends and NewCo becomes an established business that is capable of standing on its own and thriving alongside CoreCo's other businesses.

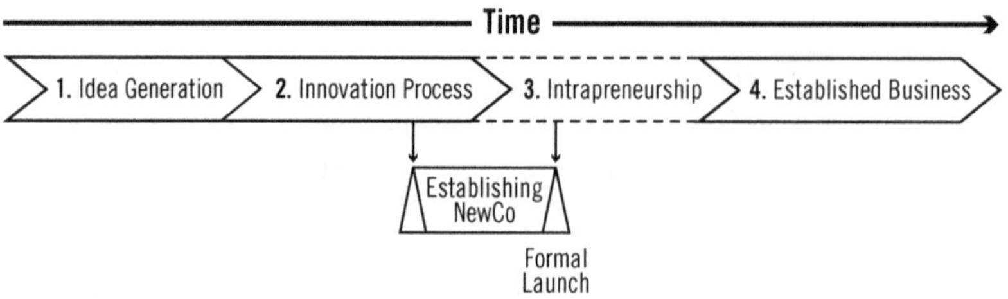

Figure 1.2 Establishing NewCo

The duration of each phase varies as a function of CoreCo's experience at generating ideas and running an innovation process. Also at play is its history of launching NewCos and whether or not they have been successful, how close NewCo's targeted customers and market are to CoreCo's existing ones, and the complexity and uniqueness of the new business idea. For these reasons each phase can take several weeks to several months. For example, a CoreCo that is expert at generating new ideas and managing an effective innovation process, and has had several successful ventures with various NewCos and is now launching a startup into an adjacent market that is close to its core markets, will navigate phases 1, 2, and 3 much more rapidly than a CoreCo with limited experience of phases 1 and 2, no experience of launching NewCos, and is developing a startup for a market that is very different from its own.

The focus should not be on establishing precise timelines for these pre-launch activities. Instead, the intrapreneur should make sure that the sequence of steps is well understood by the key people at both CoreCo and NewCo and that the important activities and labors that must be addressed are completed in a timely manner commensurate with the level of business complexity to be faced.

Choosing the moment a NewCo is launched and handling the corporate exposure this will attract are major intrapreneurial challenges (timing and preparation are covered in labor 8). At this stage, however, what is important to note is that the decision to establish NewCo will occur towards the end of the innovation process. The innovation team will develop its idea to the point where it can demonstrate its application and broad business potential. It will already have validated that the new business idea fits within CoreCo's overall strategy, developed a preliminary business model to demonstrate how NewCo can make money, and finalized a business case to provide CoreCo with the risk-reward insights it needs to make a decision. Once the CoreCo leadership team is convinced that the business opportunity warrants setting up NewCo, a sponsor is confirmed. Her responsibility will be to ensure the startup's success.

Establishing and formally launching NewCo entails eight steps:

1. Naming the sponsor
2. Selecting the intrapreneur
3. Setting NewCo business objectives
4. Identifying the gatekeeper
5. Defining the strategic plan
6. Preparing the elevator speech
7. Securing the buy-in of CoreCo's executives
8. Developing and launching a communications strategy

The culminating event is NewCo's formal launch, which is usually marked by an internal announcement. This is when the broader CoreCo organization is made aware of NewCo's expected contribution to the corporate strategy and NewCo's own business goals. It is crucial that the announcement includes details about everyone's role in supporting the startup.

When to Appoint the Intrapreneur

Do not wait until you have decided to formally launch your new corporate business to appoint your intrapreneur. If you do, a huge learning opportunity will have been lost. A wealth of information is available during the first two phases, when ideas are being evaluated for their business potential and preliminary plans are being drafted to validate the financial benefits, necessary investments, and business risks. The intrapreneur needs this information. The period spanned by the first two phases is also when he gains an understanding of which aspects of CoreCo can be leveraged to accelerate the startup.

The best time to appoint the intrapreneur is when the innovation has been validated to the point where a business leader is required to begin the transition towards intrapreneurship. These are the pre-launch months, when NewCo is facing a steep learning curve and the intrapreneur can begin to take ownership of the innovation and become excited about its business potential. By taking part in early fundamental activities, for example, participating in drafting the initial business model, he will develop a strong business foundation. This will allow him to make better and faster decisions when NewCo starts to grow in earnest. The intrapreneur's involvement can be part-time during this phase, but the commitment will become full-time once NewCo is ready to be launched.

A Few Final Words

If you are NewCo's intrapreneur, you have been charged with a great responsibility. Taking ownership and displaying leadership early on is key to building the confidence of those who put you in charge. Always keep in mind that others have staked their reputations on NewCo's success, so be sure to keep them informed of your progress and let them share in your successes. Make the effort to establish and maintain a solid relationship with your sponsor, which means keeping the lines of communication open. Trust between the two of you is essential if your goals are to be met, and do not wait too long to ask for her help. Remember your allies and supporters and share the limelight when warranted. Finally, do not get trapped into trying to please everyone. You will not have the time.

If you are a business leader launching, sponsoring, or supporting a new line of business within your corporation, be very careful when selecting your intrapreneur. Look at the criteria I outlined earlier and use it to objectively evaluate each candidate. CoreCo may have leaders who are proficient at what they do, but they may not be qualified to drive the launch of a new business. Even creative innovators within CoreCo who have come up with brilliant ideas, products, or prototypes and are keen to run their own business may not be qualified, though they might be ideal candidates for the intrapreneur's team.

COMING UP NEXT....................

You now appreciate the difference between an intrapreneur and an entrepreneur, and you are clear about the characteristics and skills the intrapreneur must possess.

You realize the importance of communicating his role to CoreCo early and often, and how the elevator speech presents and reinforces those messages.

Your next responsibility is to avoid the temptation of finding a quick fix for your NewCo leadership needs, which is covered in detail in labor 2.

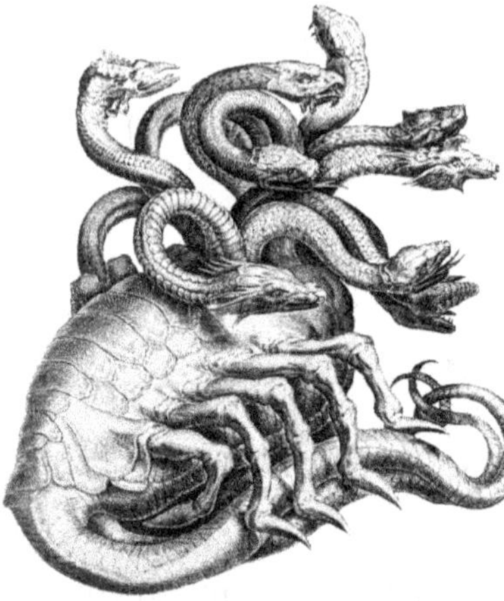

The Lernaean Hydra

Standing guard at the entrance to the underworld was the Lernaean Hydra, a serpent-like creature with poisonous blood that terrorized the surrounding countryside. Killing the Hydra became Hercules' second labor, and he advanced on its lair with flaming arrows drawn. When the Hydra emerged, Hercules attacked its heads, but for each head he crushed with his club, two grew in its place. The struggle seemed hopeless but Hercules refused give up. He called to his nephew, Iolaus, for help, and together they used a torch to burn the Hydra's open wounds so no new heads would grow. Finally, Hercules cut off the Hydra's last remaining head, which was immortal, with a golden sword he was given by Athena. He buried it under a giant rock, and his second labor was complete.

LABOR 2

The Dangers of the Quick Fix

The tendency to find a quick fix for NewCo's leadership needs when launching a new venture within a corporation is like dealing with the multi-headed Hydra. As unqualified candidates for the job of intrapreneur surface and are turned away, more crop up. The need for a quick fix often arises because CoreCo has waited too long to begin its search. Having decided to launch a startup and feeling very excited about this initiative, CoreCo wants things to move quickly and will be after NewCo's sponsor and the corporation's HR leader for results. Soon the sponsor and HR leader are playing catch-up. Having failed to consider what was discussed in the previous chapter, the corporation opts for a quick solution to the problem. While this may be expeditious, it is also highly dangerous.

One of the more common mistakes behind the quick fix phenomenon is the assumption that the innovation is so good that it will sell itself. If this is the case, the thinking goes, a "good enough" team is all that is needed to take the new product to market. This is a major error in judgment. Great ideas do not build successful businesses, great leaders and teams do. This important point has a parallel in the world of venture capitalists (VCs), where VCs follow a generally accepted rule when deciding on which startups to invest in: they would rather back an A-type entrepreneur with a B-type idea, than a B-type entrepreneur with an A-type idea. The same is true of corporations, and if CoreCo wants NewCo to succeed it must identify and attract an A-type intrapreneur.

A-type intrapreneurs are not necessarily the innovators at your company who develop or promote the products or services that could one day lead to a NewCo. These individuals are what I refer to as NewCo subject matter experts, and they may very well play a significant role in the new venture and even become part of its leadership team. But if they have not demonstrated the characteristics and skills described in labor 1, they are not qualified for the monumental task at hand.

Sometimes pretenders present themselves as intrapreneurs. Perhaps they were encouraged to step forward by an executive who is a supporter or mentor but does not understand the requirements of the job, or by a manager who wants their champion leading the charge for political reasons. Or they may be volunteers who see this opportunity as a shortcut to leading their own business. Like Hercules, who faced two new heads for each Hydra head he destroyed, the corporation runs the risk of facing two new intrapreneur pretenders for every candidate who is turned away. This is due to the excitement that trickled down from the executive team as word got out that CoreCo is launching a NewCo. Several CoreCo managers will feel the allure of the startup's potential and what running a successful new business might mean for their career advancement.

7 Types of Intrapreneur Pretenders

Over the course of my career I have seen seven types of intrapreneur pretenders who can come from anywhere in the organization. They include the Eager Innovator, the Enthusiastic Product Developer, the Excited Business Development Manager, the Efficient Process Improvement Leader, the Individual High Performer, the Political Player, and the Forced Conscript.

1. **The Eager Innovator** is the engineer, programmer, or designer who led the innovation and produced the prototype that eventually became the product or service on which NewCo's business plan is based. This person demonstrates great passion for her innovation and she likely put a lot of sweat and unpaid time into advancing the technology. Being technically savvy, she orchestrated an impressive and convincing presentation that wowed her audience and showed how her idea can impact or even revolutionize the given market. She was a big part of getting the idea through each step of the innovation process, and was even an armchair product manager, doing research on competitive products and putting together high-level numbers for market potential. Very good at dealing with customers on technical issues, she might appear to be a first-rate candidate.

If your team confuses innovation with intrapreneurship, it stands to reason that it will mistake an innovator for an intrapreneur. The crucial difference is that an intrapreneur has what it takes to turn an innovation into a profitable final product that penetrates its market and generates sustainable sales and profits for the benefit of the corporation. This involves a higher level of personal and business risk-taking, navigating CoreCo to gather support and leverage resources, leading sales and business development, creating strategies, building up an organization, and adapting to the market's needs. Many innovators are not qualified for or comfortable with these activities. To make an objective assessment of the Eager Innovator's ability to lead NewCo, evaluate her against the criteria in table 1.1.

A business team that confuses innovation with intrapreneurship will mistake an innovator for an intrapreneur.

2. **The Enthusiastic Product Developer** was given a prototype or saw an innovative process demonstration and turned the new technology into a product. He might have done this without a direct mandate, scrounging bits of budget from here and there to fund the effort. Nonetheless, he turned the R&D into something that will meet a need in the marketplace. Because of his product development background, he spent quite a bit of time understanding the market's requirements and can speak to them convincingly. He confidently talks about competitive products, recounting dozens of their features and explaining why the innovation will do a better job addressing customer needs. He has also thought about how this one-off product prototype can be produced in larger quantities, and in addition has developed an estimate of startup and production costs and potential selling prices. Engaging and committed, he may seem like a good choice to lead NewCo, but first he must demonstrate the characteristics and skills required of a successful intrapreneur.

3. **The Excited Business Development Manager** was tasked to look at an innovation idea and assess its market potential as part of the review process. As she familiarized herself with the market she became increasingly convinced that the innovation would do well in it. She read various market studies and arranged for a few demos from the product leads so she would better grasp the technology. Having been trained in market analysis, she created complex spreadsheets to simulate the market and determine NewCo's growth. She can discuss pie charts in great detail

and create exhaustive PowerPoint presentations, and she comes across as knowledgeable about how the new innovation will make money. She has always dreamed of leading her own business and what better way to start and learn than with a NewCo? Perhaps she should be considered as a candidate, but not until she has been assessed as having the other necessary skills to make it as an intrapreneur.

4. **The Efficient Process Improvement Leader** is very good at finding novel ways of driving internal performance metrics. He has an impressive track record of improving operational results by lowering costs and knows how to analyze data and tweak processes to achieve efficiencies. Because of this core skill set he has a solid reputation among his peers. Like other Efficient Process Improvement Leaders, he is adept at change management, which is one of the most important skills for a successful intrapreneur. All of the above makes him an appealing candidate, but only if he also has a demonstrated track record of building teams, working in a cross-functional environment, managing operational activities, and interfacing with customers. Despite these strengths, his qualities must be compared to those listed in table 1.1 to see if he truly qualifies for the position of intrapreneur.

5. **The Individual High Performer** functions exceedingly well in her discipline. She excels at the more individual sports such as sales, business development, financial analysis, and contract negotiations. She is great with customers and can be very creative in finding solutions for getting deals done. One of her goals is to expand into a more general business leadership role, despite having never managed or led any teams of significance or been involved in growing an operation. Although she has many competencies, if she has not demonstrated the full range of critical skills and characteristics found in table 1.1, she is not qualified to lead a startup and should not be given such a pivotal strategic role.

6. **The Political Player** is one of the most difficult pretenders to spot. He may present himself for all the right reasons, but in fact his main purpose is to gain political influence or control over the new business being launched. Typically, the Political Player is not qualified to be an intrapreneur, but he is nominated anyway and may get the job as a result of the maneuvering of a powerful executive who is also an excellent negotiator. The sponsor must be on the lookout for the Political Player because his true allegiance may be to the person who helped him secure the position and not to NewCo. His objectives may clash with the sponsor's.

7. The Forced Conscript was pushed to apply for the job for reasons that are not understood by others at the company, and maybe not even by the Forced Conscript herself. She is unlikely to make a good startup leader because she is only moderately engaged, and consequently she may create a negative environment that will be felt by NewCo's team and customers. Appointing a Forced Conscript as the new intrapreneur is the equivalent of settling for a warm body. People who volunteer will always be more desirable than people who are in the position under duress, but still they must reflect the company's values, bring loads of talent, and be motivated by the many challenges of successfully launching a startup.

Five of the listed pretenders – the Eager Innovator, Enthusiastic Product Developer, Excited Business Development Manager, Efficient Process Improvement Leader, and Individual High Performer – are all engaged and motivated contributors who find novel solutions to real problems. They think nothing of going beyond their basic job description to research how innovations can be applied to real market problems. Because they are excited about their discoveries and the business potential, they get others motivated as well. In fact, their strong belief in the business opportunity and their perseverance in being heard attract the interest of CoreCo's executives and make them excited too. At the very least, people who fit these five categories are NewCo subject matter experts who should be encouraged, credited, and rewarded for their efforts. But the reward should never be placing them in charge of launching the startup if they have not demonstrated the intrapreneurial skills and characteristics discussed in labor 1. These pretenders should be given the chance to apply, but only if they have been objectively evaluated as possessing the knowledge, skills, and abilities demanded by the job.

I have witnessed companies appoint subject matter experts as NewCo leaders under the guise of rewarding them or giving them a chance to prove themselves. The real reason they were assigned, however, was the intrapreneur quick fix. Without a clear plan in place to identify and groom potential intrapreneurs, the company's HR and business leaders took a chance on a keen employee who displayed enough intrapreneurial qualities to persuade CoreCo's leaders that the startup was in good hands. Without a doubt, they *wanted* to be persuaded. I have even seen cases where the employee felt unqualified, but after some coaxing and cheerleading from HR and the sponsor decided to jump in anyway.

The bottom line is that NewCos are not launched to train employees to become business leaders. Certainly the intrapreneur will learn a tremendous amount as NewCo's leader, but to be chosen in the first place he must have relevant experience. It is too big a gamble to assume that an employee can create a prosperous NewCo without having a track record of successfully working across the organization and leading major change within CoreCo, and without having demonstrated business savvy, an aptitude for understanding customer requirements, and the ability to work with customers to solve their issues. A gamble that fails and leads to NewCo's demise will also have a seriously negative impact on the employee's career and self-confidence.

If your company does not yet have a robust system for identifying and developing intrapreneurs, at the very minimum the sponsor and HR business partner should use table 1.1 to create a checklist to evaluate potential candidates. As for the Eager Innovator, Enthusiastic Product Developer, Excited Business Development Manager, Efficient Process Improvement Leader, and Individual High Performer, why not assign them to work in NewCo? Their skills and expertise will benefit the qualified NewCo leader, who can help them develop by providing the opportunities and exposure that will fill in the gaps in their qualifications. One day these pretenders might be the leaders of future NewCos.

The Willing Entrepreneur

A different kind of quick fix is to hand over NewCo to a successful independent entrepreneur, who I refer to as the willing entrepreneur. As you know by now, there are profound differences between an entrepreneur and an intrapreneur. Even if CoreCo's executives have some knowledge of these differences, they too often overlook them to everyone's peril. Entrepreneurs similarly prefer to turn a blind eye to the possibility they might not be suited to lead their company now that CoreCo has acquired it or to lead a startup situated within a corporation. They believe they can walk into the corporate world and achieve the same success they had on their own. This is partly based on their assumption that they will have access to more funding and resources while enjoying the same latitude and flexibility that served them so well as independent entrepreneurs.

The times I have seen a willing entrepreneur join a corporation via an acquisition and not survive for long are too many to count. To compound the situation, instead of learning from these failures, some companies assume that the problem was with the entrepreneur and immediately replace the departing face with a fresh one, only to experience the same struggle all over again. It may not surprise you to learn that the "failed" entrepreneur, once he is back in the world, very often is able to successfully launch yet another startup, far away from CoreCo's constraints.

This is not to say that a successful entrepreneur can never lead a NewCo. If the acquired candidate assesses favorably against the criteria listed in table 1.1, he should absolutely be considered. Just remember that basing the appointment on past success at running an independent startup is not the way to go, as it in no way predicts future success as a corporate intrapreneur. This is because an entrepreneur who launched a business and grew it into an attractive acquisition did so in part because he was solely accountable for making all the decisions about growing the business. Entrepreneurs tend to revel in their autonomy. Until later in the game, when larger sources of funding are needed and investors are acquired who demand some accountability and wish to influence strategic decisions, they answer only to themselves for operational decision making, budgetary allocations, and spending, and they like it that way. This is in sharp contrast to an intrapreneur, who invariably faces some limitations regarding how he executes his strategy. CoreCo may offer significant leeway, but never as much as the entrepreneur is happily used to.

The following is a typical scenario: Upon joining a large corporation via an acquisition, the entrepreneur clashes with CoreCo's leaders. It turns out there is incompatibility between the entrepreneur's ego and the corporation's governance policies. This ego-governance clash is a common occurrence because neither the entrepreneur's personal needs nor the corporation's governance policies were discussed thoroughly during contract negotiations. Instead, both sides focused on getting the deal done. Uppermost in the entrepreneur's mind was to retain the roles, responsibilities, and autonomy that had made him successful, met his personal objectives, and nourished his ego. For its part, the corporation's sole interest was to retain the entrepreneur in order to benefit from his market insights, customer relationships, and in-depth operational know-how.

In this type of scenario the entrepreneur agrees to the terms and conditions of the sale of his business to CoreCo and includes demands to remain at the head of the business. Having previously experienced tremendous autonomy, he simply cannot imagine having to negotiate with other leaders regarding funding, resources, support, or any important decisions at all. On the flip side, CoreCo is in a hurry to close the deal and submits to the entrepreneur's demands.

However, CoreCo has managed not to clarify the level of autonomy the entrepreneur will be granted, or more precisely, the degree to which autonomy will be limited by existing corporate policies and procedures. To convince the entrepreneur to sell, CoreCo emphasized the availability of high levels of resources, funding, and CFMs, all of which, they promised, will accelerate the entrepreneur's ability to achieve his vision. He believes a win-win is achievable because along with the financial reward of selling his business, he will reap the intrinsic reward of achieving the vision that motivated him to launch the startup in the first place.

Unfortunately, he has underestimated the consequences of where the buck now stops: it used to stop with him, but since signing the contract it stops with someone else. This subtle shift in accountability results in a major shift in power, and before long the entrepreneur is saying his goodbyes. Of course, it is not only the former independent entrepreneur who experiences this kind of difficulty. The acquired company's chief technology officer and the heads of sales, marketing, and product development can equally feel too restricted and resentful.

Let's imagine that the entrepreneur is still looking forward to this new business opportunity. His optimism evaporates when he realizes that his autonomy has dramatically shrunk. In the first phase of his integration he is made aware of the rules of business as defined by CoreCo's governance directives, business processes, corporate guidelines, and codes of conduct. Before long it becomes painfully clear that what the entrepreneur seeks to achieve and how he plans to achieve it conflicts with the priorities and systems of CoreCo's divisional and functional leaders.

The entrepreneur begins several struggles, for example, adjusting to CoreCo's slower decision making, reconciling himself to spending more time conducting internal reporting and attending meetings instead of being directly involved in customer activities, and getting used to seeking approvals from other CoreCo functional leaders. In short, the entrepreneur needs to accept that he and his team must bend to the new demands and constraints placed on them by CoreCo managers who are focused on accomplishing their integration goals and are looking for operational efficiencies.

The entrepreneur who survives this first phase assumes that his efforts will be rewarded by the flow of incredible benefits to NewCo. When this happens he might successfully transition into his new role of intrapreneur and continue to grow NewCo. When no such benefits accrue, the entrepreneur's struggle escalates as he experiences slower decision making due to the need for more approvals, manpower redundancies that lead to layoffs, the transfer of work from "his" company to a larger CoreCo function, and the imposition of new corporate policies relating to IT, financial reporting systems, purchasing controls, HR hiring and retention practices, legal and contract structures, and other CoreCo business processes. These changes can leave the entrepreneur so frustrated and disheartened that he does not make the shift to intrapreneurship, and this ultimately puts NewCo in a precarious position.

There is no magic bullet that can solve this situation. The former independent entrepreneur must manage his expectations by being more realistic about what will change personally and professionally as his business is integrated into the corporation. The corporation, on the other hand, while taking advantage of the wealth of knowledge and influence the entrepreneur has accumulated, must be more transparent about what he can expect as a CoreCo employee. It must also try harder to create a more attractive situation for him. This means not only recognizing his desire to see his vision through, but finding ways to satisfy, at least to some extent, his ego. Making sure the agreement covers the range of these concerns is basic risk mitigation.

Some of you may be thinking, "Shouldn't this have been uncovered and documented during the due diligence phase prior to the acquisition?" Yes, it should have. But the reality is often very different. Many of the world's largest consulting firms have produced studies that show the culprit behind the failure of a large number of acquisitions is poorly conducted due diligence activities.

Intrapreneurship Is a Full-Time Job

One final quick-fix trap to avoid is to appoint a part-time intrapreneur who continues with his CoreCo responsibilities while taking on the leadership of NewCo. This trap occurs when CoreCo's leaders assume that the members of NewCo's small team could not possibly be as busy as their CoreCo colleagues, who are managing much larger P&Ls, departmental budgets, and resources. This kind of thinking stems from an entrenched belief that permeates many large corporations, which imagine that level of activity is directly proportional to an organization's budget size and number of employees. It is a false correlation. People who have not worked in a startup environment have no idea what is involved in launching a new business.

With minimal resources to count on – very little infrastructure and few people, if any, to delegate to – the corporate startup team has to do everything themselves, and soon everyone is accustomed to wearing several hats. As tasks arise, new processes must be defined on the spot. This can become a frustratingly time-consuming exercise when CoreCo department leaders are resistant to developing new approaches to address NewCo's business activities. Add to this the unfortunate reality that the CoreCo functions who are tasked to support NewCo tend to prioritize the core business, which they view as their primary responsibility, and relegate NewCo's needs to the back burner.

I have worked in all the key areas of a large corporation and led major change initiatives. I have managed CoreCo organizations with several hundred employees, and I can tell you that I was never busier than when leading the launch of a new business with a tiny fraction of those employees. If you are the sponsor of a startup, do not think that NewCo can be a part-time assignment added to the intrapreneur's CoreCo role. This would be a gross underestimation of the work that needs to be done. Part-time intrapreneurs deliver part-time results and make part-time progress. Just prior to the formal launch, free up your intrapreneur completely so he can be 100 percent dedicated to NewCo.

COMING UP NEXT.....................

Now that the intrapreneur has been rigorously assessed against objective criteria and his appointment has been properly timed, the next step in preparing for NewCo's formal launch is to ensure that two CoreCo leaders with clout are assigned to support him.

The first is the sponsor, who we met briefly in the last chapter but whose role warrants much more discussion. The second is the gatekeeper. These two key appointments, along with other important allies, are the topics of labor 3.

The Hind of Ceryneia

Hercules' challenging third labor was to bring King Eurystheus the hind of Ceryneia. An unusually beautiful deer with golden horns and hooves of bronze, the hind was so swift that it could outrun even the fastest arrow. Hercules knew he must take special care with this labor because the hind was sacred to Artemis, the goddess of the hunt, and he was fearful of incurring her wrath. After tracking the animal for one year Hercules was finally able to wound and capture it. He draped it over his shoulders and began his journey homeward. Along the way he was confronted by Artemis, who became very angry. Hercules pleaded with her and told her about the oracle and his many labors. Taking pity on him, Artemis gave Hercules permission to carry the hind to the king.

LABOR 3

The Sponsor, the Gatekeeper, and the Allies Needed to Survive

Intrapreneurship is a team sport. As we already know, the intrapreneur is the intrepid leader who takes full responsibility for the trajectory of NewCo. But the truth is, he cannot achieve his goals alone. Having the help of influential supporters within CoreCo is crucial to transforming the innovation into a profitable business. Equally crucial is identifying allies within the corporation who are invested in NewCo's positive outcome. We can compare the intrapreneur's third labor to the third task completed by Hercules, when the help of Artemis made the difference between success and failure.

It would be naive to believe that in a corporate environment everyone will be in favor of launching NewCo. Certainly there will be a large number of people who back the startup, but CoreCo will also be home to a contingent of doubters, detractors, naysayers, and downright resistors. There may even be a saboteur in the mix. Finding out who these people are is similar to Hercules' pursuit of the hind of Ceryneia in that they can be hard to track down. The intrapreneur's ability to identify the influential supporters, the allies, and the critics, and deal effectively with the latter, will be key to NewCo's survival.

Fortunately, NewCo's new leader has two trusted supporters to help him with this task: the CoreCo sponsor, who is accountable for NewCo's success, and the CoreCo gatekeeper, who is responsible for guarding NewCo against unwanted help and protecting it from unnecessary interventions by the corporation. The sponsor and gatekeeper also play a role in helping the intrapreneur secure new allies to the NewCo cause.

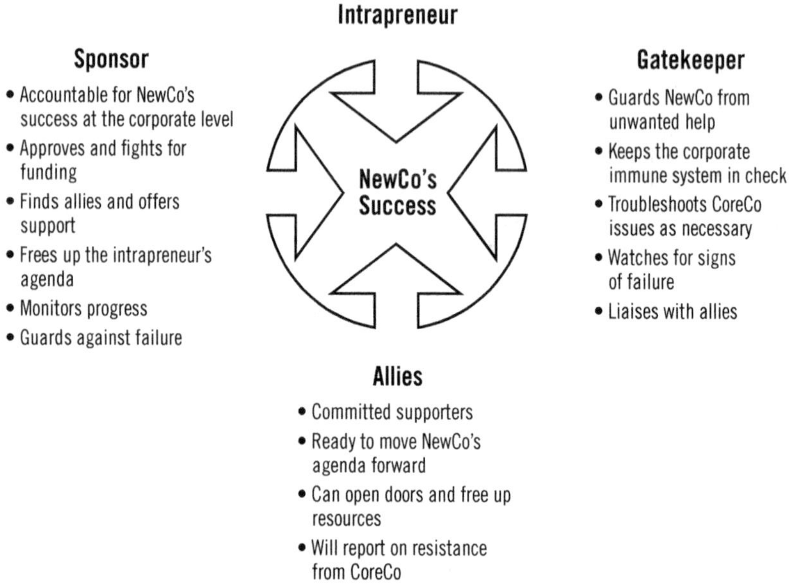
Intrapreneur
Sponsor
• Accountable for NewCo's success at the corporate level
• Approves and fights for funding
• Finds allies and offers support
• Frees up the intrapreneur's agenda
• Monitors progress
• Guards against failure
NewCo's Success
Gatekeeper
• Guards NewCo from unwanted help
• Keeps the corporate immune system in check
• Troubleshoots CoreCo issues as necessary
• Watches for signs of failure
• Liaises with allies
Allies
• Committed supporters
• Ready to move NewCo's agenda forward
• Can open doors and free up resources
• Will report on resistance from CoreCo

Figure 3.1 Roles of the Sponsor, the Gatekeeper, and the Key Allies

The Influential Sponsor

NewCo's sponsor is either self-appointed, meaning she is the CoreCo executive who made the strategic decision to create NewCo, or she is appointed by a senior executive within the company. This happens towards the end of the innovation process phase discussed in labor 1 and prior to the appointment of the intrapreneur. As the most senior executive at CoreCo who is directly involved in NewCo, she is in charge of selecting the intrapreneur and is accountable for the startup's s, setting the business objectives, and approving the budgets. If the sponsor initiated the transformation of the innovation into a NewCo, and if the new market is very different from CoreCo's, she might be the corporation's CEO or COO. If the startup falls within the market of an existing division, she might be the divisional president, general manager, or vice president. In come cases, when NewCo needs to be isolated from divisional bias and short-term financial or operational pressures, the chosen sponsor will be the leader of a centralized new business development organization that is independent of the company's other P&Ls or divisions.

There are various pros and cons to consider when deciding on the appointment of the sponsor. Here are some examples to help you clarify what will work best in your organization.

1. Several years ago we launched a technical support outsourcing service for our existing airline customers. Because its goal was to generate a new source of revenues for our division, the startup was established within the division and the sponsor was the divisional president. As one of the division's most senior executives, I volunteered to become the intrapreneur.

2. When launching an e-learning business line that offered simulation-based training solutions to our existing customers, I took on the role of sponsor and was responsible for appointing NewCo's intrapreneur. This made sense because the new line of business provided complementary solutions to customers we already knew well.

3. A few years later I was appointed by the CEO to be the intrapreneur for a healthcare business aimed at entering a completely new market. The startup would leverage our expertise in simulation and simulation-based training, and we decided it should be positioned outside existing P&Ls and divisions to shield it from interference. We placed it in the new business development and strategy group, whose executive vice president became the sponsor. NewCo's isolation allowed it to grow in size and financial materiality and to nurture a unique business culture that reflected the healthcare industry. Once it achieved critical mass and an attractive level of sales activities, it was transferred to report directly to the CEO.

The subject of where to place NewCo within the CoreCo organization is covered in labor 9. This is a challenging and very important decision, and is intricately linked with who is chosen to execute the role of sponsor. But there are other factors to consider when selecting the best sponsor. When it comes to ensuring NewCo's success, who has the biggest incentive? Who will make the time to support NewCo? Who is innovative and flexible enough to employ the business management techniques and measures of performance that are suitable to a startup environment, even if they fall outside CoreCo's usual practices? Who has the know-how and commitment to coach and develop the intrapreneur?

The role of the sponsor is to:

- Select the intrapreneur
- Communicate the objectives for setting up NewCo and ensure the intrapreneur remains aligned with them
- Approve and fight for funding
- Make sure the business objectives and strategic plan are progressing

- Determine that the measures of performance are suitable
- Spot behaviors or key decisions that might lead to failure
- Free up the intrapreneur's time from meetings that are not pertinent to NewCo's progress
- Work with the gatekeeper when CoreCo attempts to meddle or makes unrealistic requests
- Mentor the intrapreneur, for example, help him develop and refine his business acumen and leadership skills

Keeping the lines of communication open is imperative for NewCo's success. First and foremost this refers to communication between the sponsor, the intrapreneur, and the gatekeeper. If you are the sponsor, be careful not to rely on alternative channels to access information or opinions regarding the startup's progress. This is not to say that you are prohibited from informing yourself on matters related to NewCo. You are right to gather information from every credible source, but avoid allowing these sources to dictate how to best support NewCo, and never negotiate with them. All information should first be validated and discussed with the intrapreneur and gatekeeper, and final decisions must be left to the intrapreneur.

Alternative communication channels that bypass the intrapreneur and gatekeeper can result in unwanted political activity and give detractors too much access. As the sponsor, make sure that NewCo's leader and gatekeeper know that if your influence is required, they should not hesitate to ask for it. This is extremely important in the early stages, when the startup is struggling to remain independent from the company's other activities and when CoreCo's formal and informal rules regarding NewCo are being established.

A Gatekeeper with Clout

The *Merriam-Webster* dictionary defines a gatekeeper as "1. one who tends or guards a gate, and 2. a person who controls access." This exactly describes the role of the corporate gatekeeper, who invariably is a senior executive whose ideas and opinions carry real weight. The gatekeeper's primary task is to support NewCo by controlling access to it and barring access if necessary. He will be busiest when a high level of unwanted corporate interference is present. The gatekeeper's intervention can be triggered by his perception of unwanted or detrimental CoreCo activity or by receiving a report of such activity from the intrapreneur, the sponsor, or other allies. Regardless of the source of information, the gatekeeper should check with the intrapreneur prior to intervening to validate that an intervention is warranted and that he should be the one to carry it out.

The role of the gatekeeper is to:

- Aid the intrapreneur in vetting CoreCo departments that wish to "help with" NewCo
- Verify that functional assistance offered by CoreCo is actually necessary
- Make sure that groups granted access commit to adapting or inventing new business processes as required by NewCo
- Ensure that the sponsor and other senior executives allow NewCo to modify its strategic plan or execution as it adapts to lessons learned from its market
- Intervene with fellow CoreCo executives if resistance, sabotage, or inadequate support is perceived
- Work with the sponsor to spot and avoid potential for failure
- Be on the lookout for signs NewCo is isolating itself from CoreCo
- Coach NewCo's leadership team

The gatekeeper must be someone who is comfortable intervening when corporate stakes are high or internal politics are boiling over. In other words, his greatest asset is his clout. He gets his clout from the support he receives from the CEO or sponsor, who has granted him the authority to intervene as required, including approaching CoreCo's executive leadership team regarding, for example, roadblocks that were set up in HR. The gatekeeper's senior position makes him an ideal partner if the intrapreneur and sponsor need to recalibrate expectations. He can also be influential when it comes to securing funding and defending NewCo's separate and distinct status. The gatekeeper must have the unreserved support of the sponsor.

Although the gatekeeper's role does not qualify as a full-time job, his responsibilities are demanding. He can be called into action at any time and for any reason, from giving advice when not enough progress is being made in leveraging a CoreCo competency to handling interference that cannot be managed by the intrapreneur alone to neutralizing an overactive corporate immune system that is getting out of hand. Any number of internal threats to NewCo's survival might surface for which the intrapreneur will require the gatekeeper's intervention.

However, he cannot be someone who is overly political, because too political an approach often leads to compromises and reaching compromises is not in the job description. By trying to appease some colleagues and avoid creating friction with others, the political gatekeeper risks negotiating half-measures that can delay or even hurt NewCo's progress. His job is only about getting NewCo the support it needs, the way it needs it, when it needs it, so long as it is in line with NewCo's strategy. It is also about turning away any help that is unnecessary.

The stakes are high and the gatekeeper must be exactly that, a gatekeeper. He must watch out for internal threats so the intrapreneur does not have to, and instead can be free to focus on NewCo's external business realities. I am not suggesting that the intrapreneur should evade dealing with internal issues. On the contrary, as NewCo's leader he must be aware of each issue as it arises and tackle it. If his colleagues have learned to appreciate his role and mandate (labor 1) and he was thoroughly vetted before being chosen (labor 2), he should be well suited to addressing conflicts that come from inside the corporation, clarifying his role and responsibilities as needed, and securing the internal support so vital to NewCo's success. But the intrapreneur must feel no compunction about calling on the gatekeeper for support if an issue is taking too much of his focus from the business of running NewCo, or it becomes clear that the mediation of someone more senior is required for an issue to be resolved.

The Sponsor as Gatekeeper?

The role of sponsor should not be confused with that of gatekeeper. The sponsor is the senior executive who is responsible to CoreCo for NewCo's success. She typically approves the startup's budgets and is accountable for ensuring that NewCo's business results meet CoreCo's expectations. The gatekeeper handles interference and obstructions when asked by the intrapreneur to do so. Neither the sponsor nor the gatekeeper runs NewCo, but they watch over its operation to make certain it progresses in line with expectations.

There are situations when the sponsor might decide to also act as gatekeeper. I did this myself some years ago when we launched a new line of web-based simulation training solutions to augment our high-end and high-fidelity simulator solutions, an example I used earlier. Our market analysis also showed that the two products could be sold separately. We wanted to go directly to market but realized that web-based simulation training solutions required a sales channel, a financial model, after-sales support, and contractual terms that were different from what we were used to in our core business. I was the sponsor for that initiative and assessed that I could also fulfill the role of gatekeeper. I had the knowledge, operational know-how, influence, and understanding of possible internal roadblocks to execute both roles effectively.

As a general rule, however, the more a startup is projected to be financially material to CoreCo's overall results and the more it will require broader CoreCo support from departments that the sponsor does not directly manage and control, the more it will need a separate gatekeeper. Working together, the two should remember the following advice: every minute the intrapreneur spends internally at CoreCo is a crucial minute he is not devoting to NewCo's new customer base or to refining its offering and strategy. When in doubt about where the intrapreneur should spend his time, the gatekeeper and sponsor should encourage him to spend it with NewCo's customers.

The intrapreneur must focus on understanding the customers' needs and refining the offering.

When to Meet and How Often

The frequency of the meetings between the intrapreneur, the sponsor, and the gatekeeper is a function of the importance of NewCo's success to CoreCo's overall results. How senior executives assign their precious time sends a very strong message to the rest of CoreCo's leadership team, who will conclude that the sponsor and gatekeeper are having regular meetings with the startup's intrapreneur for a very good reason. The message is a simple one. If NewCo's success is important for the sponsor and gatekeeper, then it must be important for everyone else in the organization.

How often these meetings take place should not be related to NewCo's modest size. This is a common mistake you would be wise to avoid. In the pre-launch and launch phases, a startup's size is dwarfed by the size of the sponsor's other divisions, businesses, and core functions. But it is precisely when NewCo is small and struggling to establish itself – and therefore existing in a higher state of flux – that the sponsor and gatekeeper need to support it the most.

To provide the right level of support, which the sponsor and gatekeeper can do only if they are grounded in NewCo's evolving reality and have a clear grasp of the issues and challenges, they need to meet regularly with the intrapreneur to hear his perspectives, whether on the new market or the customers' receptivity to the value proposition. In addition, these meetings are an opportune time for the sponsor and gatekeeper to provide the intrapreneur with feedback from their own internal networks, perhaps regarding potential risks to NewCo the intrapreneur may not be aware of. A weekly 45-minute meeting should do the trick.

Items on the agenda might include:

1. **Recent successes.** Many leaders are reluctant to talk about achievements that might be considered small in the grand scheme of things, but it is important from an information standpoint and also for morale that the intrapreneur become comfortable speaking about NewCo's successes, no matter how modest.

2. **Recent unexpected roadblocks.** The intrapreneur might feel reluctant to mention roadblocks, worried that talking about colleagues or superiors who are failing to provide the agreed-upon support puts him at fault for not handling the situation properly. But with the goal of keeping NewCo's progress on track, the sponsor should encourage the intrapreneur to describe any major difficulties and how they were dealt with, and the gatekeeper should not hesitate to remind the intrapreneur that he is ready to help.

3. **Is NewCo getting all the assistance it needs? Is the sponsor's input required?** These key questions reinforce the point that the sponsor is on hand to provide help and support. Most CoreCos juggle numerous priorities, and the sponsor must see to it that NewCo's needs do not fall to the bottom of the priority list.

4. **Customer reaction to the innovation/business idea.** It is important for the intrapreneur to share customer feedback so the sponsor can be aware of a possible need to adapt and modify NewCo's strategy in the future.

5. **New key points.** By sharing what he has learned about the new business, the intrapreneur not only keeps the sponsor and gatekeeper up to speed, he deepens their knowledge of the ways the startup differs from the core business, which will be crucial when the time comes to provide support that is different from what CoreCo is used to. Throughout this book I will continue to stress the need to encourage learning in every phase of a corporate startup.

Three main criteria must be kept in mind for these meetings to be successful. First, they should be informal in nature and not require the intrapreneur to prepare a presentation in advance. The last thing the busy intrapreneur wants or needs is to spend time preparing PowerPoint slides and updating spreadsheets. Discussions on business objectives such as financials, sales pipelines, budgets, and KPIs are out of the question. There will be plenty of time to explore these topics at the more formal meetings that will be part of NewCo's meeting governance in the future, which we look at in the book's final chapter on page 232. Second, everyone must attend the meetings: sponsor, gatekeeper, and intrapreneur. It is essential for these three central players to remain on the same page. Third, I cannot overemphasize the importance of providing the intrapreneur with a safe environment where he can have open exchanges with the sponsor and gatekeeper without fear of judgment or retribution, particularly if the news is difficult.

Genuine Allies Are Welcome

Hercules could not have executed his 12 labors without the help of numerous gods, goddesses, and mortals. The intrapreneur needs the same kind of wide-ranging and reliable support from various allies within CoreCo. By allies, I mean formal and informal leaders throughout the organization who can be instrumental in moving NewCo's agenda forward, freeing up resources, and influencing others to become engaged in NewCo's mission. Allies, by definition, are stalwart supporters of NewCo.

They play two vital roles. First, they are the advocates who are ready to go above and beyond the call of duty to help NewCo succeed, despite facing their own corporate limitations such as budget cutbacks, resource restrictions, and time pressures. Because of their numbers and passionate commitment, they are the perfect emissaries for NewCo and can be effective at positively influencing the people within CoreCo who determine how well NewCo will be supported. They can also be persuasive when other CoreCo employees are needed to execute the corporate force multipliers strategy.

Second, allies are the eyes and ears of NewCo within CoreCo. When they become aware of resistance within the corporation or spot a saboteur, they try to redress the situation and, if necessary, hurry to warn the intrapreneur or gatekeeper before the resistance creates too much damage. As we know, there will always be someone in CoreCo, and maybe more than one, who will refuse to embrace the idea of NewCo. The expression "forewarned is forearmed" comes to mind. Like Artemis with the hind of Ceryneia, the sympathy and helpfulness of allies play a significant part in the intrapreneur being able to complete his labors.

Allies you want include the CFO and the head of HR. Others who will prove valuable, depending on the type of market NewCo is entering, are CoreCo's heads of legal and contracts, marketing, product development, and engineering. Finally, if you plan on entering a specific geographic region, you probably want to engage the general manager or vice president responsible for that region. He or she should be able to open doors for you. Allies are the unsung heroes of NewCo's success, and it is up to the intrapreneur to make sure they do not remain unsung. They must be rewarded along the way and their contributions trumpeted. Remember the emphasis I placed on teamwork in labor 1? This is where it comes in.

Celebrate Often

Sometimes NewCo's leader will feel alone, especially when faced with difficult decisions. If you are that leader, do not let this isolate you from your team and your allies within CoreCo. Take the time to validate your ideas with the people who support you and want NewCo to succeed. Always remember that NewCo's success not only depends on gaining traction in its market, it requires gaining acceptance in CoreCo. For this reason celebrate often and give others credit for their contributions. Even the smallest successes, especially in the early days, should be applauded. This lets people know that progress is being made, promotes a sense of accomplishment, and builds stronger team dynamics.

COMING UP NEXT....................

With the undertaking of labors 1, 2, and 3, three critical roles have been filled, ensuring that a powerful triad – made up of the intrapreneur, the sponsor, and the gatekeeper – is in place that is well qualified to lead and support the corporate startup.

By building this strong team, CoreCo has demonstrated its ability to bet on A-type leaders to bring its innovation to market. Now is the time to confirm that realistic expectations have been set.

Labor 4 demands that CoreCo replace preconceived notions of performance associated with successfully managing and growing an existing business with an approach that is suitable when launching and growing a startup. Even the sponsor may have to modify her ideas. Providing clear objectives to everyone concerned will set NewCo up to succeed.

The Erymanthian Boar

For his fourth labor Hercules was ordered by King Eurystheus to bring him the fearsome Erymanthian boar, which descended from Mount Erymanthus every day to strike fear into the local villagers and destroy everything in its path. Uncertain how to proceed, Hercules approached his old friend Chiron, a kindly and wise centaur, to seek advice on capturing the boar alive. As instructed by Chiron, he chased it around the mountain until it was so frightened and tired it hid behind a tangle of bushes. He then used his spear to drive it into deep snow, where it became trapped. Hercules captured the boar with a net and brought it back to the king.

LABOR 4

Creating and Mastering Expectations

During the weeks leading up to the launch, NewCo will receive increasing levels of exposure within CoreCo. In an ideal world the intrapreneur's elevator pitch will do its job and the leaders of various departments and their teams will understand the startup's objectives. But it is never an ideal world. In the real world some or many of CoreCo's business leaders and team members will have misheard the elevator speech based on their own biases or needs. They will have walked away with perceptions that will grow into expectations that bear little or no resemblance to NewCo's actual objectives. Perhaps their expectations relate to the benefits they will derive from NewCo or the contributions they might be asked to make. Almost certainly they will conflict with other unrealistic expectations that are floating around the organization.

The intrapreneur needs to be aware of inaccurate expectations early so he can manage them. If he fails in this labor, they may morph into monsters that create havoc at inconvenient junctures, and he will waste a lot of time chasing them down in the hopes of correcting them. He will begin to feel like Hercules running after the Erymanthian boar. But like Hercules, he can corner and tame them with a plan. As its first task the plan must identify the different types of expectations and then strategize on how to address them and effectively communicate the relevant ones. I have found that corporate startups typically face three categories of expectations: formal, informal, and perceived.

Formal Expectations

In most cases a startup's formal expectations, also called objectives, are specified early in the game by the sponsor, who uses them in her initial meetings with CoreCo, hoping that CoreCo will agree to invest its limited time, money, resources, and management efforts in the new business. They are also invaluable when crafting the elevator speech. After the launch the sponsor uses them again to measure NewCo's success and therefore the intrapreneur's and her own success. Formal expectations are also an important weapon when it comes to fending off informal and perceived expectations that will spring up in any number of locations in CoreCo's upper echelons.

The intrapreneur needs to be aware of CoreCo's formal expectations from the earliest possible date. If they were not given to him by the sponsor, he can find them in a variety of documents that were created back in the beginning, possibly as early as the strategic planning or idea generation phase, when CoreCo first drew up its list of interesting ideas. These were then whittled down during the innovation process to a handful of the most attractive ones. What would eventually become NewCo was selected as the top prospect because it was assessed as having the highest potential for making a financial contribution to the company's top and bottom lines while carrying an acceptable level of risk.

The strategic plan created by CoreCo during the innovation process likely contains an overview of the formal expectations. They may also reside in the document used by the company's innovation group to track various ideas. Or they may be in the summary presentation made to the management team or to CoreCo's board of directors when seeking approval to establish NewCo. They may even be found in the sponsor's performance objectives, because the sponsor is held accountable for delivering on NewCo's strategic promise. If you are the intrapreneur and you have not yet reviewed any of these documents, do so immediately. Without them you are already a step behind.

Setting SMART Objectives

Once the formal expectations have been located they need to be properly documented. According to best practices on business objectives, they should be SMART, meaning Specific, Measurable, Attainable, Relevant, and Time-bound. SMART became a popular tool in project management and employee performance management following an article written in *Management Review* by business consultant George Doran in 1981, though the criteria are widely attributed to a concept developed in 1954 by Peter Drucker called management by objectives. It remains an excellent tool that the intrapreneur would be wise to use.

The next step is for the intrapreneur and sponsor to meet to discuss and agree on the SMART objectives. Working together they will further refine them to achieve ultimate specificity. This will eliminate misunderstandings during future performance evaluations. At this stage the intrapreneur must be as proactive as it gets, because achieving crystal-clear clarity about NewCo's objectives will allow him to successfully construct a detailed NewCo strategy from CoreCo's original strategy, which was actually more of a framework. He will also begin to refine a business model that will eventually meet CoreCo's expectations regarding performance metrics such as revenue, profit, market share, return on investment, sales objectives, cost of goods sold, return on assets, return on capital, and contribution to earnings per share.

The most difficult issue for CoreCo when setting objectives for its startup is to refrain from copying the objectives it uses to track its established businesses. They are almost certainly unsuitable for an early-stage NewCo. The line of thinking among CoreCo executives goes like this: "If our business objectives are good enough for CoreCo's main businesses, why aren't they good enough for the startup?" The answer is fairly straightforward. CoreCo is a long-standing business that is efficient and profitable, with an established culture and an approach to setting business objectives that has been fine-tuned and validated over years or decades of operations. NewCo is a small, unproven startup with an immature business model and a product that has yet to be tracked. These are two very different animals.

My experience launching several NewCos is that a great deal of learning goes on in the early post-launch phase that is invaluable for understanding how to succeed in the new market over the long-term. (I discuss this phase at length in labor 7.) With this in mind, tracking a corporate startup's progress in its first 18 to 24 months must be less about P&Ls and more about validating the new product or service, gaining customer insights, and achieving a deeper knowledge of the market. Other activities that are critical following the launch of NewCo include confirming key assumptions with customers, figuring out how the product will make money, developing distribution channels, hiring core positions, and updating budgetary projections as new insights are gained.

Prior to the launch of NewCo, the intrapreneur and sponsor must tackle the following formal expectations and agree on an unambiguous definition of each one:

- NewCo's mission, strategic intent, and goals (the output of the ABS model covered in the last chapter on page 234)
- A budget for the first three years and a commitment to reviewing it on a quarterly basis with the goal of adapting to the learning taking place
- KPIs and other metrics to track NewCo's progress during each gMmilestones to track the learning that is expected along the way
- A set of limited reporting requirements and formats that reflect NewCo's startup status (more on this in labor 7)
- The roles of the sponsor and gatekeeper (if the gatekeeper has not been assigned, agreement on who that person will be)
- The assignment and transfer of specific resources (talent) from CoreCo to NewCo and the authority to hire key positions from outside CoreCo when necessary
- The corporate force multiplier (CFM) strategy, or if this is premature, a general appreciation of what will be required from CoreCo with an agreement to refine the requirements at a later date (for more information about CFMs see labor 10)
- The level of management and decision-making autonomy that will be given to NewCo's intrapreneur

Making Startup Objectives Relevant

Of the five SMART criteria for setting objectives, the R, for being relevant, can be a challenge for a corporate startup. The problem is that NewCo is often launched into an area that CoreCo does not really comprehend. Nonetheless, CoreCo develops assumptions regarding NewCo's market, and whether or not they are relevant, these assumptions greatly influence its view on how to grow NewCo effectively, how NewCo will make money, what makes NewCo's customers tick, and how NewCo competitors will behave.

There is a way for CoreCo to properly assess how similar, or more importantly dissimilar, the new market is to its existing core market, as you will see in labor 8. It is of fundamental importance that CoreCo recognize the dissimilarities. The more a new business resembles its parent's core business, the more inclined the corporation is to assume it can reuse the performance metrics associated with its existing business model. In other words, it may believe, in many cases wrongly, that it knows exactly which performance metrics to impose on NewCo via the objectives, and that this will make the new business successful. A sponsor who is unaware of the differences between the startup and parent will impose objectives that are irrelevant to NewCo. When this happens the intrapreneur has to work extremely hard to correct metrics that are wrong. The result of all that hard work? Valuable time is lost.

A venture I was involved with in aviation pilot training provides an example of the challenges of getting relevance right. Early on we set aggressive revenue growth targets that were premised on assumptions we had made about increasing the number of hours our flight simulators had to be in service. These assumptions came from the perspective of the parent company, which was used to dealing with performance metrics based on manufacturing asset utilization, as well as from external benchmarking on simulator leasing (we benchmarked other industry players to determine a simulator usage target, then we established that target as one of our KPIs). We set a primary KPI that tracked optimized simulator usage time and devised a reporting system that showed weekly simulator usage as a percentage of hours of operations versus total available simulator time.

Sales incentive plans were created that essentially rewarded salespeople for signing up customers to lease our assets. We quickly realized it would be a struggle to meet return on capital employed (ROCE) and return on net assets (RONA) targets. Evidently, in this new line of business the revenue and profit generated per asset mattered more than hourly usage. This was because one asset could get more usage, but at a much lower hourly revenue rate than another asset that was not running as often but generated more money for the business. Our primary KPI led us to develop a sales incentive plan that focused on selling simulator time rather than generating the most revenue per device.

This realization allowed us to shift our mindset from simply filling simulator time to creating activities that would generate higher revenues. We added pilot-training packages, got busy upselling our instructional system design capabilities, included classroom time and the use of our quality management programs, and handled regulatory approval requirements. The result was a new set of offerings that took the focus from leasing simulator time and put it on selling higher-value activities. This led to higher-priced training events and considerably more revenue per hour. We learned that while the original KPI used to track simulator usage was important, it needed to be coupled with an even more critical KPI: the average revenue per simulator hour.

Similarly, our simulator usage was being tracked against a baseline of 16 hours of availability per day. This was a carryover from our manufacturing culture, which ran two eight-hour shifts every day. We eventually realized that pilots could train the way they fly, meaning at all hours of the day or night. By adjusting our baseline measurement to reflect this we were able to drive more simulator usage over a 24-hour period.

These two examples demonstrate that all too easily CoreCo's realities can result in the use of metrics that ineffectively, and sometimes wastefully, track NewCo's success. If you are a member of CoreCo's executive team, give the people at NewCo leeway to validate whether the established KPIs are relevant to the new business or not. If they are irrelevant, it is best to realize this early on. Relevant KPIs are essential to getting NewCo to focus on the right issues and develop the right business model and revenue-generating engines.

Here are two common examples of objectives being set poorly due to missing the R in SMART. The first relates to R&D and product development expenditures. CoreCo may have well-established business metrics that include how R&D expenditures are set as a percentage of total revenue. These percentages have been validated to work for CoreCo, yet they become the baseline for NewCo. A benevolent executive might add an extra 10 or 20 percent of funding to the base metric in recognition of NewCo's needs, but that number is likely irrelevant.

As a startup, NewCo requires a very large percentage of its expenses assigned to R&D and product development, certainly much larger than the ratios CoreCo is used to in its core businesses. This is because NewCo's innovative solution requires significant prototyping, testing, and customer validations before making it to the marketplace. NewCo must estimate its R&D and product development needs on a stand-alone basis using an activity-based costing approach. Then it must set the targets appropriately.

In every NewCo I have worked in, I have battled this corporate mindset surrounding R&D and product development funding. Each time, as a consequence of having to convince the corporate parent to adequately fund the work required, we faced serious delays. In some cases our first-to-market strategy was hurt, which had a negative impact on our revenue growth and profit margin projections. All this can be avoided if the sponsor appreciates the differences between the startup and parent and vigorously defends NewCo's budgets.

The other common budgeting battle that impacts the setting of objectives is marketing expenses. In my view this is the most underestimated and undervalued aspect of NewCo budgeting. When it comes to assigning NewCo's marketing expenses, CoreCo is again tempted to use percentages similar to the ones it applies to its mature businesses. These can take various forms such as a percentage of sales, percentage of cost of goods, or percentage of total costs. It seems obvious that taking this approach leads to grossly underestimating the budgeting needs of a startup, but CoreCo will be tempted to take it anyway.

This underestimation can be exacerbated by the degree of variation between NewCo's market and CoreCo's. CoreCo is a running business with a recognized brand, a well-known suite of products or services, a good understanding of the marketing activities that generate better returns, an established credibility, and a generally healthy and mature marketing ecosystem. Naturally, its annual marketing budget reflects all of the above.

NewCo's marketing environment is a far cry from CoreCo's. As a startup it is still establishing its presence in the new market and must position its product or service with a new customer base. On top of this, it must conduct tests to validate its go-to-market strategy, which requires additional marketing efforts. In some cases even further marketing is necessary to distinguish the startup from the parent company to avoid any confusion in the marketplace. Considering NewCo's need to establish its own distinct identity, it makes sense to approve and fund broader marketing activities than CoreCo is used to. NewCo's marketing budgets must reflect these differences in business reality. Starting with metrics from CoreCo's business model is simply not going to work.

There are many other examples of objective-setting that can get NewCo in trouble early, such as determining initial targets for cost of sales or cost of goods sold when your new product or service is still immature, or adopting quality metrics that are irrelevant in a startup environment, where validating the prototype with early adopters occurs frequently. Everyone involved must take the time to make certain that the selected objectives are relevant to whichever phase the startup is in. The best way to test their relevance is to determine which metric or KPI will be used to calculate progress and assess success.

Miscalculating Time-Bound

The other letter in SMART that can cause difficulty for a corporate startup is the T, for Time-bound. As with Relevant, it is an excellent idea to get Time-bound right. Even the most relevant objectives can end in major confusion if the time element is improperly set.

In the world of business everyone knows the expression "time is money." In fact, time and patience are rare commodities in the corporate world. Business leaders generally have short horizons, especially in North American companies. I have extensive experience in Asia, South America, and Europe, where a more long-term view of business investments is the norm because value is measured with a longer horizon in mind. But regardless of the valuation of time, every startup is given a timeline for results.

Unrealistically short time expectations for your SMART objectives will lead the intrapreneur to strive to achieve a business objective earlier than should be reasonably expected for a startup. What the intrapreneur actually needs is enough time to focus on urgent issues. Without clear and reasonable guidance from the sponsor, time expectations that are too short will result in a lack of focus and poor prioritizing of business activities. The last thing the intrapreneur wants is to be under the impression that a medium- or longer-term goal was set when CoreCo's executives are thinking short-term.

Another expression that might be less well known is "time kills all deals." Launching a new business within a corporation is the outcome of a deal made with the parent company, which believes that investing in this new venture will lead to financial gains. Once the deal is made the clock starts ticking, and too much time is a killer. The sponsor must be careful not to be so generous with CoreCo's time expectations as to diminish the intrapreneur's sense of urgency.

The Time-bound aspect of SMART is usually what gets the discussions going when the sponsor and intrapreneur negotiate objectives. In most cases the sponsor will not simply be guessing, she will be starting with assumptions that were set by her CoreCo business development and financial teams, which will have simulated the projections for the startup's revenues and costs. They will probably have completed a SWOT analysis (Strengths-Weaknesses-Opportunities-Threats) to achieve a general understanding of the competitive landscape and how to differentiate NewCo. They may even have added provisions to their cost assumptions that allow the intrapreneur some wiggle room. To their way of thinking, they have given NewCo a comfortable plan with plenty of cushion and the breathing room needed to succeed.

Unfortunately, these assumptions were made by people who likely never worked in an intrapreneurial environment. Furthermore, they may know very little about the new market being targeted. Their expertise might come from their experience creating business cases for launching new or improved products or services that will replace aging ones, or launching incremental innovations within existing product lines. In both cases there are many fewer unknowns than with a startup.

Estimating the time element of NewCo's SMART objectives is a major challenge. What level of maturity is the NewCo product or service starting at? How ready is it to go to market? What growth assumptions were used for NewCo's early years? When are the first sales projected to take place? How quickly will the business become profitable? What discounted pricing was modeled to reflect the market penetration strategy? Which of CoreCo's resources are being leveraged? If these and other pivotal assumptions have not been thoroughly vetted, then the T in your not-so-SMART objective will become your business case's Achilles heel. NewCo will be labeled "not fast enough," I guarantee it. Do not get me wrong, this is not to imply that NewCo should be given a blank check, time-wise. Time pressures will always be part of the deal, but do not compound them by messing up the Time-bound aspects of the formal objectives.

The sponsor and intrapreneur can avoid this situation by tackling objective-setting in two steps. The first step is to identify the objectives that are relevant to each phase of the startup's growth without assigning them any value or time expectation. Once the appropriate objectives have been selected and validated (remember, do not select objectives from CoreCo just to make life easier), proceed to the second step: setting value and time expectations for each one. If you are not ready to give a value and time-based target to an objective, agree to do so at a later date when more data is available. Finally, if you discover later on that a previously set objective is not suitable for your startup, do not hesitate to modify or eliminate it.

A healthcare startup I led some years ago serves as an excellent example of underestimating the time aspect. Our assumptions about our sales projections were premised on what we knew of the aviation industry's buying cycle, augmented by anecdotal information from small companies operating in what was a completely new market for us. But our assumptions seemed sound, and we used them for setting dates for our first and subsequent sales, and for creating a forecast that covered the first 24 months of sales activities.

The reality proved to be very different. It took much longer than anticipated to book our first sales due to a) the longer buying cycles of hospitals and medical schools, b) the extended approval process of these customers (approvals had to make their way up through several layers of the organization), and c) a very different contracting methodology and process. It is an understatement to say that the resulting lengthy delays in achieving our first and subsequent sales placed additional pressures on the NewCo team.

In another example, our CoreCo established P&L targets for its new software business that were based on the corporation's core business of delivering large, sophisticated equipment to the defense and security sector. The original objectives for gross profit and operating income worked well for the core business, but were ill suited for a company that sold off-the-shelf software across several industries. This led the software business to focus on reducing expenses in the wrong areas, such as product development and marketing, selling, and distribution expenses, resulting in delays in product roadmap releases and broad product adoption. These targets were eventually modified to reflect the software industry business model, and in the end the proper focus on spending and cost controls was achieved.

Informal Expectations

Informal expectations have their origins in CoreCo's senior management team. They are undocumented and informal in nature, but they are very formal in the minds of the people making them. It is a miscalculation to let informal expectations linger. Unless they are promptly corralled and dealt with, they can cause real problems. Do not mistake them for the unrealistic expectations of leaders within CoreCo who are not part of the senior management team. Those are perception expectations and are addressed in the next section.

It is inevitable that in the course of agreeing to support NewCo, some CoreCo senior leaders made informal assumptions that over time they began to believe formed part of their agreement. No intrapreneur wants what happens next to happen to them: leaders communicate their mistaken assumptions to their subordinates as part of their debrief on what can be expected from NewCo, and of those subordinates, some misinterpret their leader's mistaken assumptions and leave the meeting with their own mistaken assumptions. Imagine putting out all those fires! Some examples of informal expectations include:

- The head of CoreCo's operations, typically a COO, assumes that NewCo will make full use of CoreCo's facilities and resources to get its work done. This is an attractive assumption because it allows her to build up the organization while spreading fixed costs to a new business.

- The vice president of manufacturing believes that NewCo's production work will not leverage CoreCo's existing facilities and resources, which is good news because his production line is already running at maximum capacity and no budget increase was announced to provide the funds needed by NewCo.
- The general manager of one of CoreCo's overseas territories believes that NewCo operations in his region will fall under his responsibility and proceeds to brief his team prematurely.
- The head of sales in a given territory assesses that NewCo's target customer base is the same as her existing base and consequently assumes that she will lead NewCo sales activities in her territory. She initiates customer meetings.
- Department heads assume they will be asked to support NewCo's efforts and they set about preparing budgets to cover additional costs related to resources, travel, and other expenses.

The behaviors and activities that are a consequence of informal expectations often occur without the intrapreneur's knowledge and can lead to significant confusion in CoreCo, NewCo, and with customers. The confusion creates distractions, inefficiencies, and conflicts, all of which result in delays, and valuable time is wasted in setting matters straight.

There are a few tools the intrapreneur can use that will expose and defeat these expectations. The first is a well-executed internal communications strategy. Its priority is to make certain that the formal expectations created for NewCo are frequently and effectively communicated as early as possible, meaning immediately prior to NewCo's launch or immediately after, or both. The second tool is the CFM strategy, which is thoroughly covered in labor 10. Through the CFM strategy, which precisely identifies how relevant parts of CoreCo can be leveraged, NewCo is able to take full advantage of selected CoreCo capabilities.

Perception Expectations

These are expectations held by people working below the senior management level who asked themselves, "What's in it for me?" A different variation has people worrying that NewCo's arrival will adversely affect their workload. Like informal expectations, perception expectations can quickly become firmly lodged in the minds of the people who hold them.

Some examples include:

- Assumptions made by the director of HR regarding the employee profiles best suited for NewCo
- The strategy the head of recruiting is developing for sourcing NewCo employees, which includes thoughts on how quickly they should be hired
- Beliefs held by the head of compensation and benefits regarding pay scales, compensation, and working conditions for the type of people NewCo will engage
- Conclusions reached by the manager of facilities about NewCo's workspace and whether NewCo's employees are to be squeezed into existing facilities or located in new ones
- The head of finance's conjecture that the same business reports she prepares for CoreCo will be expected for NewCo at the same frequency
- The regional head of sales for the West Coast thinking that a series of customer meetings should be set to introduce the intrapreneur and NewCo to potential clients, and that she will make commissions from NewCo sales

These assumptions are the tip of the iceberg. Because of the number of employees involved there are many more perception expectations than there are formal or informal ones, and they begin to take shape around the time of NewCo's launch, when every supervisor and manager with a connection to NewCo will make assumptions. Some will even start working on them. As with informal expectations, strong internal communications and well-articulated CFM strategies are key to avoiding the disorder and confusion that can result from perception expectations.

Internal Communications Strategy

When it comes to countering unclear formal expectations and unrealistic informal and perception expectations, the intrapreneur's best bet is to return to NewCo's formal expectations, which by the time of the launch should be expertly honed. He must be sure he understands them clearly and succinctly, and then his job is to refer to them as often as possible: in departmental meetings, during business update meetings with the sponsor, when establishing NewCo's priorities, and when deciding on budgeting and hiring.

Even as he is relentlessly conveying NewCo's objectives, the wise intrapreneur is executing a carefully thought-through internal communications strategy. This is an indispensable tool, although I was unaware of its existence when I was first involved with NewCos many years ago. But I should have known better given that clear and timely internal communications are at the heart of change management and organizational transformation, and successful intrapreneurship necessitates change and transformation, as we saw in the first chapter.

The internal communications strategy must be developed in the weeks leading up to the launch, even though the intrapreneur is unbelievably busy during that period. Regardless, it is crucial to the success of NewCo that he carve out the time to create a strategy that targets the corporation's major groups. At a minimum, this strategy should cover the key NewCo messages that must consistently be communicated to CoreCo, prioritize the CoreCo departments that must be approached, and select the communications tools that are best suited to each of those departments. He must also pay attention to the timing of ongoing communications activities.

At the top of his priority list is to prepare a compelling presentation. Similar to the elevator speech, it will have two parts, but it will be much longer, between 30 and 45 minutes. A third part is a Q&A that can last up to 45 minutes. The NewCo presentation should be delivered in an informal atmosphere that encourages dialogue and triggers questions. If carefully crafted and executed, the presentation and Q&A session will not only prevent innumerable future misunderstandings, it will bring informal and perception expectations to the surface that the intrapreneur can immediately address and put to rest. He will never be able to tackle every wrong expectation individually, but in broad terms he can make a serious dent.

The presentation's first 20 minutes is standard and should always be used, no matter who is in the room. As with the opening of the elevator speech, its goal is to engage the audience in NewCo's vision. But it must also inform. The intrapreneur must clearly articulate NewCo's purpose, business objectives, expected rollout, and benefits to CoreCo. He needs to explain the relevance of the new market being entered and why CoreCo thinks NewCo can be successful in it. Other points include which of the parent company's core competencies NewCo will leverage and a description of the prototype or product concept. If either is available, the intrapreneur should show it to make it real in the audience's mind. Then he should end with a sentence that describes NewCo's future once it is established and fulfilling its strategic promise, for example, "NewCo will be successful when we are the preferred supplier in our region." For help putting words to the future of your NewCo, complete the ABS model on page 234.

The second part of the presentation must be tailored to the circumstances of the audience. The goal is to summarize the major differences between NewCo and CoreCo regarding products and services, customers, and markets, and to give a rundown of any similarities or differences that are particularly relevant to the department being addressed. Because the issues to tackle could be endless, the intrapreneur needs to realize he cannot address them all. Here are some examples of what to include:

- Cultural differences between CoreCo's customer base and NewCo's new customers
- How NewCo's financial model differs from CoreCo's, for example, is NewCo planning on a high-volume—low-margin business, whereas CoreCo's is low-volume—high-margin?
- New regulatory hurdles, if any, that NewCo might face
- The contrast in operational models, for example, is NewCo moving away from operating on a project basis, as CoreCo does, and instead will use a product-based model?
- Plans for NewCo to enter new territories or countries where CoreCo has never sold or operated
- New employee skill sets or knowledge that will be required for NewCo, and where these candidates will be sourced
- NewCo's go-to-market strategy and differences between NewCo's and CoreCo's sales model and cycle
- NewCo's need to secure suppliers outside of CoreCo's supplier ecosystem, if this is the case

The intrapreneur needs to remember to make NewCo relevant to each CoreCo department. For example, when speaking with human resources, details should be provided on NewCo's staffing projections. The goal is to persuade the room to accept that CoreCo's HR systems and processes may not be appropriate for NewCo, and that new ones might be required, as well as a different recruitment ecosystem.

To get HR thinking along the right lines the presentation will need to address some of the following questions: What are the hiring projections for the first 18 months, and what are the rough estimates for months 19 to 36? Will these be internal or external recruits? If external, where will they be located geographically? What expertise will be required and is this expertise different from what HR looks for today? Are there expected differences in pay scales and compensation? What expectations will these new employees have regarding their work environment?

When briefing CoreCo's finance department, the intrapreneur must highlight how NewCo will make money and grow revenues and profits. Again, the goal is to paint a picture to help the leaders in finance identify where they will need to establish new systems and processes for conducting and tracking business, and where parts of the existing finance and accounting systems and processes might be perfectly suitable.

The finance audience will likely want answers to questions like these: What about the price points of NewCo's new products and services? How do customers typically pay? What kinds of project milestones are expected? Is information available on accounts receivable and accounts payable? What level of capital expenditures is projected? Will there be new requirements for conducting business transactions via a new channel, such as web-based transactions, with which CoreCo may have no prior experience? Might revenues be generated from new geographic locations?

If the first section of the presentation shows NewCo to be attractive and interesting and an effective bridge is made to each organization with the second part, the audience will leave the presentation convinced, or at least in a cautiously optimistic frame of mind. Some may have concluded that NewCo is an exciting initiative and worthy of support, and that it will not actually affect their day-to-day job. Others will go away thinking of how they can help and will be planning the moment they jump in.

The large majority of the people in your audience, however, will be pondering, even as you are talking, the impact NewCo will have on them personally or on their group. This is because the reality in today's business world is that most employees are overworked and have too few resources. People are regularly stretched to do more with less. They will not specifically be unsupportive of NewCo; rather, they will be searching for the path of least resistance.

New initiatives create new work without reducing the existing workload. When presented with the reality of NewCo, the vast majority of employees will rapidly conclude that the best way to deal with what they perceive as more work is to make better use of their department's systems and processes. Even before the meeting is over, most of your audience members will have convinced themselves that the right way to approach NewCo is to reuse what they already have and to enforce existing departmental systems and processes.

This is why the Q&A period of the NewCo presentation matters so much. It gives the intrapreneur the opportunity to reset expectations before anybody leaves the room. Besides coming to the meeting prepared to answer a lot of questions, he should arrive with a set of his own questions he can pose to trigger conversation when there is a lull. No matter who is asking the questions, his objective is to clarify how NewCo will need to be supported.

There is no need to worry if he cannot answer every question. The best leaders are not afraid to say, "I don't know," or "We don't have an answer for that yet, but when we do we'll let you know immediately." It is always better to tell people they will have an answer later than to give information that might be misleading. What the intrapreneur needs to remember as he describes NewCo's unique business reality is that his aim is to engage the audience in the startup's vision and to separate people in the room from any informal or perceived expectations they may be hanging on to.

"The single biggest problem with communication is the illusion that it has taken place." – George Bernard Shaw

Other Communications Tools

An internal CoreCo newsletter is a good vehicle for introducing aspects of NewCo and reinforcing key messages. The focus should be on clarifying how NewCo will interface with CoreCo, and of course garnering support is a perennial goal. If there are several newsletters published during the year, one topic should be emphasized per issue with priority given to topics that have a higher likelihood of creating confusion. Needless to say, always keep articles positive.

Another priority is to create a NewCo website for internal CoreCo use. It should feature a standard presentation that describes the basics about NewCo and include a list of frequently asked questions. Short videos can also be posted that show the CEO and sponsor explaining the decision to go with NewCo, its importance to CoreCo's growth, and how CoreCo intends to support the new startup. In addition, the decision to set up NewCo independently and the benefits of doing so can be clearly explained. The website can go a long distance to eliminating speculation.

You can be sure that no matter how well a presentation is received, most of the people in the audience will grasp only parts of it. They will leave with many questions and more questions will come to mind in the days that follow as they reflect on what was said. The intrapreneur needs to schedule follow-up meetings with individual departments, but only once they have had their own departmental management meeting after the presentation. He should also request that NewCo be added to the agenda of their meeting, and ask them to collect feedback from their team. The feedback can be used in discussions with departmental heads to answer questions, address concerns, and clarify misperceptions.

Internal Speaking Engagements

The minute NewCo is given the go-ahead the intrapreneur and his team will be extremely busy. They will not have enough time to do everything on their urgent priority list, let alone address CoreCo's departments in the first few weeks post-launch. The larger the corporation, the truer this will be. But the intrapreneur will have to squeeze in some meetings anyway. As we know by now, NewCo's success depends on constantly gauging and resetting expectations. To draw from *The 7 Habits of Highly Effective People*, a great book by Stephen Covey on time management, it is smart to deal with this very important but not especially urgent issue early on rather than risk having crises surface later.

Departments that are assessed as needing the most clarification or those that will be called upon first to support NewCo should be placed at the top of the speaking engagement list. If CoreCo is spread over several local or global locations, the intrapreneur will need to travel or reach out through interactive videoconferencing solutions. When I did this, I used my time effectively by combining site visits with trips to suppliers or customers. Every time I called a regional leader to suggest a visit to their site to give a presentation on NewCo, I was warmly welcomed. People generally want to help and be part of a winning initiative.

The intrapreneur cannot possibly do all the communicating and internal speaking engagements himself. Even contemplating it would be overwhelming. For this reason he must conscript key NewCo leaders to attend the first presentations so they can learn from what he does in order to present NewCo consistently across the corporation. Making them do a few dry runs is always a good idea, as the quality of their delivery, and their ability to clearly express the main messages, truly matters. Once they are up to speed they can deliver the NewCo pitch on the intrapreneur's behalf as necessary. If travel to numerous CoreCo sites is required, the help of the sponsor can be sought.

The launching of NewCo generates an immense amount of learning. As NewCo's team becomes more knowledgeable about its customers and market, it will have a corresponding increase in insights about customer needs and the competitive landscape. When significant new findings are made the intrapreneur must update CoreCo's primary stakeholders, and he must always stay attentive to revisiting key business assumptions as necessary. He must remember the 3Fs of labor 1: Fresh, Frequent, and For everyone. They will help him avoid situations where NewCo is acting on new information while CoreCo is still working with outdated assumptions.

COMING UP NEXT....................

By this time in the book I have mentioned change management a number of times. It is one of the main activities that distinguishes the intrapreneur from the independent entrepreneur, and in fact successful intrapreneurship is heavily dependent on effectively executing change management. This is because NewCo, with its many distinctive characteristics, must find its way into the world from the foundation of a well-established corporation.

Dealing constructively with CoreCo's various systems and processes and ensuring they adapt to NewCo's needs is a major part of the intrapreneurial challenge, and as such we take a good look at it in labor 5.

THE AUGEAN STABLES

Hercules had proved to be too smart and capable, and now King Eurystheus wanted to humiliate him. For his fifth labor he was ordered to clean the stables of King Augeas, which every night held thousands of cows, goats, and sheep, and had not been cleaned in many years. Moreover, he was to complete the labor in one day. Rather than admit defeat, Hercules realized that ridding the stables of dung in a single day presented an opportunity. Without mentioning Eurystheus or the labor, he proposed to King Augeas that in exchange for cleaning the stables in one day he would take as payment a large number of cattle. The king agreed, believing that the task was impossible. But Hercules had a plan. Using his great strength he tore open the ends of the stable and rerouted the water of two nearby rivers to run through it. The torrents of water washed out the filth, astounding both kings and leaving Hercules victorious.

LABOR 5

The Long-Term Benefits of Skillful Change Management

The expectation that one person could clear the Augean stables of decades of dung in a single day was unrealistic. Not surprisingly, Hercules succeeded. He did so not only because of his supernatural strength, but because he created and executed an ingenious scheme. At first glance the intrapreneur's fifth labor appears to be just as daunting. It involves driving change across several departments in an established and successful corporation with entrenched ways of doing business. Worse, the change will not benefit the corporation in the short-term, and the department heads who will be the ones to effect it through modifying their systems and processes or inventing new ones may not grasp why it is required and therefore respond with reluctance.

But the intrapreneur knows why change is required. As we saw in the last chapter, the systems and processes that work so well for the big, robust parent company are ill-suited to the small, unstable startup. Having spent the pre-launch months analyzing NewCo's unique needs and how they can be met through leveraging CoreCo's resources, the intrapreneur is now tasked with the labor of presenting this knowledge to management in such as way as to convince them that supporting NewCo means doing things differently. Completing this labor means making sure that CoreCo executes its support as promised.

According to CoreCo's expectations, NewCo's mandate is to enter a new market and make quick and significant gains. These expectations are largely based on the idea, as presented by the intrapreneur and sponsor, that NewCo has the major competitive advantage of being able to leverage CoreCo's resources, systems, and processes as needed. So far everyone is on the same page. CoreCo has resources and know-how to share and recognizes that NewCo presents an exciting opportunity for the company.

With NewCo's launch, however, the page turns, and soon CoreCo's leaders come hard up against the fact that the leveraging strategy they agreed to requires real change. The company's resources, systems, and processes must actually be adapted to meet the needs of this insignificant new business that, moreover, may be operating in an unfamiliar market. Sometimes adapting does not go far enough, and wholesale reinvention is required. Given how much time, effort, and money is needed to effect change, you can imagine how easy it is for many leaders to resist.

Exacerbating the situation will be NewCo's bright, motivated new employees who may have been recruited from an industry whose systems and processes are quite different. Furthermore, they will have brought their own best practices and expectations regarding how CoreCo needs to support the startup if it is to succeed. I have unwittingly walked into recruiting-related problems a few times. In one instance CoreCo's market was aviation and NewCo's new market was healthcare. As NewCo's intrapreneur, I understood that we needed people who knew the healthcare market, the buying behaviors of our new customers, and the regulatory guidelines governing marketing activities. Our corporate HR team thought the only difference in this recruiting assignment was to find a headhunting firm specializing in the healthcare field, and so we did.

We had a difficult time making progress. Finally, I realized that our assumptions about compensation, retention, working conditions, and even the titles of positions had to change to attract the right talent. The healthcare industry simply did things differently. For the sake of NewCo's success, this was a reality that CoreCo had to accept.

Skillful change management can mean the difference between success and failure.

You would be wrong to think this issue only applies to a major change in market. I remember the time I needed to recruit helicopter instructors for a new training market we wanted to enter. This seemed well within our traditional CoreCo market, where we had successfully operated for years and from where we had recruited many instructor pilots. But not *helicopter* instructor pilots. It did not occur to me there was a difference between helicopter instructor pilots and instructor pilots, but as it turned out there was. At the time there was a boom in the use of helicopters in the oil and gas industries. These pilots had distinct working conditions, unconventional compensation and benefits requirements, and could not be found via our usual recruiting channels. It took us three months to understand all this and change our behaviors, and those three months cost us dearly.

Managing change does not end once NewCo is launched. In fact, more change is introduced as the startup grows and begins to place increasing demands on CoreCo. As an example, tapping into CoreCo's contracting documents, systems, and processes may not be required in NewCo's earliest days because there are still no customers or strategic partnerships. By the end of the first year, however, all this will have changed. NewCo will have started to gain traction in the market and its first sales will be fast approaching. Sales require contracts, and one industry's practices do not necessarily mimic another's. I have experienced major delays in closing deals because of underestimating the volume of modifications that needed to be made to our standard contracting terms. Those modifications had to be executed by people at CoreCo who were already working full-time meeting CoreCo's own contract needs.

It is a truth that cannot be avoided that customers in different industries will likely have different expectations, which will directly challenge CoreCo's established rules of conducting business. Areas affected include nondisclosure agreements, intellectual property rights, payment terms, indemnity, penalties, and warranty. Even greater differences can be expected if NewCo plans to do business in countries previously not served by CoreCo. External communications is another good example of where change can become an issue. NewCo's first market successes may trigger the need for press releases, but the content and hook of press releases used by CoreCo that generate a positive response may fall flat when appropriated by the startup. Or the media channels may be different. New ways must be found.

Clashes and Conflict

As you may have noticed by now, the CoreCo-NewCo stage is set for multiple clashes between business cultures, systems, processes, and organizational structures, and ultimately between people. In their book *10 Rules for Strategic Innovators: From Idea to Execution*, Govindarajan and Trimble describe three areas that drive conflict when a startup is being launched within a corporation. To keep conflict at bay in these areas, CoreCo must 1) resist applying its business definition to NewCo, whose business reality is so different from CoreCo's that it needs its own business definition, 2) forego its assumptions about the competencies required to be successful, because NewCo's success will derive from a unique business model and areas of expertise CoreCo may be inexperienced in, and 3) shift its focus from exploitation and continuous process improvement to exploring new possibilities.

This is where skillful change management comes in. The challenge for the intrapreneur is to identify the leadership teams at CoreCo whose support he will need to draw on and to convey his requirements to them in a way that is clear, firm, and produces results. Securing the internal support that will magnify the likelihood of NewCo's success while minimizing clashes and conflict is the arduous challenge that lies at the heart of effective intrapreneurial change management.

When explaining the labor of managing change, I find it useful to compare CoreCo to an aircraft carrier and NewCo to a navy corvette or Zodiac, depending on where it is on its growth curve. Basically, aircraft carriers are seagoing air bases equipped with enough runways, hangars, and repair facilities to support 80 aircraft. They measure up to 330 meters in length, can accommodate 6,000 people, and have their own nuclear power generators. Their typical mission is to supply warfare capabilities to battle zones, but they are also used to provide humanitarian aid over long periods to areas hit by natural disasters. The resources, systems, and processes of these colossal platforms allow them to be highly self-sufficient and manage large, complex operations over the long-term.

Navy corvettes are much smaller, measuring between 50 and 100 meters. They accommodate a crew of 60 to 80 people and maybe one helicopter, and are only able to stay out for two to three weeks at a time. While corvettes are equipped with a less powerful arsenal of weapons than aircraft carriers, they are much more maneuverable, making them ideal for patrolling coastlines or intercepting enemy ships or submarines. While aircraft carriers are designed to fend off sustained attacks, corvettes are more limited in their defensive capabilities and ultimately are more vulnerable.

Zodiacs are inflatable boats that are powered by outboard motors. Though they measure only a few meters in length they are very rugged and are used by the military for a variety of missions. For example, they might be sent miles up a narrow river to explore new territory. Try to operate an aircraft carrier like a corvette or a Zodiac, or a corvette like an aircraft carrier or a Zodiac, and you will have massive mission failure.

NewCo begins as a Zodiac. Its mission is to explore a new market, find its way in unfamiliar territory, and eventually create a winning formula that spurs growth. If all goes well, after a few years NewCo will become a corvette, at which time it will be able to rapidly adapt to evolving market threats as it continues to make new discoveries. Still in startup mode and relatively small, the NewCo corvette is highly maneuverable and able to pivot its original strategy in reaction to its customers' needs and changing market realities. But at this stage it remains limited in its resources and quickly becomes ineffective if laden with systems and processes developed for the CoreCo aircraft carrier. Nonetheless, it still depends on CoreCo for support and replenishment.

Unlike the navy, which trains its ship operators in the specific mission and capabilities of their ship and at the same time instills buy-in regarding how their efforts support the overall naval mission, corporations typically look out only for their own needs. While the navy provides its aircraft carriers with clear guidelines on how to effectively support its corvettes and Zodiacs, CoreCo's policies and procedures were created to optimize CoreCo alone. An example that comes to mind is the way corporations integrate new hires into their business culture and way of doing things as quickly as possible. This indoctrination rarely considers the needs of NewCo.

Even if the CEO or sponsor has given a passionate and motivating speech that details the reasons for the launch of NewCo, the need to set it up independently, and why NewCo will be given latitude to develop unique ways of conducting business, and everyone in management positions left the meeting nodding their heads in agreement, once the new reality sets in their willingness to help NewCo will likely weaken. Compounding the problem are the informal and perception expectations that were identified in labor 4, which will invariably lead to a web of conflicting expectations, not only between CoreCo and NewCo but between CoreCo's leaders themselves.

Facilitating Adaptation

It is important to differentiate between the effort required to drive change in an organization for its own benefit and the effort required to drive change *not* for its immediate benefit but to support a startup. In my experience the latter is the tougher challenge. This is because most managers and employees are motivated to improve their company's business performance to remain competitive and ensure longevity. They are accustomed to using various continuous improvement techniques to boost quality, make cycle time reductions, and optimize processes, such as business process re-engineering activities and Six Sigma initiatives.

Supporting a startup, on the other hand, has very little to do with optimizing and driving the productivity of existing business processes and everything to do with freeing up resources in a timely way and adapting or modifying business practices to meet unfamiliar requirements. The effort that must be expended to create a sense of urgency at the parent company and make sure that the people with influence understand the significance of the need for change is ongoing and extraordinary.

The many change management models that exist are well covered in the literature. They all basically aim to ensure that change is implemented and sustained. One model I have used and liked is the Kotter model developed by Harvard Business School professor and author Dr. John Kotter. He proposes eight steps: 1) create a sense of urgency, 2) build a guiding coalition, 3) form the strategic vision and supporting initiatives, 4) enlist a volunteer army, 5) enable action by removing barriers, 6) generate short-term wins, 7) sustain acceleration, and 8) institute change. In short, change requires endeavors and planning that must be adapted to the situation. Table 5.1 summarizes how the activities outlined so far in this book relate to Kotter's eight steps.

Like many things in business, the devil resides in the details, and ensuring successful change management so that CoreCo properly supports NewCo will necessitate four specific activities from the intrapreneur. Some will be undertaken in the weeks leading up to NewCo's launch and others will continue until NewCo can stand alone as a successful new business.

1. The intrapreneur must formulate NewCo's needs and communicate them to CoreCo's various managers in a way that educates them and brings them onside.
2. A central part of the educating process is for the intrapreneur to negotiate SMART objectives for CoreCo that align with NewCo's SMART objectives. They must include performance incentives that secure the continued motivation of CoreCo's managers.
3. The intrapreneur assumes the responsibility for evaluating CoreCo on how well NewCo is being supported.
4. Maintaining an open and strong relationship with NewCo's gatekeeper is key to the intrapreneur's ability to effectively execute change management.

Table 5.1 Kotter's 8-Step Change Management Model

STEPS	NEWCO CHANGE MANAGEMENT ACTIVITIES
1. Create a sense of urgency	Secure the support of the CEO and sponsor; appoint the intrapreneur; write and deliver the elevator speech; make presentations to CoreCo departments
2. Build a guiding coalition	Identify the sponsor, gatekeeper, and intrapreneur; get buy-in from CoreCo's executives
3. Form the strategic vision and supporting initiatives	Define and frequently communicate NewCo's vision and the primary differences between NewCo's and CoreCo's business needs; create and launch an internal communications strategy
4. Enlist a volunteer army	Identify as many allies as possible
5. Enable action by removing barriers	Educate CoreCo; execute the CFM strategy; set SMART objectives
6. Generate short-term wins	Highlight first NewCo sales and other milestones and celebrate often
7. Sustain acceleration	Communicate and celebrate milestones as NewCo grows; execute the internal communications strategy; accelerate the CFM strategy as required
8. Institute change	Institutionalize the systems and processes developed or adapted for NewCo

Educating people about why their support is necessary and valuable goes much further in securing their support than simply telling them about what is needed. NewCo's education campaign begins with the elevator speech and continues with the unfolding of the internal communications strategy, which includes such elements as an internal website, a newsletter, and presentations to key departments. These communication activities go to the heart of helping CoreCo grasp the NewCo mission and how it differs from CoreCo's. The hoped-for result is department heads and managers who are inspired to support the startup and remain at the ready to provide their assistance when required.

SMART Objectives and Incentives

Employees are predisposed to work with diligence when they know their performance is being assessed. Everyone has an eye on their annual objectives and how meeting them will affect their raises, promotions, and overall advancement. In the previous chapter we saw that setting SMART objectives is an effective way for the intrapreneur and sponsor to reach a common understanding of what to expect regarding NewCo, and that this is a key factor in NewCo's success. The same applies when determining NewCo's expectations of CoreCo and making sure CoreCo not only shares them but is conscientious about meeting them.

I am referring particularly to the leaders at CoreCo who will play a role in supporting NewCo. By negotiating SMART objectives with these men and women, which essentially is an educational process, the intrapreneur will ensure that they are properly enthusiastic about and focused on NewCo's success. The process will also correct any mistaken assumptions they have about NewCo's rate of growth, which are based on the idea that NewCo will be able to leverage CoreCo's resources, systems, and processes. As a result of these assumptions, CoreCo's leaders will expect NewCo to deliver positive results quickly. When success fails to materialize according to their expectations, their thoughts will run along the lines of, "Why isn't NewCo happening fast enough? What's wrong?"

Once these questions start circulating the intrapreneur can anticipate serious disappointment from CoreCo and waning interest. This scenario could be catastrophic for NewCo, the intrapreneur, and the sponsor. Fortunately, unrealistic expectations about NewCo's rate of growth are not inevitable. They can be avoided through the successful setting of SMART objectives, which is essentially making CoreCo complicit in delivering support to NewCo in a timely way and in exactly the form it is needed. With SMART objectives, CoreCo comprehends that NewCo's rate of growth is dependent on the quality of CoreCo's support.

Do not make the mistake of letting CoreCo determine these objectives alone. This will lead to misunderstandings and could even provide CoreCo's leaders with a powerful tool that allows them to establish control over NewCo. The lead player in this process must be the intrapreneur, who will be watchful that the objectives are expressed from NewCo's perspective. In this task the intrapreneur has help in the form of corporate force multipliers, or CFMs. By aligning the objectives with NewCo's CFM strategy, CoreCo's leaders will know well in advance what is needed of them, how it can be delivered, and how their actions are crucial to NewCo's success.

Corporate Force Multipliers

Corporate force multipliers™ refer to strengths, attributes, relationships, and proven capabilities that exist within a large corporation that can be leveraged by a much smaller organization that operates within it. CFMs give the smaller organization capabilities that are well beyond what could be expected of a stand-alone business of the same size. They can include, but are not limited to, people, resources, know-how, partnerships, systems, processes, assets, and technology.

The last item on the intrapreneur's checklist when setting CoreCo's SMART objectives for NewCo is to give them sufficient weight. Weight refers to the importance, usually identified by a percentage, that an objective is given relative to all the others, with the sum of all weights adding up to 100 percent. By sufficient weight, I mean that it must be comparable to the weight accorded to achieving CoreCo's own business objectives. The NewCo-related objectives must have a meaningful impact on the annual performance assessment of everyone at CoreCo who plays a role in NewCo's progress.

Once again, it is critical to sidestep the bigger-is-better trap. Just because the startup represents only a small fraction of the overall business activities and results of the company is no reason to assign CoreCo's objectives vis-à-vis NewCo a small relative weight. Doing so sends the message that NewCo is insignificant. But nothing is further from the truth, and CoreCo's leaders must realize that not meeting their NewCo-related objectives will seriously impact their end-of-year performance evaluation, rating, raise, and bonus.

Perhaps the central point to remember is that NewCo's progress correlates directly with how well the CFM strategy is executed. With poor execution NewCo risks finding itself in the dire situation of being burdened with systems and processes from the parent aircraft carrier that have no place on the smaller NewCo corvette and even smaller NewCo Zodiac. I use the word dire because nothing less is at stake than NewCo losing the many benefits it would have accrued by leveraging CoreCo's resources, systems, and processes.

Evaluation

Once CoreCo's objectives as related to NewCo are properly conceived, made SMART, weighted, and rolled out to the relevant company leaders, how well those leaders execute them will need to be evaluated. The decision regarding who will carry out the evaluations is paramount to NewCo's success. The person must be objective and willing to place the right pressure on CoreCo. This eliminates CoreCo employees and leaves the intrapreneur, who will bring care and purpose to the task. The evaluations should be conducted on a quarterly basis. In the rapidly moving startup environment, NewCo cannot let more than three months go by before formally addressing a major support issue. When someone at CoreCo disagrees with the evaluation he or she is given, the sponsor or gatekeeper will arbitrate and their decision will be final.

Keep the Gatekeeper Involved

The last element of effective change management with regard to supporting NewCo is the involvement of the gatekeeper, whose role was discussed at length in labor 3. What needs emphasizing is that the gatekeeper will need to intervene right away when progress is not being made fast enough as a result of resistance to change. The emphasis on speed is critical. A corporation can count on its large pool of talent and substantial resources to make up for lost time, but a startup is too lean to recover this way.

This is not unlike the navy corvette that runs out of fuel faster than its parent aircraft carrier. Delays in CoreCo providing the support required will lead to NewCo missing key milestones, and missed milestones cost time and burn cash. For this reason the gatekeeper must be intimately familiar with both sets of SMART objectives: NewCo's on the one hand and CoreCo's for supporting NewCo on the other. The gatekeeper must also be well versed in the CFM strategy.

COMING UP NEXT....................

The challenge of getting CoreCo resources assigned to NewCo and having people in CoreCo work in a timely way to adapt their systems and processes and maybe even develop new ones has a lot to do with individual workload and departmental priorities.

In a corporate environment there is never enough time to get it all done. Priorities are often assigned as a function of the financial significance of an activity to the results of the next quarter or fiscal year. You may not be surprised to learn that NewCo's requests often end up at the bottom of the corporate pile because, as a startup, it will not be financially relevant for quite some time.

Financial relevance is behind the concept of materiality and is the subject of the next chapter.

THE STYMPHALIAN BIRDS

For his sixth labor Hercules was told by King Eurystheus to drive away an enormous flock of man-eating birds that had made their home in a marsh near the town of Stymphalos. The birds had beaks of bronze and sharp metallic feathers they used as weapons. When Hercules arrived at the swamp, he wondered how he would complete the labor given the great number of birds and that the ground was too soft to hold his weight. Once again Athena came to his rescue. She provided him with a set of clappers that had been specially crafted to scare the birds from their nests with their loud noise. As the birds rose into the air Hercules shot them with his bow and arrow, killing many. The others few away and were never seen again.

LABOR 6

Avoiding the Materiality Minefield

Most companies have a threshold that defines when a financial event such as an investment, transaction, or level of debt becomes material to its overall performance and health. This threshold is called materiality, and companies often use it to measure whether or not a given activity is making a significant positive contribution. Typically, the larger the company, the larger the materiality limits. The difficulty with using materiality as a benchmark for NewCo is that considerable time needs to pass before NewCo will be in a position to augment CoreCo's results. In fact, NewCo's impact on the corporate P&L, balance sheet, and cash flow will remain negative for quite a while, possibly two years or more. It is during this lengthy post-launch period that NewCo and the intrapreneur will have to carefully navigate the materiality minefield.

To complicate matters, it may be hard to tell when people within CoreCo are using NewCo's insignificant results to deny it access to resources and budgets. Others may use them to question NewCo's value and future. For the intrapreneur, challenging the materiality threshold CoreCo has established for NewCo will feel like hunting the Stymphalian birds: lonely, difficult, and dangerous. He should not lose hope. The best way forward is to find opportunities that will flush out materiality arguments so they can be shot down as they become visible. They will present themselves in various forms: a manager's refusal to make a NewCo request a priority, the sponsor or CEO not giving NewCo enough airtime during a strategic meeting, a CFO not assigning someone to help with NewCo's finances, or comments made that belittle a NewCo achievement.

The intrapreneur will not always be present to hear denigrating comments or spot resistance to change that appears to be based on NewCo not being big enough to warrant CoreCo modifying a system or process. This is why he needs to know that allied CoreCo managers will shoot down materiality-related arguments themselves and keep him informed of what was said. Being proactive on this front is essential for NewCo to receive the support it requires to succeed.

Accessing CoreCo Resources

An organic growth strategy typically comes with a condition: before a new business can begin to make a positive difference to the corporation's top and bottom lines, it needs time. This is the price the corporation must pay for choosing the path of organic growth over other options. Although NewCo's results were openly projected to make a material financial contribution to CoreCo only in the outer years (say, three to five), people at CoreCo may not have fully grasped or accepted NewCo's negative impact in the early years.

The reality is that an organic growth strategy requires the parent company to provide the startup with an infusion of funds and access to resources. This will be the case until the startup has expanded its customer base and achieved a level of market success that translates into profits that can be used to fund its growth. Before reaching this critical moment of self-funding, during which time NewCo may be drawing resources from many of CoreCo's organizations, it will be exposed to materiality-based challenges.

The following is typical thinking: While still in startup mode NewCo will be perceived as requiring a disproportionate level of support relative to other CoreCo organizations that are larger operationally or generate higher levels of business. The natural management tendency of some CoreCo leaders will be to question why so much support is being given to a new business that is not making a meaningful contribution to the overall company. This line of thinking will be aggravated in CoreCo leaders who are facing poor business projections, market downturns, or budgetary pressures in their own areas.

In these situations leaders are directed to make difficult choices, even sacrifices. This can result in the argument that NewCo is getting the budget that would have been better used elsewhere. Some CoreCo people might wonder why NewCo has the go-ahead to hire while the parent is in a hiring freeze or laying off employees. Others may object when they find out that NewCo employees are allowed to travel when CoreCo's are under a travel restriction. Still others may resent having to cut their R&D activities to free up funds for NewCo's R&D. The list goes on, which is another way of saying that NewCo will find itself fighting the materiality battle on a regular basis.

Strategic Fit and Growth Rewards

One way to keep internal discord to a minimum is to explain how NewCo's growth will eventually contribute to CoreCo's results. I have found that being transparent is more effective than making vague promises about NewCo's future success. Everyone likes data. Most corporate managers will listen to viable options when shown projected growth data that reveal that without NewCo, CoreCo's growth will stagnate, decrease, or not meet shareholder expectations. They will shift their focus from the short-term tactical reality of having to invest in NewCo to the longer-term strategic benefits of NewCo's projected contributions.

Good managers understand the need to accept short-term pain for long-term gain. They will accept making sacrifices in their areas of responsibility if they are convinced that the startup embodies an exciting vision that will lead to a stronger financial footing for the corporation. Shifting the focus from short-term sacrifices to long-term rewards can be accomplished by providing CoreCo's leadership teams with a clear picture of CoreCo's financial future without NewCo.

Table 6.1 provides an example of how to capture NewCo's financial story. A table of this type will be a central component of presentations made to CoreCo. Although it reflects a parent company that has decided to launch a startup to support its growth strategy, it can easily be adapted to the financial metrics that are relevant to your business and industry. The point is to create a sense of urgency and buy-in by showing the contributions the new business is expected to make to the corporation's total performance over time.

Regardless of the business or industry you are in, your table should emphasize the following elements:

- The expectations of the owners, investors, or market analysts regarding CoreCo's growth
- The financial reality of CoreCo as it stands, without the launch of NewCo; section (2) should demonstrate if and when CoreCo is projected to fall short of its growth expectations
- The investments that will be required to support NewCo's growth
- NewCo's projected financial results on a stand-alone basis over time; to allow for a comparison, the same financial metrics should be used as in (1)

- The projected financial growth of CoreCo, including NewCo's impact, using the same categories as in (2) but restated to include NewCo's results as seen in (4)
- The net contribution that NewCo will make to CoreCo over time, showing how it eventually becomes material and helps CoreCo meet its growth expectations

You will notice that ROI (return on investments) is not listed in this table. ROI is too vague to be used in discussions about the future financial benefits of a startup to its parent corporation. Although it is an important tool when reviewing investment options and validating that the risk-reward balance is appropriate for your company, it provides few insights to CoreCo's leaders who are trying to understand why funds should go to a risky startup rather than to one of the company's more predictable (albeit incremental) innovations.

These leaders, whether they are managers, directors, or vice presidents, are not rewarded for NewCo's ROIs, nor are ROIs useful for forecasting the level of job security within the company. What matters for the intrapreneur is to provide a sense of how NewCo will contribute to profitability and other key business metrics. This will encourage people to make the leap from today's investments and sacrifices to tomorrow's rewards and employment longevity.

The information in table 6.1 must clearly represent the reasons behind NewCo's launch. For example, if the decision to establish NewCo is based on a diversification strategy whose goal is to help CoreCo weather market cycles, the numbers should reflect projected industry cycles and their impact on CoreCo. If the reasoning behind NewCo is to position CoreCo in an industry with better margins, table 6.1 should emphasize why better margins are necessary and how NewCo will contribute to improving its parent's overall profitability.

Support for NewCo must start at the top of CoreCo and be enlisted well prior to the launch, when the intrapreneur and sponsor meet with the senior executives to secure their approval to proceed. To increase their chance of success they must arrive at the meeting with their own version of table 6.1. Next they will make presentations to the managers who are subordinate to the executive team, and then to the company's departments. At all these meetings table 6.1 will contextualize the information and ground people in the short-, medium-, and long-term expectations that CoreCo can reasonably have of NewCo.

Table 6.1 NewCo's Contribution to CoreCo's Performance

	YR. 1	YR. 2	YR. 3	YR. 4	YR. 5	YR. 7	YR. 10
(1) Expectation of CoreCo's Growth • Revenue • Gross profits • Net profits • Cash flow • ROCE, RONA, EPS*							
(2) CoreCo's Current Projected Growth • Revenue • Gross profits • Net profits • Cash flow • ROCE, RONA, EPS							
(3) Investments Required in NewCo • Capital investments • R&D funding • Operational budgets							
(4) NewCo's Projected Growth • Revenue • Gross profits • Net profits • Cash flow • ROCE, RONA, EPS							
(5) CoreCo's Projected Growth with NewCo • Revenue • Gross profits • Net profits • Cash flow • ROCE, RONA, EPS							
(6) NewCo's Net Contribution to CoreCo • Revenue • Gross profits • Net profits • Cash flow • ROCE, RONA, EPS							

* ROCE: return on capital employed; RONA: return on net assets; EPS: earnings per share

Transparency about NewCo's financial projections will lead to corporate buy-in.

Materiality comes down to how much the new business will contribute to CoreCo's financial health, and at what point in time. As is almost always the case when dealing with corporate startups, the issue of time is omnipresent. If you are the intrapreneur, your presentations to CoreCo's management must clearly demonstrate when NewCo will start to make a positive contribution. In the minds of CoreCo's managers, this piece of information will translate directly into how long they will have to participate in "subsidizing" your operations. Demonstrating transparency by sharing NewCo's financial projections will go a long way to securing their buy-in and will result in their willingness to make NewCo requests a priority despite the startup's immateriality early on.

The table will need to be updated on a quarterly basis to ensure that everyone remains aware of the financial facts. While undertaking these activities, the intrapreneur must remember to properly manage expectations prior to and following the launch, as discussed in labor 4. This will be central to keeping negative materiality behavior in check.

3 Dangerous Situations

There are three situations associated with the materiality minefield that a fledgling business like NewCo must avoid at all costs: 1) losing corporate support over time, 2) accelerating acquisitions to spur growth, and 3) allowing CoreCo to impose budget cuts. Failure to avoid these situations can cause significant damage.

Maintain Corporate Support

Time marches on, and what started as an acceptable level of investment for CoreCo may one day seem less acceptable. Or CoreCo's belief in the strategic basis for launching NewCo may weaken due to shifts in the market, new business cycles, or the arrival of a new CEO who brings a different set of expectations. As time passes most startups experience unpredicted delays, which can lead to waning support from the parent company as it changes its priorities. The intrapreneur and sponsor must remain hyper alert to any potential changes within CoreCo that might affect its support. They must also stay in constant contact with the gatekeeper, who may be the first to get wind of backtracking in the company's upper echelons. Allies are also crucial sources of information.

The intrapreneur and sponsor should never tire of asking themselves these questions:

1. Has CoreCo's support for NewCo changed?
2. Has the business justification or rationale for establishing NewCo shifted?
3. Do we need to review how NewCo is positioned vis-à-vis CoreCo?
4. Do the NewCo key messages and elevator speech need to be adapted to an evolving CoreCo business environment?

If you are the intrapreneur or sponsor, seek input from your senior allies to identify who at CoreCo may be having a change of heart. Shifts in attitude must be identified early. Like Hercules, NewCo has many allies, but it also has doubters, detractors, and maybe even enemies. You must be careful of the ground on which you tread and be sure to get your information from sources you trust. You must also remain objective about your assessment of NewCo's current situation within CoreCo. By remaining objective, I mean seeing the world as it is, not as you wish it to be. Keeping an objective mind regarding NewCo's position in CoreCo will help you act promptly to ensure that the startup continues to receive the support it requires to grow.

I have found that nothing gets a parent company more excited and supportive of their new business than signing up paying customers. Use early successes with new customers to showcase that NewCo is gaining traction and market share. The commitment of paying customers, while not equated with business success, demonstrates progress and that the new product or service has value. The intrapreneur should join with the sponsor, gatekeeper, and key allies in celebrating hard-won customer contracts, new partnerships, and the achievement of product milestones. These celebrations will also play a role in your change management efforts.

Other activities that can protect CoreCo's continued support include demonstrating an early working prototype; communicating a first product delivery, large order, or international sale; announcing a strategic partnership or new distribution channel; and reporting important revenue events and profitability achievements. These are exciting watershed moments and their importance to CoreCo's stakeholders should not be underestimated. After all, these people have made many sacrifices to help NewCo succeed. Celebrating milestones reinvigorates their support and energizes employees in both the parent company and startup. Taking lots of pictures and making videos of celebrations and publishing them in company newsletters and on websites is a great way to build momentum and secure support.

Despite a successful launch and a good internal communications strategy, the original excitement about NewCo will inevitably subside as everyone gets back to business as usual. As corporate fiscal results and NewCo's P&L statements and balance sheet are shared among CoreCo's senior leaders, the impact of investing in the startup will begin to feel tangible. What everyone understood in theory becomes a grinding day-to-day reality: NewCo's financial impact is inversely proportional to the funding and other support it receives. The intrapreneur and sponsor must be on the lookout for CoreCo leaders who are questioning their original commitment. They can preempt discontent by frequently bringing out table 6.1.

Any delays, detours, or strategic pivots experienced by NewCo should be communicated to CoreCo's management team. As an intrapreneur I did this in a variety of ways with the help of the communications tools we covered previously, such as articles in internal newsletters, updating the NewCo website with the latest successes, making a quarterly presentation to CoreCo's executives to outline progress made and shifts in strategic direction or key business assumptions, and scheduling a general meeting to brief the company's managers.

It is too much for the busy intrapreneur to take on all these internal communications activities alone, so others in NewCo will have to step up and share in the workload. Without their support the intrapreneur will become too internally focused on CoreCo. The sponsor and gatekeeper will have to raise their voices as required and remind their colleagues to honor their initial commitment to the startup.

Do Not Force Acquisitions

Acquiring companies can be a pivotal aspect of NewCo's strategy and should certainly be considered. Making acquisitions for the right reasons and at the right time can accelerate growth and provide the much-needed resources and expertise that would otherwise take years to build. Conversely, doing so at the wrong time for the wrong reasons, prior to properly understanding NewCo's new market and vetting acquisition targets to ensure the best fit, creates serious risk.

Forcing an early acquisition to accelerate NewCo's growth with the goal of reaching CoreCo's materiality threshold can happen for a variety of reasons ranging from business-related to personal. But they all stem from the perception that NewCo is not progressing fast enough. For example, CoreCo may have an urgent need to accelerate NewCo's growth to compensate for an unpredicted downturn in the core business, or NewCo is suddenly presented with an attractive opportunity for a cheap, opportunistic acquisition. On the personal front, the intrapreneur may be seeking to achieve organizational relevance by growing his organization via the addition of more people and infrastructure, or the sponsor may have imprudently promised results based on unrealistic expectations, and one day realizes she has placed herself in an awkward position vis-à-vis the CEO.

There is no getting around the fact that acquisitions create hard work. Even small acquisitions come with their fair share of effort, including conducting due diligence, participating in negotiations, drafting share purchase agreements, and carrying out integration activities. These tasks can be onerous, but the danger is that they are time-consuming and will divert the attention of NewCo's lean leadership team away from executing their carefully planned strategy. For this reason the intrapreneur and sponsor must be certain that NewCo is ready to undertake such an important strategic step and that the decision was made for the right reasons: to accelerate the implementation of NewCo's product development roadmap, to deploy its go-to-market strategy, or to secure distribution channels.

In my experience acquisitions should only be considered after NewCo has had a sufficient period of organic growth and learning. During this period the intrapreneur and his team must validate the original assumptions behind the strategic plan and business model and come to thoroughly grasp how its new product or service satisfies the unmet need. What constitutes organic growth and learning differs for every NewCo and is based on the business risk assessment of the new venture.

We explore business risk in detail in labor 8, but for now look at it as a function of the number of disruptions the new product or service is relying on to succeed, for example, introducing new technology, entering a new market, or leveraging new distribution channels. The level of business risk increases with the number of disruptions because each one, whether technology, market, or channel, attracts a high level of unknowns that must be understood and planned for.

Prior to allowing NewCo to proceed with an acquisition, CoreCo and the sponsor must be sure the startup has sufficiently validated the risks associated with the new business and mitigated their threat. As part of the intrapreneur's risk-mitigation approach he must seek and find the answers to four fundamental questions:

1. Are the targeted customers willing to spend money on NewCo's product or service?
2. Will the business model lead NewCo to achieve the desired revenue and profit-growth targets?
3. Are CFMs available that will effectively give NewCo the competitive advantage it seeks?
4. Are the assumptions driving the product roadmap, go-to-market strategy, and distribution channel plans accurate?

Only when NewCo has achieved clarity on these issues will it be ready to assess the tradeoffs between making an acquisition and other options such as accelerating NewCo's internal solutions, partnering with another company, or buying a division that is relevant to NewCo rather than buying the entire company. Clarity will also put NewCo's team in a better position to conduct an effective assessment and due diligence of the acquisition targets. Even if one of these issues remains open to question, NewCo must abandon its ambition to make an acquisition, at least for the time being.

The Cost-Cutting Temptation

There may be times when CoreCo faces economic pressure in its core business and needs to find efficiencies. If this happens it should not make the mistake of pushing cost-reduction targets onto NewCo. In the world of independent startups, sustaining customer and market momentum and early product successes is essential to growth, and no one would dream of cutting costs while the fledging business is still in the early stages of technology adoption and preliminary market growth. The same is true of corporate startups. Unfortunately, some corporate leaders may not realize that sustaining early momentum is important for securing gains that were already made and accelerating market penetration. Their oversight risks sacrificing NewCo's medium- to long-term potential to achieve short-term budgetary relief at CoreCo.

If you are the sponsor or gatekeeper, do not succumb to the impulse to cut back budgets. Regardless of deficiencies in CoreCo's performance and resulting short-term pressures, NewCo's vision must not be short-circuited. Remember that the financial performance expectations you created for NewCo were realistic, and to modify them now would be extremely risky. In some cases it might equate with suicide. There is a downward spiral that you do not want NewCo to enter: cost-cutting means fewer resources, which results in slower progress than planned, which leads to poor materiality and missing the projections of table 6.1. Poor materiality becomes the justification for further cost-cutting and the cycle begins again, eventually ending in NewCo's demise.

CoreCo might try to convince you that NewCo can do more with less, but resist this idea. I have successfully used the do-more-with-less strategy when managing established medium- and large-size businesses and large-scale operations. It worked because over the years operational inefficiencies had crept in and identifying and eliminating them allowed us to optimize systems, processes, and resources, and ultimately to cut costs. Attempting to do more with less in a startup environment rarely has the desired outcome because a NewCo simply will not have built up enough business infrastructure to have developed inefficiencies and sufficient operational fat to warrant cost-cutting initiatives.

This is not to say that NewCo should not follow a lean cost model. Lean is a good way to start, but once the budgets have been established, do not cut them back for the wrong reasons. As noted above, forced cost-cutting will subvert NewCo's original growth plan or worse, send it to an early grave. Growth strategies are about making choices regarding where to invest for the future. In choosing to invest in NewCo, the corporation agreed to make short-term sacrifices in its existing businesses and operations with the goal of laying the foundation for its new startup. This decision extends to the need to protect NewCo from cost reductions. If anyone says otherwise, the sponsor and gatekeeper must intervene on behalf of NewCo.

If the corporate financial situation is so dire that cutbacks at NewCo are unavoidable, the sponsor and intrapreneur must work together to adjust NewCo's growth expectations and SMART objectives accordingly. Then they will need to convince CoreCo that doing less with less will ensure NewCo's survival during this difficult financial period, and that survival is preferable to death. But once the storm has been weathered NewCo's funding must be returned to its original level.

My last recommendation on this subject goes to NewCo's leadership team. It is a fact that many people throughout CoreCo will be making sacrifices to support NewCo. I know this because I have been on both sides of the CoreCo-NewCo fence. I have felt the pain of cutting back on resources, delaying major initiatives, driving my teams to do more with less, and even laying off staff to free up our corporate resources and budgets to support a startup. As an intrapreneur, when discussing spending and budgets with my NewCo team, I always reminded them that somewhere in CoreCo supervisors, managers, or employees were making sacrifices to ensure our success. Showing humility and empathy towards these people is especially important. Being aware of their sacrifices should motivate NewCo's leaders to be as efficient as possible when making spending decisions.

COMING UP NEXT......................

The issue of materiality in the corporate environment is real. Applying a reasonable amount of pressure to accelerate NewCo's positive financial contributions to CoreCo can be healthy when properly managed, but too much pressure can quickly lead to unpredictable behavior and poor decision making.

There are two other corporate behaviors that have to be carefully managed once the decision to launch NewCo has been made. These include the methodology used by CoreCo to gather and submit estimates for the work to be done and CoreCo's deep-rooted expectations regarding forecasting accuracy. Both are dealt with in labor 7.

THE CRETAN BULL

To complete his seventh labor Hercules sailed to the island of Crete to capture the Cretan bull. Long before, when it was given to King Minos by Poseidon, the god of the sea, it was a beautiful and gentle animal. But later Minos angered Poseidon, who in retribution transformed the bull into a raging beast that charged around the island and terrified the population. When Hercules explained his labor to Crete's king he was granted permission to capture the bull, which he did by approaching it from behind and wrestling it to the ground. Hercules drove the beast home to King Eurystheus, who became so afraid that he devised a scheme to sacrifice it to Hera. She refused, knowing that the sacrifice would honor Hercules, who she despised. Finally, Eurystheus set the Cretan bull free.

LABOR 7

The Compounding Cushion and the Forecasting Trap

Let's go back to the very beginning, when NewCo was nothing more than one of many interesting innovations within the corporate innovation process, or maybe it was a beta test for a strategic initiative. Regardless, it only attracted attention within CoreCo in accordance with where it existed on its development curve and how many resources it consumed. It was not expected to generate sales, revenues, and profits. But all that changed when the decision was made to turn it into a stand-alone business via the activities of intrapreneurship.

NewCo's stand-alone status empowers the intrapreneur and his team to determine and execute its business strategy, manage all profit and loss activities, set the operational and capital expense budgets, and lead the day-to-day operations. In return, they are responsible for making NewCo a success.

With the launch now on CoreCo's calendar, sales, revenues, and profits take on real importance, and it becomes a priority to impose the corporation's estimating and forecasting processes and systems onto the new startup. At first it might appear to the intrapreneur that this is helpful, that aligning these two crucial business management activities with NewCo's needs will be like going after the Cretan bull: attention is required but the work itself will unfold without difficulty. In fact, addressing this issue successfully is among the more challenging change management tasks the intrapreneur will face.

CoreCo must also be careful about what it asks for. Like King Eurystheus, who demanded the delivery of a bull that ultimately terrified him, insisting that the intrapreneur adopt the corporation's rigid estimating and forecasting approaches will likely lead him to focus on the wrong KPIs and make vital decisions based on poor data. The outcome will be frustrating for both the parent company and the startup, and many months of turmoil for NewCo.

What may not be apparent at first is that there is an inevitable conflict between CoreCo's tested and fixed approach to estimating and its insistence on accuracy in forecasting, and NewCo's need for nimbleness, flexibility, and learning. Two insidious outcomes can arise from this conflict. I use the term insidious deliberately, and a review of its definition is warranted. The *Merriam-Webster* online dictionary defines it as, "causing harm in a way that is gradual or not easily noticed." If CoreCo imposes the wrong estimating and forecasting processes and systems onto NewCo, NewCo will be caused exactly this type of harm: gradual and not easily noticed.

The first insidious outcome is that CoreCo will draw the wrong conclusions regarding the resources and funding NewCo requires to succeed. As we will see in the section on the compounding cushion effect, this will severely undermine the startup's ability to progress, and it may even shut it down before it starts. The second harmful outcome is covered in the forecasting trap section, where we learn that NewCo's understanding of its business reality will gradually go askew, preventing it from capturing key market data and gaining important insights early on. Fortunately, these unwanted situations can be avoided through awareness, collaboration, and shared learning.

The Compounding Cushion Effect

Prior to launching NewCo, financial estimates are created to evaluate its business case, forecast its costs, and project its P&L contributions. Most of these estimates, if not all, are calculated by CoreCo's managers. This is to be expected because in the period leading up to and for some months following its launch, NewCo does not have the organization and manpower to carry out estimating work.

As a norm in the business world, estimates are inflated as a protective measure when predicting the unknown, and NewCo's future is nothing if not unknown. This inflation can occur at all levels of approval, and as estimates move up through the CoreCo organization, each level adds a risk mitigation correction. This leads to what I refer to as the compounding cushion effect. The net result is an unrealistically steep cost curve that can kill a business case by carving away its profitability projections or by leaving very little room for creating risk mitigation funds during the financial sensitivity analysis.

Sensitivity analyses are the "what if" scenarios that are created so that CoreCo can determine the level of risk in a business case and decide whether or not to support it. They hypothesize various cost projections and take into account a range of optimistic to pessimistic views of revenue growth. For example, a sensitivity analysis might model contingencies that increase cost projections and decrease revenue projections to identify how sensitive the profits of a business case are to certain critical marketing, sales, and production assumptions.

There is a tendency for corporate risk mitigation to lead to inflated estimate cushions.

The corporate behavior that leads to inflated cushioning is depicted in figure 7.1. When CoreCo develops estimates of what is required to deliver the results expected by NewCo, but within the existing CoreCo environment, each department starts with what it knows, which is usually a number based on the department head's assumptions about NewCo. I refer to this as the source estimate. Using the source estimate as a starting point, managers add and subtract from it based on their belief of what NewCo expects CoreCo to deliver. In my experience there is usually more adding than subtracting. I have seen original source estimates increase by as much as 300 to 400 percent.

Figure 7.1 shows that a supervisor added a 35 percent initial risk cushion to the source estimate of 1,000 units. Units can represent currency, hours, staffing, or any other unit of effort. Then the supervisor gave it to a Level-1 manager who applied a 25 percent risk cushion even though she possessed only a general idea of the new venture. She then forwarded it to a director for a Level-2 review, where a further 20 percent risk cushion was added, after which it was submitted to a vice president for a Level-3 review, who concluded that a 15 percent risk cushion was merited.

All the estimates were then rolled into one business case and the finance or business development team applied the Rule of 2, which doubled the cost numbers. For the purposes of the business case, the original source estimate of 1,000 units was now 4,657 units, an almost five-fold increase and enough to kill the case. A 500 percent risk cushion may not be the norm, but I can guarantee that the compounding cushion effect results in numbers that are significantly higher than you think, and they often have a material impact on startups.

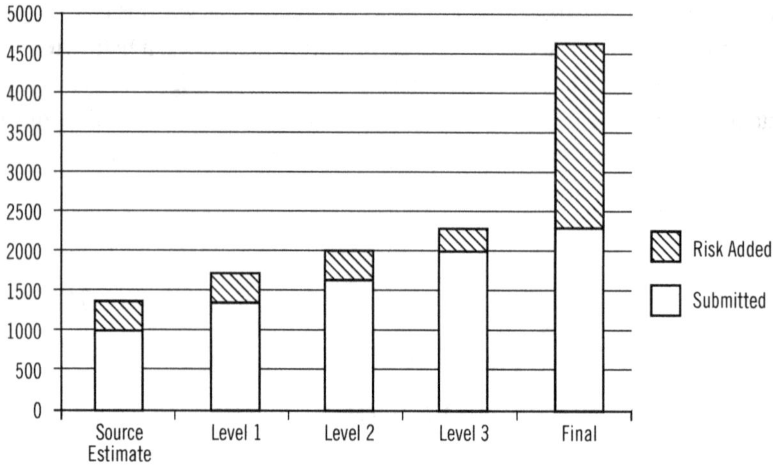

Figure 7.1 The Compounding Cushion Effect

The Rule of 2

Corporate financial analysts and business development experts who are tasked to review business cases and assess the financial risk profiles of new business proposals draw from various sources for best practices, including from the world of venture capital (VC). One frequently used VC practice is the Rule of 2, which VC companies typically bring into play when entrepreneurs come calling.

The entrepreneur who launches a startup does her best to estimate costs and revenues. She studies the market being targeted and the potential for growth, and then makes projections. For her, the expression "cash is king" means everything. Her focus is on ensuring that she has enough cash flow (often referred to as runway) to pay the bills and stay afloat.

For this reason she tends to take a short-term view. This is also why her startup will likely grow more slowly than a corporate startup, which has CoreCo in the wings covering NewCo's cash flow needs (this is a central CFM). The entrepreneur is usually close enough in her estimates to launch her business, but she underestimates the effort required to sustain growth beyond the phase associated with early adopters. When this happens she may find herself walking through the front door of a venture capital company. She has entered the period of growth that requires a lot more funding than her original investors can cover, whether they are family, friends, or angel investors.

Equipped with the market knowledge that is gained from an initial period of growth, the entrepreneur is able to refine certain assumptions and validate others. The next step is to fine-tune her business model, which may include a review by an accountant who makes sure that basic accounting principles were respected. The entrepreneur and her accountant agree that cost cushions should be added to cover any risks. This is very different from the example illustrated in figure 7.1. Here, only one level of cushions is added when finalizing the business model.

VCs know when they are dealing with an optimistic entrepreneur. To protect their interests in these cases they developed a rule of thumb to capture the overall risk associated with investing in an independent startup. The Rule of 2 states that for a startup to be successful it will generally require twice the investments it thinks it needs, take two times longer to reach its investment goals, and achieve half the projected revenue. In other words, two times the investment, two times longer, and projected revenues divided by two. After applying the Rule of 2 to the entrepreneur's business case, the VC evaluates if the business is still worth investing in.

The difficulty with the corporate estimating process is that CoreCo's business development and financial analysts, like VCs, apply the Rule of 2, but without having a clear grasp of the successive cost cushions that were included in the submitted estimates. As figure 7.1 demonstrates, an original source estimate of 1,000 units can easily swell to 4,657 units as a result of CoreCo's layering of risk cushions from the many levels of inputs, reviews, and approvals. This sharply contrasts with the case of a VC applying the Rule of 2 to an optimistic entrepreneur. In that scenario, the same original source estimate of 1,000 units, which turned into 1,350 units after the entrepreneur and her accountant added a 35-percent cushion, became 2,700, a more realistic and promising number.

The culture of overestimating can have serious ramifications. One, as mentioned earlier, is that a potentially profitable new venture gets rejected at the embryonic stage because the compounding cushion effect made the cost assumptions prohibitive. Or the launch is approved, but with the potentially devastating caveat that the intrapreneur must reduce NewCo's demand for resources and support because they are deemed too expensive, when in reality this may not be the case but a result of the inflated cushions. It could be a fatal mistake for the sponsor or CFO to direct NewCo to "make the business case work" by decreasing its requirements (costs) while maintaining its original revenue projections so it can hit acceptable ROI targets. In short, CoreCo must not let the compounding cushion effect go unchecked.

There is something else that CoreCo, the sponsor, and the intrapreneur must be on the lookout for: a demand from CoreCo's estimating departments that NewCo reduce its expectations on them if NewCo wants them to reduce their estimates. But forcing NewCo to ask for less support from CoreCo in exchange for CoreCo shrinking what are essentially overly inflated risk cushions is unworkable because nothing was said about a corresponding cut in NewCo's estimated rate of growth. This takes us back to the pitfall of asking NewCo to make its business case by doing more with less.

The only way for CoreCo to address this situation is to find out if the problem resides in NewCo's needs or in CoreCo's estimates of the work it must undertake to satisfy those needs. Not solving the problem will set up NewCo for a very slow and difficult, if not impossible, start. If it is too early to validate the estimates because NewCo has not had enough exposure to its customers and market to be able to define what it needs from CoreCo, then a preliminary budget can be approved based on best estimates, with the understanding that it will be reviewed and refined at a later date.

Capture Risk Separately

The compounding cushion effect is characteristic of the culture of "underpromise and overdeliver" that is so prevalent in corporations today. This flawed culture encourages managers to inflate estimates and provide potential savings as they execute the work. In many circles this is less frowned upon than to risk underestimating now and having to increase the budget later. A corporate startup can avoid being subjected to the culture of underpromise and overdeliver by capturing risk separately. Each group submitting an estimate should be asked to isolate their best source estimate for getting the job done from the additional risk estimate they are assuming. The best source estimate must be exactly that: each manager's best assessment of the cost of providing the support requested by NewCo.

NewCo's intrapreneur and leadership team have a two-pronged role to play here. They must identify the strategies and assumptions at play in CoreCo when cost estimates are being worked out, and they must assess the costs to CoreCo of the work it is doing on its behalf. The next step is for CoreCo and NewCo to collaborate to ensure that the assumptions behind the estimates accurately reflect a common view of the support to be delivered. Finally, still working together, they make a list of the risks that might reasonably surface while CoreCo is delivering on its commitments. This is an iterative and interactive process with the goal of defining the impact in terms of cost, resources, and schedule if the risks materialize. At this point NewCo is assigned the responsibility of managing any budget associated with risk. Should risks surface at a later stage, the intrapreneur can gradually release funds to the appropriate CoreCo department to deal with them.

This fundamental risk management activity is too often missing from corporate startup environments. Separating risk from people's basic assumptions about the work required of CoreCo to support NewCo results in a much clearer picture of that work. Furthermore, in the process of documenting the potential risks (each with its own cost, resource, and schedule impact) CoreCo and NewCo have begun a conversation that will help clarify perceptions, assumptions, and expectations. This baseline of communication and collaboration will last for the lifetime of the startup. In my experience this approach leads to lower cost estimates and consequently an increased level of buy-in and collaboration from CoreCo's leadership teams.

Identifying the risks involved in supporting NewCo and applying a separate estimate for each validated risk has another benefit: people begin to think more profoundly about the differences and similarities between existing CoreCo activities and what can be expected of NewCo. In addition, it provides the finance and business development teams with more realistic data to conduct sensitivity analyses. If done properly a NewCo launch is based on realistic source estimates with well-understood risk profiles. The estimating and operational focus shifts from "underpromise and overdeliver" to "realistically estimate risk and effectively manage it." This fundamental cultural shift must be adopted if you want to increase the chances of NewCo's success.

NewCo will eventually develop the internal expertise to arrive at its own definitions of the work that is required of CoreCo, and by then both organizations will have a few years of validated historical data to draw on that will help them accurately estimate the costs of that work, something that was not available in NewCo's early days. When this happens the compounding cushion effect will diminish. However, there may still be valid reasons to request CoreCo departments to support NewCo, even following its transition from being a startup to being another one of CoreCo's established businesses. This is especially true of larger corporations with matrix organizations that achieve significant cost savings by having their divisions leverage centralized functions.

The Forecasting Trap

The purpose of forecasts is to provide objective and reliable estimates of the investments and operational expenses required to run a business. They help managers calculate important business parameters such as revenue growth, market share, and the costs associated with selling, delivering, and supporting goods and services. Managers are also better able to estimate ongoing research and development needs and product development funding. Established corporations use forecasts to achieve the maximum level of accuracy for projecting future business performance, and to help calculate the risks associated with a business so they can take necessary corrective actions.

The difficulty with CoreCo rigidly applying its forecasting process onto NewCo is that it forces the startup team to spend an exorbitant amount of time and effort trying to achieve levels of accuracy in their forecasts that are simply untenable so early in the game. CoreCo's insistence is generally well intentioned and stems from deep-rooted habits associated with analyzing the data and metrics of successful established businesses. Because the forecasting process is used throughout its divisions and business units, as well as for tracking its own incremental innovations, CoreCo is predisposed to applying the same methodology to assess the predictions about NewCo's performance. Once NewCo is launched, CoreCo requires forecasting information to decide whether or not to continue to invest in the startup, adjust its activities, or shut it down. From CoreCo's perspective, asking NewCo to adhere to the forecasting process of its parent company is a very reasonable request.

Some people at CoreCo might ask, "Why should NewCo not be held to the same standards we are?" The reason is simple: the two businesses are profoundly different. CoreCo developed its exacting methodology as a result of years of learning about its customers and markets, which led to validated assumptions that drive its forecasting models. NewCo is a new business operating in a unique market or market sub-segment, and it has acquired very few insights. This is an inherent reality of the startup environment, and CoreCo will have to accept it and demonstrate flexibility early on.

NewCo's forecasts of its financial results cannot have the same level of accuracy that CoreCo is accustomed to when projecting the financial outcomes of its core businesses. Nor can they capture the accuracy achieved in forecasts associated with making investments in incremental innovations within an existing CoreCo business. Accuracy will be achieved over time, but the very nature of launching a new business is one of assumptions and educated guesses, as represented in figure 7.2.

At the root of the assumptions behind an accurate forecast are the experiences and insights that a company gains of its market over time, and given that NewCo is just entering its market, its management team is short on both. In fact, NewCo's team will remain in a period of critical learning for the first 12 to 24 months. Their initial assumptions will be based on general insights, market surveys, and industry studies and research, which they will complement with anecdotal customer validations and feedback. Any predictions they make will be nothing more than educated best guesses.

CoreCo can expect that the assumptions behind NewCo's business model and growth projections will go through various iterations according to the five steps in figure 7.2. It is the iterative aspect of this process that leads to learning, and learning leads to improved accuracy and predictability.

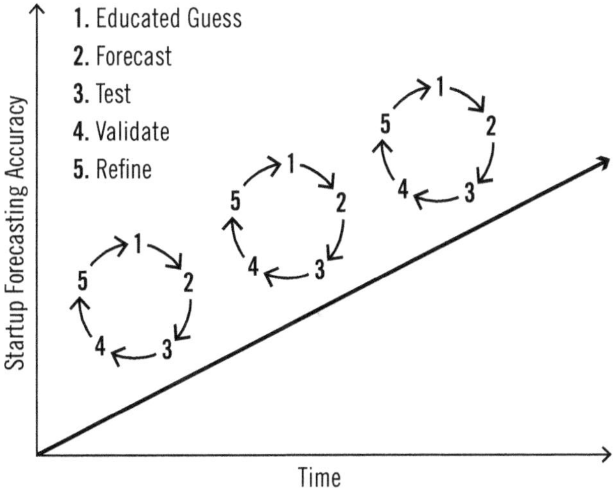

Figure 7.2 Iterative Learning Cycle

1. NewCo's initial educated guess is formed using raw data and subjectively validated assumptions, some of which were likely made during the innovation stage and in the weeks leading up to NewCo's launch. As time goes by these best guesses will be increasingly based on objective and validated data and will become more accurate.

2. The educated guess is combined with available data to form assumptions that are used to project trends for the metric of interest. These trends will cover a broad spectrum of activities related to every aspect of the startup's business, including customer buying behaviors, sales cycles, contracting and purchasing protocols, product adoption rates, and development costs.
3. Over time the NewCo team will increase its interactions with its new customers and build on their knowledge of how the proposed solution will address the unmet needs. It is through these interactions that the startup's business model will be tested and refined. At the same time NewCo will learn how it can drive revenue growth in a profitable and sustainable manner.
4. As NewCo tests its forecast, it will be able to link customer behaviors and feedback to the forecast's educated guess. This will provide a deeper appreciation of customer decision making and buying patterns, and will help bring increased accuracy to future forecasts.
5. Each iteration of this five-step process will lead to further refinements to the educated guess. Eventually the educated guess will become a solid assumption and, in most cases, a solid objective data point, leading to improved accuracy and predictability.

CoreCo, the sponsor, and the intrapreneur must remain alert to the possibility that some of CoreCo's leaders assume that NewCo is dealing with the same customers and markets as CoreCo. Such an assumption includes the idea that the same customer behaviors apply, which predisposes CoreCo to push NewCo to circumvent the iterative process shown in figure 7.2 and conclude prematurely that its business assumptions are valid.

There are many examples of companies that have made this mistake and subsequently were unsuccessful. Think of large legacy airlines that launched their own low-cost airline service to compete with thriving low-cost competitors only to struggle because they failed to ascertain that this sub-segment of the market behaves very differently when choosing a low-cost carrier. How about phone companies that tried to compete with the iPhone by adding more features to their existing smartphones without first taking into account the social aspects of the market sub-segment Apple had targeted (some say created)? What about car manufacturers that introduced higher-end luxury vehicles under their existing brand only to find few takers because they had missed the fact that people who buy luxury cars have unique buyer personas and buying behaviors?

I have made this mistake myself. When launching a new computer-based training business for the aviation industry, we assumed that we were targeting the same customers as in our core business and would face the same issues. We knew aviation training and we knew pilots, so how different could selling computer-based pilot training solutions be? We soon discovered that the airlines that were willing to be early adopters and transition some of the training conducted on a full-flight simulator to a computer-based platform needed a very different value proposition and purchasing model than what we originally proposed. What's more, we thought that we only had to convince the heads of training and their purchasing agents. These individuals obviously had to support the product and value its benefits, and the business case had to make sense to them before we could discuss contractual terms, but our biggest obstacle turned out to be convincing the airline's chief information officer and information technology director that our web-based solutions were robust, safe, and compatible with their IT infrastructures. This had a major impact on contracting and added significant delays to our ability to close deals, which, consequently, impacted our forecasting accuracy.

If you want to understand the forecasting trap, you need to grasp the magnitude of the learning challenge faced by a corporate startup. To start, let's expand on two primary business functions that anyone working at a CoreCo will be familiar with but might take for granted: creating and refining the business model and executing the launch of a product or service. The first depends on defined macro functions and the second on a wide range of essential micro activities.

Getting the Business Model Right

In their book *Confronting Reality: Doing What Matters to Get Things Right,* Larry Bossidy and Ram Charan present their concepts regarding what makes an effective business model, which inspired me to create figure 7.3. The three lists under the main titles – External Realities, Internal Activities, and Financial Targets – are not comprehensive; rather, they provide a sample of the most common points to consider in a business model. Each corporation will need to tailor it to its own situation.

On many occasions I have adapted Bossidy and Charan's iterative process when building or validating business models for both established businesses and NewCos. I have found it to be applicable to any product, service, or market. In other words, it works. Bossidy and Charan demonstrate that all business models require ongoing validation based on a series of iterative reviews that look at the business's internal activities, external realities, and desired financial target. The key to this process is to do it frequently, questioning and validating all aspects of the model and how they must interact to achieve success. This is fundamental to figuring out how to get where you want to go, and to focusing on the elements that will confirm that once you get there, you have reached your financial objectives.

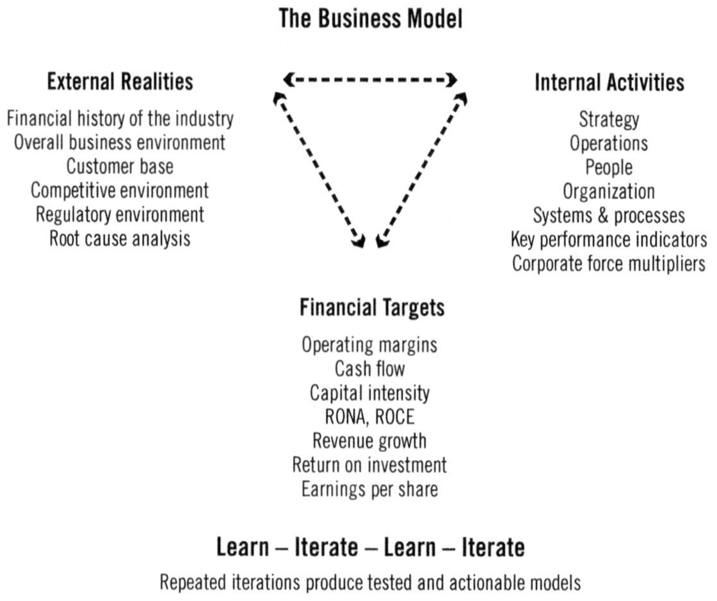

Figure 7.3 Summary of the Iterative Process

In NewCo's early phases iteration should be done weekly because so many discoveries are made when dealing with early adopters. As NewCo begins to grow and shifts from its early adopters to a broader market, the intrapreneur will become increasingly convinced that the business model is valid, meaning fewer changes will be made to its basic assumptions. At this point the frequency of iteration can switch to monthly, and later to quarterly.

With only a very preliminary and basic command of its external realities, each NewCo starts with a rudimentary understanding of the business model that will be required to succeed. This is reasonable given that the leadership team has not had much time to interface with customers and learn the dynamics of the new market, industry, and competitive landscape. Compounding the issue is the reality that a startup uses relatively immature internal processes that have been developed to address the needs of early adopters, and at the same time are developing others on an ad hoc basis to address activities and challenges as they surface. Finally, as we know from studying the compounding cushion effect, it is often the corporation that sets the startup's financial targets, which are based on a still-untested view of how the startup can make money in its market. Forecasting expectations for a NewCo must take all of this into consideration.

It bears saying again that it is the iterative aspect of this model that is fundamental to developing an accurate macro-level view of NewCo's business. Getting the business model right is far from being a one-time process. By repeatedly iterating the business model of projects I have worked on, I have made many discoveries that resulted in critical adjustments that allowed us to achieve success.

In one case it led us to redesign our internal systems and processes and to change our performance metrics to reflect the reality of our new market. In another case it helped us reach a much better understanding of the sub-segments of our market, and consequently we refined our market strategy and shifted our product development focus from the early adopters to the needs of the broader market. In a third case it resulted in a notable shift in our corporation's targets for returns on net assets (RONA), returns on capital employed (ROCE), and cash flow as we validated the asset-intensive nature of the new business with its requirements for large investments of fixed assets and working capital in exchange for generating more substantial cash flows. In all these examples we had to revise our initial financial targets to reflect the insights we had gained on how to achieve sustained and profitable growth.

Key Pre-Launch Activities

The micro-level activities associated with the launch of a new product or service present a different kind of learning challenge. The best way to impress upon you the magnitude of this challenge, which for NewCo is to achieve the level of market knowledge that CoreCo has of its core markets and products, is to draw from marketing models. Over the years I have found that the Pragmatic Marketing Framework™ does a good job of mapping the tasks that must be executed prior to going to market. It identifies 37 such tasks under seven broad categories:

1. **Market tasks:** technology assessment, competitive landscape, distinctive competence, win/loss analysis, market problems
2. **Focus tasks:** product roadmap, product portfolio, distribution strategy, market definition
3. **Business tasks:** innovation, product profitability, buy/build/partner, pricing, business plan
4. **Planning tasks:** status dashboards, use scenarios, requirements, user personas, buyer personas, buying process, positioning
5. **Programs tasks:** referrals and references, lead generation, thought leadership, launch plan, program effectiveness, customer acquisition, customer retention, marketing plan
6. **Readiness tasks:** channels training, sales tools, collateral, sales process
7. **Support tasks:** channel support, event support, special calls, presentation and demos

It is important to comprehend the scope of the tasks that must be completed when introducing a new product or service. If you have a role to play in managing CoreCo's expectations of NewCo's forecasts, the above list will give you a sense of the work required and the customer and market insights that are necessary to achieve profitability. Each of these 37 tasks represents a grouping of marketing activities that must be undertaken to transition a new product or service from an idea or prototype to a successful launch, and then to ensure it thrives in the marketplace. The level of effort will vary according to each case, and in some instances certain tasks may not be required, especially if the launch is of a new service rather than a product or technology. Regardless, do not underestimate the amount of work involved.

CoreCo is able to effectively execute these activities because it has a profound knowledge of its products, markets, and industry. This knowledge is accumulated over years or even decades and is embedded in the company's established systems and processes. It is this maturity that enables CoreCo to achieve a relatively high level of forecasting accuracy and business predictability when introducing incremental innovations or new products or services to its customer base.

In contrast, many unknowns characterize NewCo's startup environment. The number of discoveries NewCo makes will increase as it delves deeper into its market and deals with more customers. Remember that every one of the 37 activities comes with a high degree of uncertainty and demands wide-ranging learning. Chipping away at the uncertainty that exists across every one of these micro-level activities will take considerable time and require NewCo to make several iterations of its business model. Only then will it begin to stabilize its assumptions and provide a level of accuracy that CoreCo will find acceptable.

Avoiding the Forecasting Trap

The forecasting environment that will benefit NewCo in its early phases reflects the uncertainty in two sets of activities: those that inform the macro-level business model and those undertaken at the micro level leading up to the launch. The forecasting process must encourage learning, knowledge sharing, and frequent validation, and it must allow for necessary adjustments. There will be trial and error. Yes, I said error. CoreCo must tolerate the presence of error and make sure that the people involved learn everything they can from it. Errors are part of the learning cycle for any startup. The intrapreneur, sponsor, and gatekeeper are responsible for creating a safe environment where errors can be discussed and resulting discoveries can be shared. This is an indispensable ingredient in ensuring that NewCo learns quickly and uses its learning to establish a solid foundation for future projections.

The iterative learning cycle is a process of continuous improvement that over time leads to forecasting that is substantially more accurate. Rushing the cycle means that NewCo is cutting corners and building its business model on top of a weak foundation of improperly validated core business assumptions. Rushing also pushes the startup to finalize its solution too early and scale its operations prematurely. It is asking for poor results. Conversely, letting it go on for too long leads to wasting precious time and money. Worse, it prevents NewCo from making pivotal modifications to its key assumptions early on, with an outcome no one wants: stagnation. It is up to the intrapreneur, sponsor, and the head of NewCo finance to make sure that the iterative learning cycle is managed properly and that NewCo demonstrates the ability to make better assumptions over time.

Do Not Leave Learning to Chance

As with any important performance indicator, you must track the progress of NewCo's learning. This can be achieved by defining metrics that show two kinds of improvement: in the quality of the business model's key assumptions as measured by a reduction in assumption changes and a shift from validating broad assumptions to refining validated ones, and in the speed of learning as measured by a reduction in the frequency of broad changes in assumptions about the business model. Setting up the right metrics to track progress in these areas requires a keen understanding of the main assumptions underpinning NewCo's business model. If these assumptions are imperfectly identified, testing and reviewing them on a regular basis will be of little use.

Every time NewCo's team iterates the business model in figure 7.2 after they have executed the activities in figure 7.3, NewCo's forecasts should demonstrate increased accuracy and predictability. This is an indication that NewCo's management team is improving its awareness of, and comfort with, vital elements of the startup's financial engine for profit and growth. If this is not happening, or if you are the sponsor and you find that NewCo is not progressing well in the quality or speed of its learning, you will need to meet with the intrapreneur and find out why learning has stagnated. It is never too soon to get NewCo back on the learning curve.

Learning from Errors

I stated earlier that corporate patience does not mean that NewCo gets a blank check for burning cash. The same goes for learning. Learning must not be used as an excuse for repeatedly missing forecasts. Negligence, incompetence, and errors due to laziness are unacceptable, and repeated errors that would have been avoided if sound learning had taken place must not be tolerated. The learning from errors I am referring to relates to errors that were based on original assumptions that were reasonable, but were nonetheless educated best guesses. These types of guesses necessarily result in hits and misses. Celebrate and learn from the hits. Highlight the misses and learn from them too.

It is unwise to sweep misses under the carpet. Rather, it is precisely by recognizing what caused these misses that you will refine your business assumptions and begin to improve the accuracy of your forecasts. Only through the confirmation or invalidation of key assumptions will NewCo be able to continuously perfect its business model until it gets it right.

Dealing with Lumpy Data

A discussion on the need to adjust CoreCo's expectations regarding NewCo's forecasts would not be complete without highlighting CoreCo's unease with lumpy data. I have noticed over the years that financial analysts are generally uncomfortable with forecasts that look chunky or clumsy, meaning the data is not represented by the smooth slopes or curves we all like to see in charts. The term for this is lumpy data. The desire for smooth data is sensible given that slopes or curves are needed to analyze patterns and behaviors and to predict trends. CoreCo's tendency is to view any data that does not look coherent and predictable as a missed projection or a forecasting inaccuracy.

At first glance the bar graphs, line charts, and spreadsheet columns representing NewCo's business results will very likely appear irregular. This is because the progress NewCo is making with early adopters is typically slow and its expenditures, sales, and revenues have almost no critical mass behind them. This type of variability can be expected of a new business dealing with new customers, so you must resist the temptation to adjust the data to make these lumpy forecasts look more predictable. Both CoreCo and NewCo need to accept that the startup environment is a far cry from CoreCo's well-ordered world.

By adjusting data to make it look less lumpy, you are robbing CoreCo's stakeholders on three counts: from sharing in the lessons learned in NewCo's early days, from keeping pace with the adjustments being made in its business assumptions, and from appreciating the challenges NewCo is facing. You also risk giving CoreCo the impression that NewCo's forecasts are on the predictable side when actually they are still unstable. All of the above can lead CoreCo and NewCo to develop a diverging view of the business and its market, which will become the source of confusion and future conflicts.

If, by chance, NewCo ends up delivering results that are in line with the fluid-looking forecasts, then no one is the wiser and the issues behind the lumpy data never manifest. But reality tells us this scenario is unlikely. If it does happen it is by pure luck, and luck is no way to manage business initiatives.

The problems caused by artificially adjusted data can be quite serious. One problem is that CoreCo executives get accustomed to being presented with smooth projections and conclude that NewCo's growth pattern is following an expected trajectory. Therefore they will not ask important hard questions and will miss the chance to share in the lessons that were learned about success factors like customer buying behaviors, pricing, distribution channels, product development focus, and NewCo spending. After a few review cycles, when NewCo's business continues to be lumpy and its lumpiness is finally exposed, CoreCo might assume that NewCo's reporting is faulty. It may take this as a sign of poor management or erratic market behaviors and demand major reviews, impose adjustments to the business, or go as far as deciding on leadership changes, all of which might be unwarranted.

If you are an executive who is involved with a startup, you can thwart the temptation of its leaders to present you with smoothed-out data by following these four steps:

1. Have NewCo's management team present its results only to CoreCo's senior people. It is a mistake to rely on subordinates who have a cursory grasp of NewCo's business and few insights to help them interpret the data. Subordinates are not accountable for NewCo's success, so their stakes are low.
2. Assign a financial leader to NewCo from the onset. This must be a senior person at CoreCo who gets how a business is run and makes money. Look for someone who has demonstrated the ability to work as a business partner and has the curiosity needed to analyze data and provide insights that explain trends. He will answer to the intrapreneur and grow with the team, and over time will become deeply familiar with all aspects of NewCo's business reality. His main responsibility will be ensuring that an accurate financial view of the startup is presented every time. He can explain lumpy data and the similarities and differences between NewCo's and CoreCo's business models. He will also be an invaluable resource to NewCo's intrapreneur, chief technology officer, and head of product development in that he can provide them with objective reports on the progress actually being made and inject a sobering view into conversations among overly enthusiastic leaders whose excitement might lead them to overlook key business data.
3. Remember to leverage the sponsor and gatekeeper. Both play a primary role in influencing the perceptions of CoreCo's executives, and they are well positioned to educate their colleagues on the nature of NewCo's business environment. Their input will also help CoreCo gain insights into how NewCo's customers make their buying decisions.
4. If the data presented looks too coherent, question it. It is my experience that in the early days of a startup, if the data looks too good to be true, it probably is. I have asked my NewCo teams many times to dig deeper into the data and come back with more specificity.

COMING UP NEXT....................

The difficulties associated with estimating and forecasting that are covered in this chapter require solutions that are best developed by CoreCo and NewCo following a collaborative approach. These issues will arise immediately after the decision to launch NewCo, and as the startup grows they will require increasing attention from the intrapreneur and his team.

This is why properly timing NewCo's exposure to the realities of the business world is a critical step in its successful evolution, and the topic of labor 8.

The Mares of Diomedes

On the shores of the Black Sea there lived four magnificent wild mares that belonged to the brutal king of Thrace, Diomedes. For his eighth labor Hercules was commanded to capture the mares, which were known to be savage because they fed on human flesh. First he had to successfully battle their grooms and guards. When this was done and the horses were under control, he was attacked by a band of local soldiers who were determined to recapture them. Hercules asked his companion, Abderos, to watch over the horses so he could fight the soldiers. Abderos was unprepared for this task and was soon devoured. After killing the soldiers and their king, Hercules fed Diomedes to the beasts, knowing that eating him would make them calm. Hercules was now able to lead them back to King Eurystheus.

LABOR 8

Preparing the Startup for Corporate Exposure

The intrapreneur's eighth labor is to correctly time NewCo's exposure to CoreCo. This is similar to Hercules' struggle to capture the wild mares in that exposing NewCo will immediately trigger attempts by the corporation to reign in the startup and force existing business practices onto it. Furthermore, for the intrapreneur to avoid the terrible fate of Abderos, the sponsor must work closely with him to ensure he is well prepared to successfully tame the resistance of any dissenting CoreCo department heads. The intrapreneur can easily become overwhelmed during these initial weeks, making it harder to know which are the surrounding threats he should turn his attention to first. Only by wisely prioritizing his time will he be able to pull off a successful launch.

The major benefit of a carefully timed NewCo launch is gaining access to the full range of CoreCo's resources. If improperly timed NewCo's lifespan could be very short. Executing a launch too early – before the innovation has sufficiently matured and while NewCo's leadership team is still unprepared for the corporate pressures to come – can lead NewCo to buckle and yield to CoreCo's insistence on sales and revenues. Feeling pressured, the intrapreneur might release an improperly validated product onto the market. On the other hand, delaying the launch for too long can result in the innovation's premature extinction as the excitement around it sinks to a disastrous level because progress is too slow. The question that will preoccupy the sponsor and intrapraneur is: How long should we keep this new business idea quiet?

One approach is to allow NewCo to stay under the radar for as long as possible, which usually means until CoreCo's senior leadership team becomes emphatic about establishing hard deadlines. Working under the radar has the advantage of delaying the triggering of the corporate immune system. This corporate reaction is not only real, it is powerful, and can have many negative consequences that must be expertly handled, so much so that it is the focus of labor 11. I have experienced the corporate immune system within my own organizations when launching NewCos, and have witnessed it across other corporations when I was helping create joint ventures and strategic partnerships. It will cause havoc if improperly managed.

Even though the intrapreneur will have to face CoreCo's immune system at some point, it is reasonable to want to avoid it for as long as possible. But putting off the formal launch for this sole reason can be bad for NewCo, for example, potential partners or early adopters may disappear. The better approach is to be proactive, which includes assessing the readiness of the product or service and the innovation team behind it to transition out of the innovation phase. This assessment is based on grasping the advantages and disadvantages of both delaying the launch and setting a firm date for it. These will be explored later on in the chapter.

There will come a time when CoreCo's expectations of seeing hard deadlines can no longer be deferred, or the work being done on the new product or service begins to interfere with other CoreCo activities, creating friction. Either or both of these situations will cause the intrapreneur and sponsor to evaluate if NewCo requires broader access to CoreCo's resources. If it does, it is time to launch. As we saw in earlier chapters, one of the main competitive advantages the corporate startup brings to its market is its ability to access the parent company's resources and know-how. NewCo's urgent need to leverage CoreCo to accelerate its progress is what tips the balance in favor of proceeding to the formal launch.

NewCo's launch should simply be viewed as another activity that will help accelerate its growth. Prior to making the important decision regarding timing, the sponsor, the intrapreneur, and CoreCo must share a deep understanding of the tasks involved. Like Hercules taming the four wild mares, there are four areas that might spin out of control if they are not thoroughly understood in advance. The intrapreneur, the sponsor, and CoreCo's leaders who are involved in NewCo must:

1. Fully appreciate what a formal launch entails
2. Have a thorough knowledge of the phases of the innovation process
3. Be informed about CoreCo's assessment of the startup's risks
4. Comprehend the work that is required to properly launch a new product or service

1. Understanding the Formal Launch

The message at the heart of the formal launch is as follows: a new business is being established at CoreCo that will be distinct from and independent of the corporation's other businesses, and it will enter a new market or a new segment of an existing market that previously was not served by the corporation. CoreCo's executive leadership team will deliver this message in two ways: through a corporate strategic commitment and an official declaration. The corporate strategic commitment acknowledges that NewCo is part of the corporation's strategic plan with clearly stated medium- and long-term expectations, and that budgets and resources will be assigned to it as necessary so it can meet financial objectives that are material. The official declaration is an internally directed statement whose purpose is to clarify the startup's vision and goals and mobilize support among CoreCo's various leadership teams.

Three criteria must be expressed at the time of the formal launch: the need to establish a distinct entity within CoreCo, the assignment of budgets and resources commensurate with the entity's financial objectives, and the commitment of support not only from senior managers, but from everyone in the corporation. These announcements are never taken lightly. They send a strong signal, and managers throughout CoreCo will begin to formulate expectations and think about the role they will play. It is extremely important that the launch does not take place until NewCo is ready to deal with the fallout.

2. Phases of the Innovation Process

To know when to time the launch we must review how innovations are managed within successful intrapreneurial organizations. This will spell out how much development work on the new product or service can be done during the innovation phase, and how many marketing activities can be completed. Most innovation processes include a series of tollgates. The tollgates are actually checkpoints where the innovations are objectively evaluated for whether they should receive further funding, be put on pause, or terminated. This leads to the gradual pruning of initiatives. In the world of corporate innovation various methods have been developed to manage the innovation process. One of the most successful is the Stage-Gate® process created by Dr. Robert Cooper, a widely recognized expert in the field. Dr. Cooper has written many books, including the best-selling *Winning at New Products* and *Portfolio Management for New Products*.

The Stage-Gate process reproduced in figure 8.1 tracks the progress of ideas from selection through investigation, development, and launch. It can be adapted to fit the nature and complexity of any product or service being evaluated and allows the innovations to move through the process at various speeds. Each gate has a pre-established set of objectives and business criteria that are used to make assessments and comparisons. The conclusions determine whether the innovation progresses to the next level, is sent back for more analysis and validation, or is terminated.

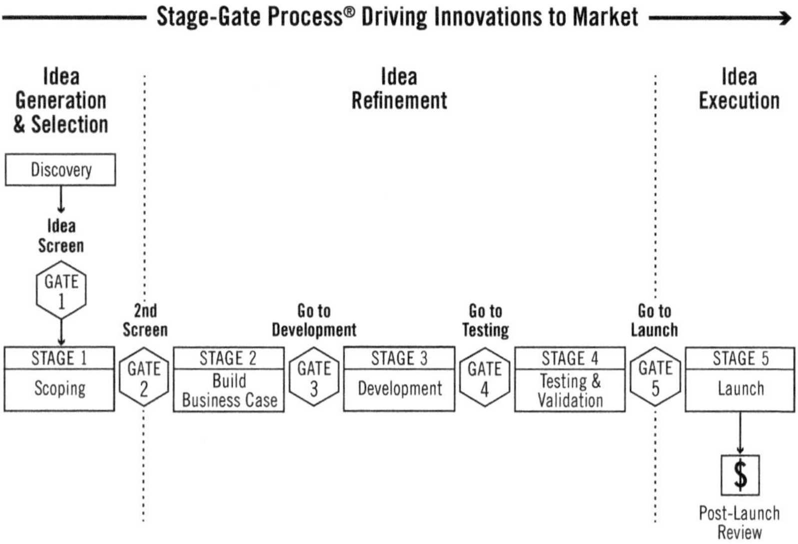

Figure 8.1 The Stage-Gate Process

According to Dr. Cooper, the launch of a product or service takes place after leaving gate 5. I am in full agreement, that is, if we are talking about launching in an existing business or line of business within CoreCo. Intrapreneurship, however, adds a level of complexity. Remember, a major difference exists between an innovation being launched in CoreCo's core markets or customer segments and one being launched via the creation of a NewCo. The difference is that the latter is confronted with a much higher degree of product and market uncertainty, and this dictates the need for additional effort prior to the formal launch if NewCo is to be rolled out successfully.

3. Business Assumption Risk

From CoreCo's perspective the decision to transition from the innovation phase to NewCo's formal launch is primarily one of assessing and managing the risks inherent in its business assumptions. The higher the level of risk associated with the new business, the longer the incubation and validation periods should be. It is critical to use these periods to assess risk and develop risk mitigation strategies to minimize the possibility of risk becoming reality. To evaluate the business assumption risks, corporations gauge the number of disruptions a new product or service is relying on to succeed.

As we saw in labor 6, it is generally accepted that there are three business activities that lead to disruption: introducing new technology, entering a new market, and leveraging new distribution channels. Each disruption is accompanied by a high level of unknowns, so the business assumption risk is lower if only one is anticipated, and substantially more if two or all three – technology, market, and channel – are present. For example, introducing a new technology by leveraging CoreCo's existing distribution channel into a well-known customer base is less risky than introducing a new technology into an unfamiliar market using untested distribution channels. It makes sense that the riskier a new business idea, the longer it remains in the innovation phase.

The best way to deal with the many unknowns associated with NewCo is to draw on sound risk assessment practices. Risk assessment is all about anticipating what could reasonably go wrong with your initiative and preparing accordingly. For this reason best practices in risk management suggest that once risks are properly identified and documented, they must be systematically assessed for their impact potential and probability of occurrence. The impact potential captures the effect the risk will have on NewCo's business objectives and the probability of occurrence evaluates the likelihood it will materialize. In each case, the higher the estimated impact, the higher the rating assigned. The end result is a ranking of risks with the ones with the highest estimated impact and probability of occurrence at the top and those with the least at the bottom.

With this list in hand you can prioritize your risk mitigation efforts and begin to assign contingency budgets to cover potential risk mitigation activities. These mitigation activities will help you prepare for the eventual NewCo launch by allowing you and your team to focus your energy on the risks with the highest ranking. They need to be understood and planned for prior to the launch for it to be successful. The lower-ranked risks can be tolerated for the time being and managed post-launch.

An efficient way to determine which business activities carry risk, and how much, is to conduct an objective review of the 37 marketing activities that were covered in labor 7. Revisit the seven broad categories on page 128 so you will not be tempted to underestimate the level of effort required to successfully launch a new product or service.

After conducting the review NewCo's focus should be on the activities that are likely to carry the most risk based on the type of disruption being introduced, whether technology, market, channel, or all three. For example, if technology disruptions will be significant, special attention must be paid to the risk assessments of the activities related to technology evaluation, product roadmap, innovation, and customer requirements. If channel disruptions will be problematic, NewCo's team must review the risk assessments of the activities pertaining to distribution strategy, pricing, buying personas and process, and overall market readiness. Ultimately, for CoreCo to authorize the launch, the innovation work must have progressed sufficiently to satisfy CoreCo that this is a business worth investing in and that the future rewards outweigh the potential risks.

Every CoreCo will view risk differently based on its level of corporate risk tolerance, and this will influence its decision on when to proceed with NewCo's launch. Keep in mind that the more disruptions the startup introduces, the greater the number of business assumption risks the NewCo team will have to face. This higher level of unknowns means there will be less corporate knowledge for NewCo to draw on when launching its new product or service. If this is the case more time will be needed in the innovation phase, time that will be well spent mitigating the business assumption risks.

4. Work Required to Launch

When working through the 37 activities it can help to use a color-coding system, with green indicating completion, yellow for tasks you have started for which good preliminary data exists but further validation is needed, and red for those not yet begun or only barely begun. If you are using this system and you have set a date for the launch, it will be because there are no or very few red activities left and the activities that received a high impact-probability rating that are critical to NewCo's initial success are all marked in green, meaning they have been completed. The remaining tasks, marked in yellow, have been validated as carrying an acceptable level of risk and show they are making good progress.

Do not attempt to complete all of the activities prior to the formal launch. Even though an effort of that magnitude sounds commendable, it would be inefficient. Certain activities require in-depth market knowledge that can only be gained from working closely with early adopters. Trying to complete them prematurely will result in having to redo the work, which amounts to wasted time and money. Conversely, leaving too many activities marked in yellow before the launch is ill advised because it demonstrates poor knowledge of the customers' needs and what is required to launch successfully, have an impact, and make money.

The Soft Launch

What the future NewCo requires prior to its launch is a period of time that mimics the early stages of an independent startup, when activities are focused on validation and efficiency. These activities go beyond what occurs internally within a corporation. The independent startup takes the basic solution, often referred to as a minimally viable product (MVP), to an early adopter group that is willing to contribute money and/or time to improve it. The efficiency stage that follows focuses on gathering customer feedback and using it to refine the business model and turn the MVP into a production-ready solution that is easily repeatable. Customer feedback is equally essential when fine-tuning sales and distribution processes in preparation for the scaling of business activities that comes with a broad market launch.

Every early-stage corporate startup should face the same customer and market challenges as its independent counterpart. This means giving it time to complete validation and efficiency work before moving to the formal launch and the challenges of rapidly scaling its operations. I call this period the soft launch, which in figure 8.1 would constitute a new gate situated between gates 4 and 5. The soft launch phase is a period of further incubation focused on working with early adopters. It provides NewCo with time to validate its disruptive new product or service, build momentum with early users, and achieve some successes prior to being given broader market exposure.

Prior to the soft launch, the innovation team works with seed funding and receives support from within CoreCo by calling in favors from colleagues in various departments who are happy to contribute time and expertise. Because these resources are fairly limited, several of the 37 activities remain marked in red during this period, there are a small number of greens, and the majority are yellow. Eventually the innovation progresses to the testing and validation phase. If it continues to show great promise, further funding is authorized and preparations are begun for the soft launch.

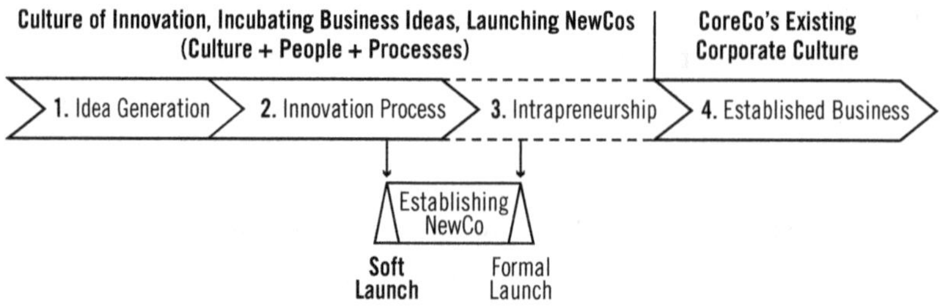

Figure 8.2 The Soft Launch and Formal Launch

The additional funding that comes with the soft launch buys more resources, which enable the team to proceed with important engineering and product development while doing testing and validation of its MVP with early customers. Working with customers allows the team to verify certain assumptions in the preliminary business model and gain insight into how the business idea will make money. Another advantage is that during these weeks or months the intrapreneur and sponsor can seek new access to the corporation's business systems and processes. They also give the intrapreneur more time to work with the innovation team to advance many of the 37 marketing activities so that red ones become yellow and yellow ones become green. Near the end of the soft launch phase CoreCo will be given one last checkpoint, when it will conduct a final business risk assessment prior to proceeding with the formal launch.

I want to emphasize that a soft launch is a validation and learning phase and not a trial period. Do not proceed to a soft launch unless you are convinced there is a high level of certainty that the initiative will move to a formal launch. If you are convinced, the ideal time to assign the intrapreneur is just prior to the soft launch phase. During this period the newly assigned intrapreneur will further assess the market, refine assumptions, and acquire valuable experience that will help him take ownership of the startup, set the right expectations, and prepare NewCo for its formal launch.

A soft launch is a great opportunity to get the innovation out of the lab and into the hands of a few early adopters who can begin to use it and provide invaluable feedback. These early adopters are typically in a hurry to possess new technology, and for this reason they have a higher tolerance for errors or defects associated with an MVP. They are also very motivated and will work with the team to help specify if the innovation can become a profitable business. Customers who are willing to spend their valuable time and resources validating a new idea are a clear indication that the idea has potential. How big the potential is yet to be determined. In this early-adopter period NewCo must be unafraid to seek brutally honest reviews, which are essential for refining the innovation. Once the intrapreneur and sponsor decide NewCo is ready for a larger group of early adopters and, subsequently, a broader market, the launch date can be set.

There is no perfect time for formally launching NewCo and inviting corporate scrutiny. In fact, it might be less risky to slowly inch the innovation forward while working under the radar. But it could be riskier still to forego NewCo's access to serious funding and the corporation's vast resources and extensive toolkit, which will be the case without launching. The formal launch has to happen and the hard decision must be made as to when. Taking everything into account, the time to trigger the launch is when the sponsor, the intrapreneur, and CoreCo's executive stakeholders have assessed that NewCo has proven its business potential and developed acceptable mitigation plans to address the more serious business risks. Everyone agrees that the innovation is ready to be established as a stand-alone business and will benefit from receiving exponentially more funding, resources, and access to the corporate force multipliers (CFMs) necessary to quickly scale its business activities and operations.

Market readiness means different things to different corporations. A common marker is that the product or service has reached the point in its development when it can be exposed to a broader customer base. It has been validated and sufficiently honed to move the solution from an MVP or stable working prototype to a production-ready solution. It will have undergone a series of preliminary validations with end users who reported that their unmet needs were met and some early adopters will have already paid for the early versions of the NewCo solution. Early optimism – that one day a larger customer base will pay for the product or service – has become certainty.

Launching NewCo positions it squarely on CoreCo's radar. This triggers significant benefits, not the least of which are resources and broader support. But the drawbacks can be overwhelming if the launch is not properly timed and managed. See the two tables on the next page for a breakdown of the advantages and disadvantages of delaying the launch and deciding to go for it.

Table 8.1 Delaying NewCo's Launch

ADVANTAGES	DISADVANTAGES
Innovations can be validated and refined with little interference	Access to people and equipment that will advance the project is delayed
More time to verify if the product or service will achieve buy-in from CoreCo's executive leadership team	Access to greater funding and abundant resources is delayed
Early support can be sought within key CoreCo groups, which will help sell the idea later on	Key CoreCo groups have little opportunity to engage with NewCo or offer support
Work environment is open and collaborative rather than threatening	People who hear negative rumors maybe become naysayers
Formal financial objectives and business goals can be faced another day	Unrealistic expectations regarding what can be achieved by NewCo can develop
Strong ability to control the message and prevent information leaks	Potential external partners may pass on the project because they perceive it is not a CoreCo priority
Creation of a cohesive team environment and sense of excitement	Agreements with potential clients may be delayed because the innovation appears insignificant and not a CoreCo commitment
Maximizes learning, leading to a better understanding of the investment requirements if the innovation becomes a NewCo	Feedback is unavailable from large volumes of customers, which is required for learning and validation
More MVP iterations lead to more validation, and more marketing tasks can be completed	CoreCo's interest wanes, leading to less support, delays, and extended timelines
Flexibility can be maintained in how the work is carried out	Limited resources lead to limited learning opportunities
CoreCo has more time to identify and evaluate potential candidates for the role of intrapreneur	Internal perceptions arise that this is someone's pet project and a waste of time

Table 8.2 Launching NewCo

ADVANTAGES	DISADVANTAGES
The innovation and intrapreneurship teams feel a sense of urgency	Formal perceptions create pressure to hit financial targets, and informal and perception expectations begin to take shape (labor 4)
Supporting departments within CoreCo feel excited and committed	The corporate immune system is activated (labor 11)
More resources (people and equipment) and financing become available to NewCo	Leaks to NewCo's competition become more likely
NewCo has greater exposure to CoreCo employees for potential transfers to NewCo	NewCo's small team must deal with CoreCo's expectations and constraints
CoreCo executives declare their support	Flexibility in the way NewCo operates decreases
Potential partners and customers recognize NewCo's credibility, facilitating agreements and partnerships	More CoreCo department heads want information, leading to more meetings and meddling
NewCo can access more internal channels for ideas on how to leverage CoreCo	Some CoreCo department heads jump in to help, leading to delays
NewCo has the formal go-ahead to leverage CoreCo as necessary	CoreCo's shareholders scrutinize NewCo and apply pressure to deliver unrealistic short-term results

Corporate Expectations Risk

There is one more component for CoreCo, the sponsor, and the intrapreneur to consider when determining the timing of the formal launch. It relates to the importance of NewCo's contribution to CoreCo's overall corporate business strategy and financial results, as outlined in table 6.1 on page 105. I call it the corporate expectations risk. The intrapreneur would be wise to actively participate in assessing this risk because it will directly impact his ability to comprehend and capture the formal expectations covered in labor 4.

To effectively assess the corporate expectations risk, it is necessary to understand how three elements come together to create the best opportunity for NewCo to succeed within its corporate environment. These elements are CoreCo's time expectations for NewCo to start showing positive results, NewCo's financial materiality to CoreCo, and NewCo's market similarities to CoreCo's core businesses. In other words, how quickly is NewCo expected to make money and does CoreCo have the patience to wait? How much money is NewCo projected to make and will it matter to CoreCo's overall business results? How similar to CoreCo's market is NewCo's market and will CoreCo give NewCo the operational flexibility it requires to succeed? The way these three variables interact will influence the decision of whether or not to launch a startup.

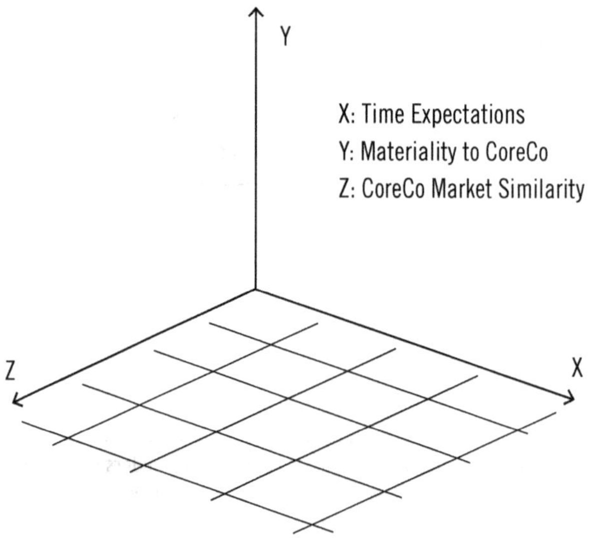

Figure 8.3 The Time-Materiality-Market Similarity Variables

Time Expectations to Success (X-axis)

This represents how much time CoreCo has given NewCo to succeed. The focus is on "how quickly." At what rate does CoreCo expect NewCo to grow? The faster the expected growth rate and the shorter the assigned timeframe, the more effectively NewCo must leverage CoreCo's CFMs. This time element, which we first saw in the SMART objectives in labor 4, varies for each NewCo. Although every corporation defines success differently, for itself and for NewCos it establishes, most definitions include annual market penetration objectives, each with its own rate of year-over-year growth. Examples include number of customers or users to be signed, market share objectives, and financial objectives that can include revenues and profitability.

Materiality to CoreCo (Y-axis)

This axis represents CoreCo's expectations regarding NewCo's materiality. We covered the financial aspects of materiality in labor 6, which refers to a certain threshold at which point NewCo's financial results become relevant to CoreCo's overall performance. It has nothing to do with comparing NewCo's results to its previous results; rather, the focus is on the contribution to CoreCo's larger financial picture. This long-term goal was captured in table 6.1, and is usually defined in terms of revenue and profit contributions, and in metrics such as margins or earnings per share contributions. Materiality also considers the investments required to get NewCo up and running. These can be in the form of capital and operational costs and are always weighed against CoreCo's investment risk tolerance. For this reason investments vary greatly across companies. The investments required might be so material that CoreCo decides to delay the formal launch so it can raise new funds to finance the startup.

There is another element to materiality: the amount of management time and mindshare CoreCo expends on NewCo. This area of materiality is often ignored, which is easy to do because it is rarely seen in timesheets, operational expenditure spreadsheets, or ROI calculations. But management materiality has significance. If CoreCo's leaders are spending a large number of hours on NewCo, they have less time to run CoreCo's other businesses. This must be considered when timing NewCo's launch. The financial aspects of materiality are key, but management attention must also be considered. In some cases CoreCo can decide to delay NewCo's launch because there are urgent strategic and operational issues that require its management focus.

CoreCo Market Similarity (Z-axis)

This refers to the level of intimacy CoreCo has with NewCo's target market. If a corporation wants to avoid wrongly assuming that a new market segment will behave similarly to its existing ones, it must identify which of the following three categories NewCo's market falls into:

1. **Same market, same segment.** If NewCo's target market is the same as CoreCo's and in the same segment, the amount of learning required of NewCo's management team to work effectively will be low, and CoreCo will feel less pressure to modify

or reinvent its systems, processes, and organizations. The business assumption risks related to NewCo will also likely be low.

2. **Same market, different segment.** If NewCo's target market is the same as CoreCo's but it exists in a different segment, NewCo will have to face the challenge of leveraging more of CoreCo's resources, processes, and systems. Modifications to some of CoreCo's business practices will be required and there may be a need for a few new business processes. The business assumption risks related to NewCo will likely be moderate.
3. **Different market, different segment.** If NewCo's target market and segment are outside of CoreCo's existing ones, CoreCo will feel strong pressure to modify or reinvent a greater number of its business practices. A new market brings an unfamiliar business culture, meaning a different set of rules, processes, and systems, possibly even surprisingly different. A lot more work will be required of NewCo's team to understand this market, and more time will be needed to complete the 37 marketing activities. This scenario carries the highest level of business assumption risks.

The Best Time to Launch

Determining the optimal time for the formal launch equates with giving NewCo the maximum chance for success. Every NewCo is unique, so you must study the advantages and disadvantages and find the balance that fits your situation. If you are the sponsor or intrapreneur, the best time for the launch will be a function of when you feel most ready to face the risks associated with CoreCo's time expectations, sufficient validation has taken place to prepare NewCo to scale its operations to meet CoreCo's materiality expectations, and NewCo and CoreCo agree on how different the target market is from your parent company's.

To help you know when you are ready, I have further broken down the analysis you must undertake into three matrices: time expectations versus materiality to CoreCo, materiality to CoreCo versus CoreCo market similarity, and time expectations versus CoreCo market similarity. The remainder of this chapter will focus on learning how to use these matrices to bring more objectivity to the decision of when to launch. As a byproduct you will gain insight into how the corporate immune system will likely react (as will be discussed in labor 11), and your team will have the opportunity to revisit the 37 pre-launch marketing activities and reprioritize them if necessary. Finally, everyone who is weighing in on the decision of when to launch will come away with a clearer appreciation of NewCo's upcoming business challenges.

Time Expectations versus Materiality to CoreCo

The more an innovation is projected to be financially material to CoreCo, the more it makes sense to transform it into a startup, and the more likely it is that NewCo will require resources from CoreCo. This demand will trigger increased interest and attention from management. The four quadrants in figure 8.4 can help you determine where your innovation fits relative to the other innovations being evaluated, and whether or not it warrants becoming a NewCo. Your analysis will also yield clues regarding the scope of CoreCo's immune system reaction.

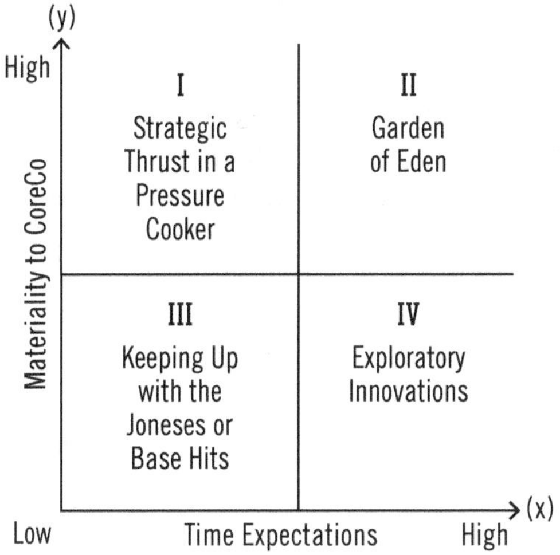

Figure 8.4 Time Expectations versus Materiality to CoreCo

Quadrant I – Strategic Thrust in a Pressure Cooker

Quadrant I captures initiatives that have been assessed as high materiality-low time. This is where you will typically find innovations that have been placed on the CoreCo fast track. I refer to them as Strategic Thrust in a Pressure Cooker ideas because their high materiality means they form part of CoreCo's strategic objectives. If time-wise they are on a short leash it is usually because CoreCo is feeling market pressure or has a small window of opportunity to enter a market. Either way, CoreCo urgently wants them to perform and grow. If you have an innovation that falls into this category, review it immediately for a NewCo launch, though if it is still being led informally or forms part of someone's secondary objectives, you will need to reconsider. Another choice is to accelerate the process of appointing a full-time intrapreneur.

If you choose the latter, you will need to re-evaluate the innovation to assess its market readiness and to understand how CoreCo's CFMs can be successfully leveraged to meet the aggressive time expectations. But you must also revisit the time expectations to determine if they are realistic. Chances are, this initiative is already on the company's radar and its immune system is active to some degree. If its future results have been included in the growth forecast for CoreCo's inner years, the immune system will be on high alert. How similar the new market is to CoreCo's will also influence its activity. The more different it is, the stronger the response of the corporate immune system.

Quadrant II – Garden of Eden

Quadrant II identifies initiatives with high materiality-high time expectations. I call these Garden of Eden innovations because they have the potential to deliver a substantial financial impact and therefore typically receive good funding and support, and they have been given lots of time to succeed. For these innovations, the immediate pressure is off. Being in this quadrant usually means that several key CoreCo people believe that the innovation is the company's next homerun. However, the absence of urgency might indicate a lack of alignment at CoreCo's senior executive levels. An alternative scenario is that a change in CEO or sponsor relegated the idea to the back burner, but someone still believes in it and is keeping it alive.

Innovations that fall into the latter two categories must be reviewed for strategic alignment. If they seem to truly have the potential for material impact within CoreCo, consider accelerating them through the innovation process. Should they prove worthy, their next stop is quadrant I. But if the decision is made to maintain the status quo, put them out of their misery because they are draining resources and energy. Ideas in quadrant II receive medium attention from the corporate immune system because of the low time pressure they are under.

Quadrant III – Keeping Up with the Joneses or Base Hits

Quadrant III is home to initiatives in the low materiality-low time category, meaning they do not form part of CoreCo's strategic objectives, but nonetheless CoreCo urgently wants them developed and incorporated into the company's portfolio. Quadrant III innovations are of two types: Keeping Up with the Joneses and Base Hits. The former may have come about because of market pressure that required an immediate response, or they could be CoreCo's answer to customers who have communicated that its core offerings have fallen behind the competition. Other possibilities are that they were developed in response to a competitor that entered the market with a unique solution, or to solve an obsolescence problem that needs prompt attention. Base hits, on the other hand, are ideas that are genuinely innovative and could be successful in a new market if they had sufficient materiality to impact CoreCo's financial results.

Keeping Up with the Joneses ideas typically belong in CoreCo. Think of them as roll-ups that will do well in one of CoreCo's existing product lines or segments, and not as candidates for a NewCo. Their low materiality does not warrant the additional overhead that accompanies getting a startup off the ground. Base Hits should be terminated because they consume resources, funding, management time, and mindshare without offering substantial returns. The corporate immune system will have only a modest reaction to initiatives in quadrant III because even though there is urgency to get them moving, they have little materiality. From CoreCo's perspective they are business as usual.

Quadrant IV – Exploratory Innovations

Quadrant IV is the basket that holds initiatives in the low materiality-high time category. I call them Exploratory Innovations because they are in the early stages of the innovation process and are on the receiving end of moderate funding from CoreCo. If your company has a healthy innovation culture, Exploratory Innovations are critical because it is important to have a range of ideas at various stages of development that are proceeding through the tollgates of the innovation process. They should be reviewed regularly for continued funding. If yours is an unhealthy innovation culture, these early-stage innovations can be money and time wasters, and are possibly nothing more than pet projects that will never achieve visibility or provide real results. Upon completion they will end up sitting on a shelf. If this is the case, they should be identified and removed. Innovations in this quadrant typically do not trigger any response from the corporate immune system.

Table 8.3 Summary of Quadrants I, II, III, and IV

I. HIGH MATERIALITY LOW TIME	II. HIGH MATERIALITY HIGH TIME
Strategic Thrust in a Pressure Cooker Typically: • Forms part of CoreCo's strategic objectives • CoreCo has high expectations • Significant funding and sponsorship is available • High need for both Stage-Gate evaluation and Pragmatic Marketing	**Garden of Eden** Typically: • Believed to be a business homerun • Strong commitment by some but not all CoreCo leaders • Receives significant funding and other resources • Possible source of political conflict
Consider: • Verifying that the expectations are realistic • Validating if it will make a successful NewCo • Appointing an intrapreneur	**Consider:** • Getting broader executive buy-in • If the high-time rating is a function of insufficient resources
Immune system reaction: High	**Immune system reaction: Medium**
III. LOW MATERIALITY LOW TIME	**IV. LOW MATERIALITY HIGH TIME**
Keeping Up with the Joneses or Base Hits Typically: • CoreCo feels urgency • Represents a market differentiator for CoreCo • Addresses a customer perception or helps retain customers	**Exploratory Innovations** Typically: • CoreCo feels no commitment • Seed funding is available • Might be someone's pet project
Consider: • Rolling it into one of CoreCo's existing business lines • Terminating due to no evidence it will provide sufficient returns	**Consider:** • Conducting a thorough review • Deciding to augment or stop funding • Evaluating the health of your innovation process
Immune system reaction: Medium	**Immune system reaction: None to low**

Materiality to CoreCo versus CoreCo Market Similarity

Comparing CoreCo's expectations of NewCo's materiality to the assumptions about its market similarity with CoreCo's is an effective way to validate the degree of overlap between the startup's customer base and the corporation's. The wider the overlap, the more reassured CoreCo will be about the quality of the assumptions that underlie the NewCo business case. The narrower the overlap, the more work will be required by both NewCo and CoreCo to understand the new market and how NewCo can succeed. The four quadrants in figure 8.5 will help you decide if creating a startup is a good idea or if the innovation should be tucked under an existing CoreCo business.

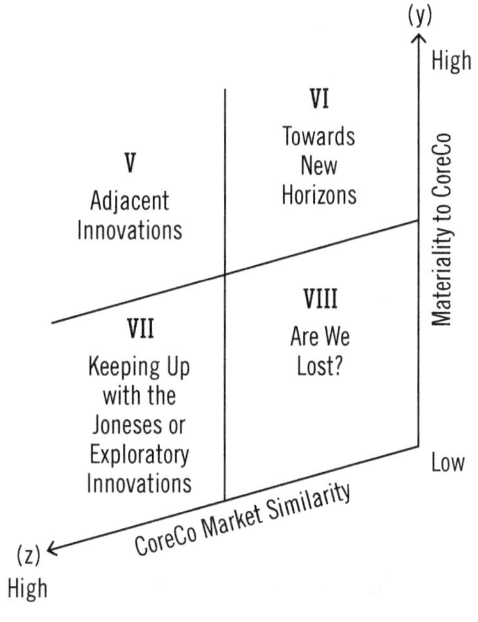

Figure 8.5 Materiality to CoreCo versus CoreCo Market Similarity

Quadrant V – Adjacent Innovations

Quadrant V identifies initiatives in the high similarity-high materiality category. Before you get too excited about innovations in this quadrant, make sure their high ratings are well supported. If they are, you are dealing with what I call Adjacent Innovations, because they are likely destined for a segment already addressed within one of CoreCo's existing markets. High similarity usually points to high market intimacy, meaning

CoreCo believes it has a deep appreciation of the market because it has successfully done business there for many years. Given this familiarity, many of the 37 marketing activities will already have been completed and marked in green.

Adjacent Innovations can be good candidates for stand-alone NewCos due to their materiality. If t his is the decision taken, they are best positioned within an existing business segment because of the similarities between their market and the business segment's. The corporate immune system will be out in full force due to its assumptions about these similarities, even if they are not as strong as they appear. Because CoreCo's existing systems, processes, and resources have proved successful in the past, it will want to impose them on NewCo. The gatekeeper will have to be on constant alert.

Quadrant VI – Towards New Horizons

In quadrant VI you will find initiatives in the low similarity-high materiality category. These have been assessed as having a high potential financial impact on CoreCo, despite the fact that the market is not well known. I refer to these as Towards New Horizons ideas because they usually represent opportunities for CoreCo to enter an adjacent market by repurposing existing products or services that have been successful. These ideas are seen as running the greatest risk because of the market unknowns. They can, however, yield impressive financial rewards, and they are a great opportunity for diversification. When NewCo's leaders are executing the 37 activities with the new market in mind, they will notice that it takes more time for activities to go from red to yellow and eventually to green.

These initiatives are best served by a two-step launch. The soft launch will give CoreCo time to make a thorough assessment of what is required to succeed and what the risks are, and hopefully this will lead to reasonable expectations. At the same time NewCo will make critical progress in exploring and completing several iterations of the business model, which will further its understanding of the challenges of going to market. The NewCo management team must leave no stone unturned in its preparations for the formal launch.

While all this is happening be on the lookout for a condition known as analysis paralysis. It often plagues innovations aimed at an unknown market. Corporations have a tendency to want to cover all risk angles and may spend an inordinate amount of time analyzing the business case and conducting in-house validations in the hopes it can mitigate all risk and guarantee the innovation's success. But there are no guarantees when launching a new business. The best you can do is weigh your temptation to delay the launch against the consequences of too long a delay, which could result in the initiative running out of steam, not enough material progress being made to warrant continued support, or competitors using the time to better prepare themselves for your market entry.

Where initiatives in quadrant VI are concerned, CoreCo's immune system will be at its most active due to the high perceived risk. It will want NewCo to use many of its existing systems, processes, and resources, even before validating whether or not they are applicable to the new market. CoreCo's behavior reflects a mix of risk mitigation on the part of its functional departments, not enough time for department heads to truly comprehend the new startup, and the typical resistance to change that was discussed in labor 5. Whatever the reason, the gatekeeper must be working the front lines, making sure NewCo's leadership team is spending as little time as possible battling the corporate immune system and as much time as possible managing NewCo's business opportunities.

Quadrant VII – Keeping Up with the Joneses or Exploratory Innovations

Quadrant VII is for high similarity-low materiality ideas that I refer to as Keeping Up with the Joneses or Exploratory Innovations. They are similar to what you saw in quadrants III and IV. The fact that CoreCo will be intimate with this market points to one of two scenarios. The first is that CoreCo is simply keeping up with the Joneses, in which case the innovation should be dealt with similarly to quadrant III initiatives and be absorbed within an existing CoreCo business. The second is that these innovations are exploratory in nature and may or may not be aligned with CoreCo's innovation strategy. They should be dealt with like quadrant IV items, meaning reviewed regularly for continued funding or terminated. Where Keeping Up with the Joneses are concerned, the corporate immune system will be on medium-to-high alert, and for Exploratory Innovations, the alert will be low.

Quadrant VIII – Are We Lost?

Quadrant VIII captures initiatives in the low similarity-low materiality category. CoreCo knows very little about this market and sees only low financial potential in these innovations, which is why I refer to them as Are We Lost?. Why is CoreCo even bothering? One answer might be that it is developing intimacy with these ideas to better assess their materiality. If this is the case, give them more oxygen as part of your innovation

Table 8.4 Summary of Quadrants V, VI, VII and VIII

V. HIGH SIMILARITY HIGH MATERIALITY	VI. LOW SIMILARITY HIGH MATERIALITY
Adjacent Innovations Typically: • Innovations are well validated • CoreCo has high intimacy with the market • Good fit with existing CoreCo markets	**Towards New Horizons** Typically: • Seen as a bigger strategic gamble with high potential rewards • An opportunity for CoreCo to diversify • Executive support is not unanimous
Consider: • Launching as a NewCo • Positioning within a division or business unit • Not jumping to conclusions about customer behaviors	**Consider:** • Getting broader executive buy-in • Assigning more resources to complete the market assessment • Organizing a soft launch
Immune system reaction: Medium to high	**Immune system reaction: Low until the launch, then high**
VII. HIGH SIMILARITY LOW MATERIALITY	VIII. LOW SIMILARITY LOW MATERIALITY
Keeping Up with the Joneses or Exploratory Innovations Typically: • Enhances CoreCo's portfolio • Addresses a customer perception or helps retain customers • May be new concepts for an existing product line	**Are We Lost?** Typically: • Somebody's pet project • The innovation process is poorly managed
Consider: • No need for a NewCo • Including as part of an incremental innovation strategy • Stopping because it has no future value	**Consider:** • Stopping because it has no future value • Asking if precious resources are being wasted
Immune system reaction: Low to high	**Immune system reaction: None to low**

process, but be sure to review them frequently to avoid wasting valuable time and energy should supporting them not be warranted. The corporate immune system will likely ignore these activities because they are not worth the effort at this early stage.

Time Expectations versus CoreCo Market Similarity

Figure 8.6 is an effective tool for analyzing CoreCo's time expectations in relation to what is known of the target market. This analysis will help identify ideas that might have unrealistic expectations and innovations that stem from broad-stroke conclusions and overly optimistic assumptions about CoreCo's ability to enter a new market.

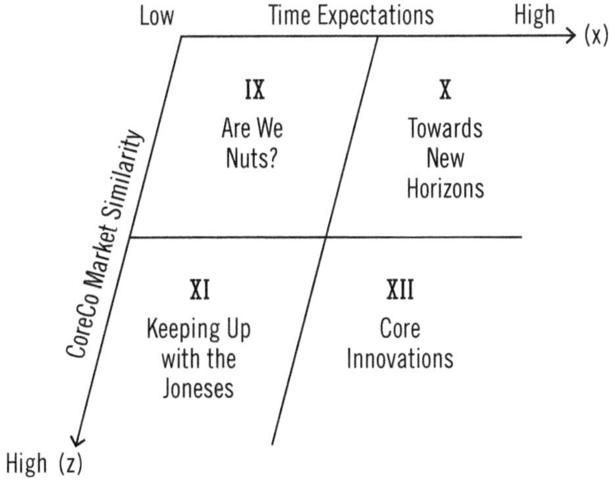

Figure 8.6 Time Expectations versus CoreCo Market Similarity

Quadrant IX – Are We Nuts?

Quadrant IX indicates what I call Are We Nuts? ideas, which sit in the low time-low similarity category. These are presumably well-validated innovations that may eventually have a high financial impact on CoreCo (which could explain why they are under time pressure), but in a market CoreCo knows nothing about. Instead of rushing to set up a business in a field where much remains to be understood, CoreCo's innovation team needs to gather a lot more information about the market before considering a launch. It must also revisit what is probably an unrealistic time expectation. With such a low intimacy rating, a soft launch strategy definitely has to be part of the game plan. The corporate immune system reacts aggressively in these situations, and even more aggressively the higher the materiality rating.

Quadrant X – Towards New Horizons

In quadrant X you will find high time-low similarity innovations that have been assessed as having little to no urgency and are aimed at a market CoreCo knows next to nothing about. I also refer to these as Towards New Horizons because they are very like the innovations that fall in quadrant VI on page 153. These are usually opportunities for CoreCo to enter an adjacent market with products or services that are successful in its core market. They should be dealt with in the same manner as described in quadrant VI: be given extra time to be well validated during the innovation phase. Should they be approved to become a NewCo, they would benefit from a soft launch. The corporate immune system will be relatively tame as long as results are due far off in the future.

Quadrant XI – Keeping Up with the Joneses

Quadrant XI identifies low time-high similarity innovations. They face extreme time pressure from CoreCo and fit very well in its core market. They have a lot in common with the Keeping Up with the Joneses ideas in quadrant VII and should be dealt with accordingly.

Quadrant XII – Core Innovations

Quadrant XII is where high time-high similarity ideas come home to roost. Because CoreCo is very familiar with the market, it has decided to give these innovations plenty of time to be developed. They are usually exploratory in nature and are aimed at ensuring CoreCo maintains a competitive advantage in its core segments over the long-term. I call them Core Innovations because there is a low likelihood they will become startups; rather, they will remain innovations that are later introduced into one of CoreCo's existing businesses. They elicit very little attention from the corporate immune system.

Table 8.5 Summary of Quadrants V, VI, VII and VIII

IX. LOW TIME LOW SIMILARITY	X. HIGH TIME LOW SIMILARITY
Are We Nuts? Typically: • Little is known about the customers or market • The time pressure is significant • Results are expected fast • Could be an executive's pet project	**Towards New Horizons** Typically: • Believed to be a business homerun • Strong commitment by some but not all CoreCo leaders
Consider: • Getting a better understanding of the time constraint • Buying more time • Moving to a soft launch	**Consider:** • Getting broader executive buy-in and accelerating the time expectations • If the high-time rating is a function of insufficient resources
Immune system reaction: High	**Immune system reaction: Medium**
XI. LOW TIME HIGH SIMILARITY	XII. HIGH TIME HIGH SIMILARITY
Keeping Up with the Joneses Typically: • CoreCo feels urgency • Represents a market differentiator for CoreCo • Addresses a customer perception or helps retain customers	**Core Innovations** Typically: • CoreCo has high expectations for a future competitive advantage • Part of a major strategic push into new markets • Significant funding and sponsorship is available
Consider: • Letting go of the idea it will be a NewCo • Rolling into one of CoreCo's existing business lines • Exploring why expectations were too high	**Consider:** • Focusing on innovation work to validate the idea or terminate it • Tracking if significant to CoreCo's future • Absorbing it into an existing unit when ready
Immune system reaction: Medium to high	**Immune system reaction: Low to medium**

Post-Launch Expectations

Making a formal announcement that NewCo is launched is simply an event in time, but CoreCo's leadership team will immediately want to see that things are moving. The intrapreneur and sponsor must persuade CoreCo to recognize that not much changes in the days following the launch and that CoreCo's leaders must remember there is a sizeable time gap between the launch and the day NewCo operates at the capacity that will allow it to make good progress.

Before that can happen NewCo needs to be given a budget to work with and then must acquire enough staff to get the work done. Transitioning from innovation to intrapreneurial activities also requires resources. If employees are coming from CoreCo, replacements will need to be found before they can be transferred. If employees are coming from outside, the recruitment and hiring processes will take time. In some scenarios the search for talent will mean targeting a different industry, and HR may have to adapt or even reinvent its acquisition processes and compensation packages. Make sure to include these possibilities in your post-launch schedule and consider them when setting your NewCo SMART objectives.

These and other ramping-up activities are necessary and time-consuming, and the gap between launch and operating on all cylinders is real, but a post-launch silence that extends for too long will unnerve CoreCo's executive leaders. After all, the intrapreneur and sponsor sought broad corporate exposure so that CoreCo would turbo-charge NewCo by significantly increasing its support. The launch also reflected CoreCo's decision to give NewCo the level of autonomy necessary to succeed. But if the parent perceives a lack of progress, it may be tempted to wind down its support or question its decision to launch the new business. This is why the intrapreneur and sponsor must not get ahead of themselves and rush a formal launch. Rather, they should take advantage of the soft launch phase to secure early victories that can be shared.

An early victory can be as simple as making progress with potential new customers. Having even a small number of customer prospects a few weeks away from signing, or one or two partner initiatives under way that will be concluded in three to six months, allows NewCo to not only demonstrate successes prior to the launch, but to celebrate successes not long after it if the customer signings or partnerships are secured in those first weeks or months. This will reassure NewCo's supporters. Early victories are one of the main strengths of the soft launch strategy.

COMING UP NEXT......................

Having determined to shift gears and move the new product or service from the safe but limited environment of the innovation process into the unpredictable world of corporate startups where expectations are high, you must decide where to position your new business within the corporate organizational chart.

The status NewCo is granted will be the first major visible demonstration of its importance to CoreCo's executives and to the sponsor, and it will telegraph to company employees the level of autonomy and support NewCo will receive. There will be political ramifications. Making this decision is another difficult labor, as you will discover in the next chapter.

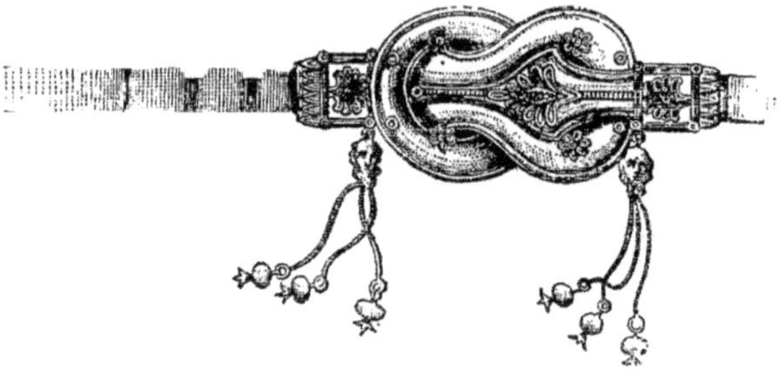

Hippolyta's Belt

As queen of the Amazons, Hippolyta led a tribe of fierce female warriors. She wore a belt across her chest to carry her weapons, and this belt was the object of Hercules' ninth labor. He was to bring it to King Eurystheus as a gift for his daughter. Hercules and a band of his friends sailed to the land of the Amazons. Realizing he was no match for Hippolyta's great army, he invited her onboard the ship to convince her to give him the belt. After hearing his story she eventually agreed, but the goddess Hera had other plans. She disguised herself as an Amazon warrior and convinced Hippolyta's followers that Hercules intended to harm their leader. The warriors rushed to the ship, ready to do battle. When Hercules saw their approach he killed Hippolyta and stripped her of the belt. The Amazons were eventually driven back and Hercules and his friends sailed home.

LABOR 9

Rules for Designing and Positioning the New Business

Organization design within a company is often rife with partisan negotiations and corporate politics. It is not unlike Hercules discussing his purpose with Hippolyta while Hera sows dissent in the ranks and advances her plot to foil him. While the sponsor, intrapreneur, and other key allies are openly debating the pros and cons of each option, they must remain keenly aware of negotiations that might be occurring in the background between people who may fear losing organizational control or power, or others who may not have the best interests of NewCo in mind. Once the sponsor decides to establish NewCo as a separate entity within CoreCo, she must move swiftly to prevent her plans from being obstructed. As we will see in this chapter, organizational decisions speak louder than words in the corporate world. They send an unmistakable message to the rest of CoreCo regarding how much autonomy NewCo will be granted and how it will be supported.

A discussion on the best way to design NewCo's structure and position it within CoreCo requires a review of sound organization design principles. There are many theories that address selecting a structure that will provide an organization like NewCo with the power and authority that are necessary to achieve its goals and deliver on its strategy. My intent here is not to give you an in-depth review of organization design, but to highlight that the sponsor and intrapreneur must be sufficiently versed in organization design theory before they make decisions about how NewCo's structure will function and where the startup will fit in the corporation.

In his book *Designing Organizations: An Executive Guide to Strategy, Structure, and Process*, Jay Galbraith, one of the world's leading experts in organization design, states, "Organization design decisions significantly affect the executive's unit. By choosing *who* decides and by designing the process influencing *how* things are decided, the executive shapes every decision made in the unit. The leaders become less of a *decision maker* and more of a *decision shaper.* Organization design decisions are the shapers of the organization's decision-making process."

Galbraith also points out that organizational structures do not get things done, people do, and I fully concur. It is ultimately people who are well rewarded for optimizing the right processes and sharing the right information who advance their company's strategy. This idea is reinforced by a fundamental Six Sigma concept I learned years ago: customers do not get their needs met by working with a company's organizational chart; rather, they work through its systems and processes as managed and executed by its people.

The Star Model™ reproduced in figure 9.1 was developed by Galbraith to represent the need to strike the right balance between each element of an organization design. It shows that decisions about structure must be derived from a company's strategy and then designed to support it. The strategy is based on a number of strategic business objectives (SBOs) that identify the imperatives that need to be accomplished for its successful execution. To accomplish these SBOs, the leaders of a company require people with the right skills and mindset, reward systems that motivate the workforce, effective business processes that allow the sharing of information that will get the work done, and an organizational structure that establishes where the power to make decisions resides and facilitates how the work is conducted. Together, these define acceptable behavior, drive performance, and shape the organization's culture.

Decisions about a company's organization must be made with a view to how the structure will co-exist with and influence each of the other elements in the model. Understanding NewCo's strategy, structure, and business processes, as well as the level of autonomy it needs to succeed, will help in identifying the types of knowledge, skills, and abilities required of NewCo's future employees. Only when CoreCo and NewCo truly appreciate the profile of the people they want for the startup will they be able to determine the reward systems that will attract and retain them.

The key to getting NewCo's organizational structure right and to properly positioning it within CoreCo resides in having a thorough grasp of NewCo's business process requirements. This will entail numerous discussions and debates between the sponsor, the intrapreneur, and the people at CoreCo who are helping with the design such as an HR organization design expert. In some cases outside experts are also hired. Using the conclusions that are drawn about the business processes NewCo needs to be successful, the group will identify the existing processes and support systems within CoreCo that can be reused or adapted. Where there are holes, new processes and systems will be created. Ultimately, the leadership teams both at CoreCo and NewCo will come to accept how the intrapreneur can best be supported to get the work done, achieve the SBOs, and ultimately fulfill NewCo's strategic promise.

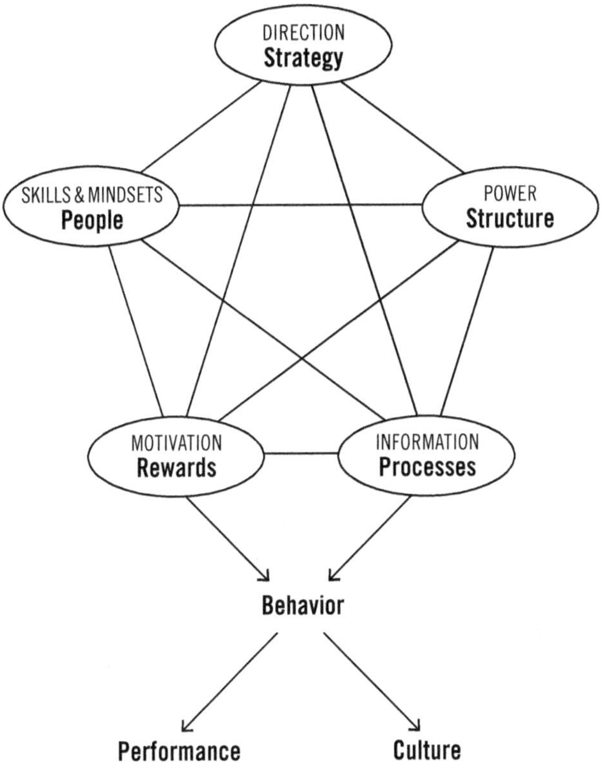

Figure 9.1 Organization Design Affects Behavior

The discussions on organization design happen in the weeks preceding the formal launch. If a soft launch approach is followed, they take place during the soft launch phase. But before these discussions can begin, significant progress will need to have been made in five important activities that will generate great quantities of essential information. As progress leads to completion and more pertinent facts and data become available, the discussions will mature and eventually yield the optimal organization design.

1. Developing NewCo's business model
2. Working through the 37 marketing activities, starting with the ones that are most relevant to your particular NewCo
3. Assessing NewCo's readiness to move to the formal launch
4. Analyzing CoreCo's time expectations versus materiality to CoreCo versus CoreCo market similarity
5. Defining the CFM strategy (covered in labor 10)

The goal when determining NewCo's organization design is not to justify a big, heavy structure that mimics CoreCo's long-established departments. The goal is to create a lean startup structure capable of moving and adapting quickly. This can be achieved by striking the right balance between developing NewCo's internal capabilities and leveraging the capabilities that already exist in CoreCo. As NewCo's business process requirements evolve over time, so will its organizational structure.

Autonomy versus Efficiency

As the sponsor, the intrapreneur, and their cohorts weigh launching the startup against keeping it within CoreCo's traditional business structure, they must consider one last element: the level of decision-making autonomy they believe is required for the initiative to succeed in the new market. The higher the level of autonomy required and the greater the difference in business models, the stronger the need for NewCo to stand alone as its own business with the ability to design its own processes, systems, and organizational structure. This may point the organization design away from maximizing NewCo's efficiencies and savings by heavily relying on CoreCo's business processes and structure, and towards allowing a more autonomous NewCo organization that executes key business processes on its own.

In setting up NewCo as a separate business unit, CoreCo is deciding to decentralize. This gives NewCo more flexibility when reacting to its customers and when developing and refining its business model. It is strategically advantageous for NewCo to be able to make decisions faster and shape its systems, processes, and reward systems more freely. To succeed, the startup must be built to correspond to its startup environment and the new market it will be working in. CoreCo's decentralization does not mean that NewCo will have to forego efficiencies. These will be achieved by leveraging CoreCo where it makes sense through CFMs. But there will be trade-offs. CoreCo will have to tolerate the partial or whole duplication of some functions, which no doubt will trigger the corporate immune system.

Positioning NewCo within CoreCo

There are four options to consider when deciding on how to position NewCo in the corporate organizational chart. These are presented in figure 9.2 as NewCo 1, NewCo 2, NewCo 3, and NewCo 4. NewCo 1 represents startups with a market or customer segment that is substantially different from its parent company's as would have been concluded in the analysis outlined in labor 8. In other words, these customers are used to a business culture, measures of quality, levels of service, and sales and marketing interactions that differ markedly from what CoreCo's customers are used to.

This points to the probability that much tailoring of CoreCo's existing systems and processes will be required. If you are the sponsor or intrapreneur, you can reduce corporate immune system activity with an organization design that sends the clear signal that things are being done differently now. For example, you might have NewCo 1 report directly to CoreCo's CEO or to a CoreCo divisional president. Conversely, the more similar NewCo's market and customers are to CoreCo's, the wiser it would be to position it lower in the organization, as a NewCo 2 or 3. This will send the message that the company expects the startup to leverage it as necessary using a variety of CFMs.

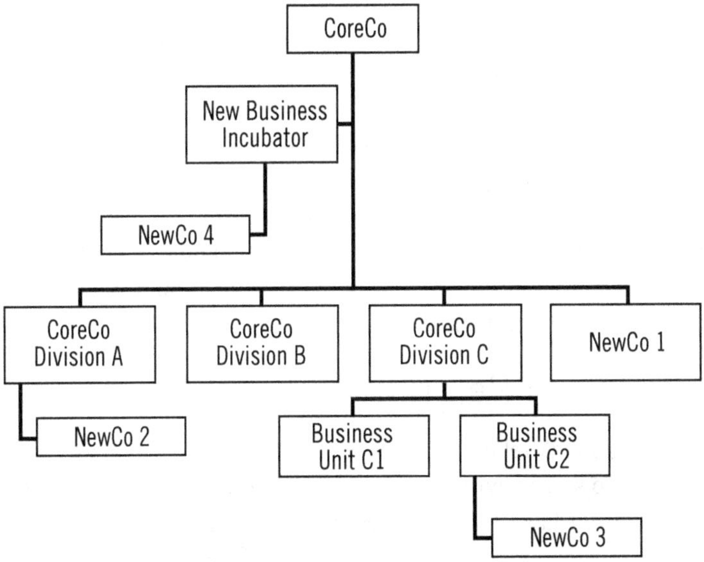

Figure 9.2 Organizational Structures

Typically the sponsor has the final word regarding where NewCo is placed in the organizational chart. This is because she is the most senior person at CoreCo to have an intimate knowledge of the startup. For example, she may be the head of the division where NewCo was developed as a strategic initiative. If that is the case strong consideration will be given to NewCo reporting to the sponsor as per NewCo 2. The same can be said of NewCo 3, which was likely developed as a strategic initiative for CoreCo's Business Unit C2. In terms of efficiencies, having NewCo report to a division or business unit can be quite attractive when launching a new product or service within an existing segment or creating a new joint venture company.

The fourth option is to launch NewCo 4 while it is still focused on its startup activities by placing it in a staff position and away from a line organization. This will shield it from having to demonstrate business results and will communicate to everyone at CoreCo that it will not be managed in the same operational fashion as the company's other organizations. This is a good option if NewCo 4 is taking the soft launch route because it will have the chance to grow and gain critical mass prior to being relocated to a NewCo 1, 2, or 3 position at the time of the formal launch.

As the Organization Grows

Regardless of the original decisions that were made about NewCo's organizational structure and its position within CoreCo, business realities will change as NewCo transforms from a startup into a more mature business. These changes will influence NewCo's structure. The first influence relates to business growth. As NewCo scales up its sales, marketing, product development, production, and delivery activities, it will require increasing support from CoreCo departments such as legal, contracting, purchasing, and human resources. Decisions that led to NewCo's inaugural organization design will have to be revisited. For example, should CoreCo's departments continue providing these services or should NewCo develop its own departments to handle them?

The Evolving Relationship

The organizational relationship between NewCo and CoreCo will also evolve. NewCo started with a high level of CoreCo centralization because it simply did not have the resources to do its own work. But as it grows and acquires more market knowledge and increases in organizational size, it might make sense to transfer certain functions from CoreCo to NewCo. The reverse is also true. Some functions that started under NewCo's control in order to give it more decision-making authority might create efficiencies if provided by CoreCo now that NewCo is more mature. Imagine that NewCo starts in a NewCo 4 position to incubate the business and give it time to learn and mature. One day the sponsor and intrapreneur recognize that NewCo has made sufficient progress to stand alone as a line function, and they transition it to a NewCo 1 or 2 position, where it will operate more efficiently. Or the startup is placed as a NewCo 3 for a period of time to complete certain market validation activities, and when these are done it is relocated as a NewCo 2 to have more access to CoreCo. It comes down to the question of where NewCo needs to be to have the decision-making authority that will allow it to achieve its goals and deliver on its strategy. When in doubt, go higher in the organization, not lower.

Becoming Independent

The interdependence between CoreCo and NewCo will change as NewCo progresses to maturity. A corporate startup goes through three growth phases following its formal launch: infancy, adolescence, and adulthood. Just as a child requires nurturing from its parent, but in varying degrees depending on its age, NewCo requires nurturing from CoreCo as it evolves from infancy to adulthood. But the degree of fostering is the inverse of what transpires between actual child and parent. When NewCo is in its early stages of growth, it needs the least help from CoreCo. In fact, it is at the launch that CoreCo must let go. This might be the opposite of what managers are used to, but CoreCo must resist its natural corporate instinct to intervene in the day-to-day running of baby NewCo.

CoreCo must take an arm's-length approach early on to allow NewCo's management team to create an environment that is conducive to experimenting and learning. The CoreCo parent is there to provide a solid framework and general rules, but it must let NewCo make its own decisions about how to behave in its new business environment based on what it has discovered from interfacing with customers. Remember, one of the most important ingredients contributing to NewCo's growth will be its ability to learn quickly and to modify its strategy and execution plans as necessary.

NewCo's growth will begin to accelerate as it experiences market successes, secures new partners, wins new customers, and generates revenues. This is its adolescent phase, and its dependence on CoreCo will accelerate commensurate with its growth. The reason is straightforward. Despite being incredibly busy, NewCo will not have sufficient work to warrant budgets that will allow it to replicate functions that already exist in CoreCo such as HR, purchasing, production, and legal. As a teenager, NewCo will seriously start to activate its parent's CFMs to enable it to meet the demands of its expanding customer base.

Following the launch, CoreCo must let NewCo learn to walk on its own.

As NewCo matures it will need to develop its own internal departments to keep up with its growth. Employees will have to be hired and processes and systems will have to be worked out. At the same time some of CoreCo's departments that were not made use of earlier will now be approached for assistance. This state of affairs will last until NewCo reaches adulthood. It will know it is all grown up when it has a full grasp of its business model and the organizational structure it requires to succeed. It will also be able to strike the right balance between the systems and processes it can handle on its own as permanent functions and activities it continues to delegate to CoreCo.

Adulthood is when equilibrium is achieved, meaning that NewCo and CoreCo have a shared appreciation of NewCo's business reality. Unless a major economic or business event occurs that changes NewCo's status as a young adult, it will maintain its autonomy with CoreCo's blessing. Eventually, NewCo will no longer be considered a new business, but one of the corporation's many running businesses with more or less the same interdependent relationship.

Each NewCo evolves through infancy and adolescence at its own speed. Each develops a different relationship and level of interdependence with its parent company as it grows. What must be understood is that following NewCo's launch, CoreCo needs to shift from a directive to a supportive role. This is not the same as having blind trust. Proper controls that define when NewCo needs CoreCo's approval before making certain decisions must be put in place. CoreCo must also establish a system of governance to ensure that the intrapreneur comprehends the rules of the game. Finally, a reporting structure is required so that CoreCo remains informed about NewCo's business activities, key decisions, and progress.

However, none of this should obstruct the startup's ability to evolve and learn.

If you are a member of CoreCo, seek to understand NewCo's needs and make every attempt to be comfortable with how its strategy evolves as it makes discoveries in the marketplace and refines its business model. This is a good time to remember the roles of the sponsor and gatekeeper. They are well positioned to help CoreCo achieve the right balance in its evolving relationship with NewCo.

5 Pitfalls

There are five pitfalls the sponsor and intrapreneur must be on the lookout for when decisions are being made about NewCo's organization design and where it fits within CoreCo. These include taking a hands-off approach to the decision making, duplicating business functions, assuming that the innovation belongs where it was incubated, positioning NewCo too far down in the organization, and isolating NewCo from CoreCo.

1. **Do not be hands-off.** It is of the utmost importance that the critical decisions about NewCo's design and its positioning in CoreCo do not rest in the hands of an HR specialist, external consultant, or anyone else claiming to have the answers. The sponsor and intrapreneur must be at the center of the discussions, though they can call on these people for their expertise. In this way NewCo's leaders will be prepared to evaluate the advantages and risks that come with each organization design option. I have worked on several organization designs throughout my career. Some took place in the larger corporation and others developed out of the need to launch or reshape a NewCo. In every case I became involved because I knew the decisions would resonate loud and clear throughout the organization and have a lasting effect on my ability to achieve the desired results.

2. **Do not duplicate business functions.** There are two business decisions that can be wrongfully perceived as duplication. The first is when the intrapreneur creates a job title for NewCo's organizational chart that is the same as a job title at CoreCo, such as Head of Marketing or Head of Product Development. This is not duplication if the type of work being undertaken is sufficiently different, or if the knowledge or other requirements to fulfill the role are unique. But CoreCo might not see it that way and unjustifiably conclude that NewCo is guilty of duplication. If this happens the organization design will be adversely affected when NewCo's

request to create an essential job function is refused and the startup is forced to rely on a centralized CoreCo function for support.

The second situation occurs when NewCo decides to partially execute a function in-house that is similar to one at CoreCo, and to complicate matters it needs help executing it. Not only might CoreCo fail to recognize NewCo's rationale and presume duplication, it might be opposed to lending out members of its team. Essentially, the CoreCo people who are assigned the work become subservient to NewCo's management, which might provoke the department's leader to draw a line in the sand. Do not allow this. Key to NewCo's success is being able to leverage CoreCo, and turf wars inhibit leveraging. When it comes to accessing the resources of the parent company, there are no winners and losers. Everyone wins. Through dialogue and compromise, the intrapreneur must lay the groundwork for flexibility and collaboration.

Actual errors of duplication can and do happen when a NewCo is created. For example, NewCo may decide to duplicate functions rather than ask for help from CoreCo functional leaders who have shown themselves to be unsupportive and may be unpleasant to deal with. Or perhaps the intrapreneur neglected to do the work to verify that duplicating a function is necessary, and it turns out to be a waste of resources. These situations can be avoided if the sponsor insists that the intrapreneur completes all aspects of the CFM strategy prior to entering into organization design discussions.

3. Do not assume. The location in CoreCo where the innovation was created and nurtured is not necessarily where it should be positioned prior to its launch. Whether it was in a department, business unit, or division, the innovation formed part of that organization's business development or diversification strategy, but only in the short-term. Once the innovation demonstrates it can have real impact, CoreCo will re-evaluate its strategic potential and may turn it into a broader corporate initiative that demands a new location. Ultimately, the decision on where to position NewCo depends on the learning that was generated during the discussions on organization design based on the Star Model. Everything comes down to what NewCo needs to succeed. A final word of advice to anyone involved in NewCo's positioning: do your best to steer clear of unhelpful negotiations and company politics.

4. Do not go too low. It would be a mistake for the sponsor to push NewCo to the lowest level of the organization, which she might be tempted to do for the sake of convenience. Perhaps she thinks that delegating the oversight of NewCo to a subordinate leader will save her hours of work. The opposite is true. The higher NewCo is in the organization, the stronger the message to CoreCo's leaders and employees that NewCo's success is critical to the company's aspirations. Most people will want to fall in line, which means a quieter immune system reaction and less work for the sponsor.

5. **Distinct does not mean isolated.** Isolation is warranted in the early phase of the innovation process when a small team is developing a disruptive technology, investigating its applicability to targeted users, and exploring market potential. Some isolation might also be justified during the soft launch phase, when further validation of the MVP is required and more customer feedback is necessary to move the innovation along. But isolation is a bad idea once NewCo is launched. It will lead to the unnecessary duplication of functions and the burning of cash far too quickly. Another outcome will be reluctance to take full advantage of CoreCo's CFMs, which will delay NewCo achieving the criteria set by CoreCo.

It is better to think of NewCo's status as distinct. The decision to create NewCo was partly founded on the realization that its business endeavors and challenges are different enough from CoreCo's to justify giving it special status, but always in relation to its parent, which has considerable support to offer. As NewCo's intrapreneur or sponsor, you must make sure that everyone involved with NewCo shares this view, and that no one confuses "distinct" with the need for isolation. This will require the intrapreneur to display the corporate leadership traits and change management skills described in labor 1.

COMING UP NEXT........................

Several of the labors faced by the intrapreneur so far have pointed to the importance of a well-defined and properly communicated CFM strategy. This is because the effective leveraging of CFMs is informed by and affects so much of what the intrapreneur does on the road to NewCo's success. The CFM strategy is complex and requires the intrapreneur's full focus, and for these reasons it is thoroughly covered in labor 10.

THE CATTLE OF GERYON

Hercules' tenth labor proved to be more treacherous than all the others. He had to travel to the end of the world and do battle with many beasts along the way. The return journey, too, was beset with difficulties of every kind. His labor was to capture the herd of red cattle belonging to Geryon, a monster with three heads, three powerful bodies, and three sets of arms and legs, all joined at the waist. Hercules sailed to the island of Erythia in a golden vessel shaped like a goblet that was given to him by Helios, the sun. Upon arrival he was attacked by the two-headed hound that guarded the herd. He killed the hound with one blow of his club, and with a second blow killed the herdsman Eurytion. While escaping with the cattle he was confronted by Geryon, who carried three swords and shields. Hercules slayed the monster with a single arrow that had been dipped in poison. Returning home he faced many arduous challenges, but he finally completed his journey and delivered the cattle to King Eurystheus.

LABOR 10

Leveraging the Parent Company for Strategic Advantage

Like Hercules, the intrapreneur will encounter his greatest challenge to date when carrying out the tenth labor: leveraging CoreCo's corporate force multipliers (CFMs) to make NewCo strong and ensure success. The threats he will face while planning what to leverage and when will be in the form of CoreCo functional leaders who want to protect their unit from additional work or who seek to retain control over certain NewCo activities. Other leaders may resist the intrapreneur's requests because they disagree with launching NewCo in the first place or they are unconvinced that NewCo merits special treatment. Transforming these hostile forces into willing support requires a range of leadership skills, ongoing change management activities, and strong internal communications. But the challenges will not end there. More resistance will emerge when NewCo tries to execute the CFM strategy and faces repeated attacks from the immune systems of CoreCo's various functions. The intrapreneur will need to be well prepared to prevail with this very important labor, which is central to spurring NewCo's growth.

Figure 10.1 includes an incomplete list of CFMs a corporation can usually provide. The shaded bars show the degree to which three different corporate startups have decided to leverage the various capabilities of its parent company. The lightly shaded areas represent very little or no use of a particular CFM, perhaps because NewCo has concluded it is immaterial to its successful launch or it has opted to create it internally. The darker areas towards the bottom of the bars represent a higher degree of leveraging. Each of these NewCos has a distinct leveraging strategy, with NewCo A choosing to leverage more of CoreCo's resources and to a greater degree, and NewCo C deciding that its needs are fewer.

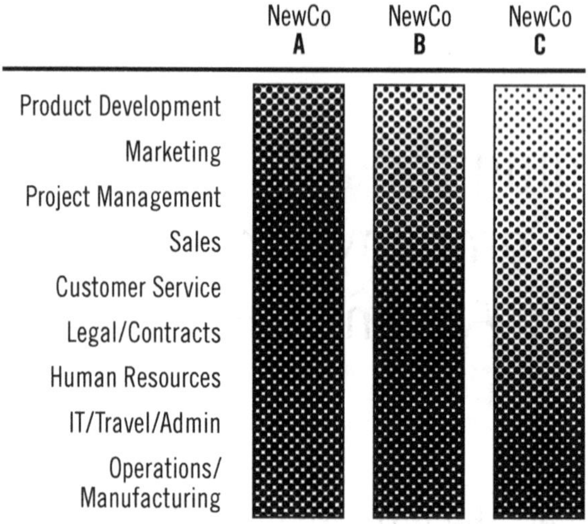

Figure 10.1 Every CFM Strategy Is Different

Identifying CFMs

Being able to leverage its parent company to accelerate growth is one of the main distinguishing factors between corporate startups and independent ones. CFMs give NewCo a significant competitive advantage and also save it a lot of time. If carried out properly, a CFM strategy will provide NewCo with instant access to a wide range of precious resources an independent startup could only dream of and would need months or years to develop.

NewCo's success depends on finalizing the scope and details of the CFM strategy prior to the formal launch. The soft launch phase is the ideal time to complete this work and conduct validation activities. Early completion allows NewCo to evaluate if CoreCo's functions are truly ready to support the startup. By clarifying which CFMs are unavailable, the risks associated with business assumptions and corporate expectations can be assessed more accurately. With this information, the intrapreneur will be well equipped to set the materiality, time, and budgetary expectations for the startup, and better prepared to defend them.

The concept of force multipliers is well entrenched in military strategy. The US Department of Defense offers the following definition: "A capability that, when added to and employed by a combat force, significantly increases the combat potential of that force and thus enhances the probability of successful mission accomplishment." In other words, the military selectively draws from existing assets to augment a unit's capabilities, giving it a multiplier effect that far exceeds what could otherwise be expected of the unit.

Wikipedia goes further in its description: "Force multiplication, in military usage, refers to an attribute or a combination of attributes which make a given force more effective than that same force would be without it. The expected size increase required to have the same effectiveness without that advantage is the multiplication factor. For example, if a certain technology like GPS enables a force to accomplish the same results of a force five times as large but without GPS, then the multiplier is five. Such estimates are used to justify an investment cost for force multipliers. A force multiplier refers to a factor that dramatically increases (hence multiplies) the effectiveness of an item or group."

I have adapted this notion to the business world and applied it to NewCos, which need all the help they can get. CFMs refer to strengths, attributes, relationships, and proven capabilities that exist in the larger corporation and can be leveraged by a much smaller organization within it. As a result the smaller organization has capabilities that go well beyond what could be expected of an independent business that is similar in size. CFMs include: people, organizations, materials, know-how, solutions, systems, processes, assets, and technology in these areas:

- Brand
- Customer base
- Sales
- Distribution channels
- Marketing
- Communications
- Geographic reach
- Customer services
- Operations
- Manufacturing
- Information technologies
- Human resources
- Legal and contracting
- Mergers and acquisitions
- R&D, IP, and technology
- Government, environmental, and regulatory
- Administration
- CoreCo executive leadership team

I am convinced that a large part of my success as an intrapreneur and business executive has been due to my ability to correctly select the CFMs my NewCos needed to grow rapidly and succeed. Let's look at some examples. When launching an outsourcing service and trying to persuade operators of aviation training centers to let us handle the operation and maintenance of their simulators, I knew that our parent company was recovering from a downturn in the economy and was under considerable financial pressure. Spending had to be carefully managed. I was short on many of the resources I needed to launch, though I was able to secure enough funding for limited sales and marketing activities and a small core team of experts from within CoreCo. I realized I would have to draw on the parent for the rest, in this case the civil aviation division. This was extremely challenging because CoreCo's business units and functions were working to unusually tight budgets, and some were undergoing cost-cutting and layoffs. Fortunately, the head of civil aviation was NewCo's sponsor and I had his full support. Furthermore, we had already agreed on our SMART objectives.

Our environment was as lean as it gets. For every dollar we wanted to spend we had to find out if there was an alternative solution within CoreCo that could be leveraged more cost effectively. This led to trade-offs. Numerous times, needing to make basic progress, we chose a less effective but acceptable solution and then dealt with the consequences later on, such as disruptions to our schedule. After analyzing the situation, I focused my CFM strategy on four CoreCo elements: sales, geographic reach, customer relationships, and finance. I wanted to sign our first customers in order to validate our value proposition and gain momentum. The experts on my team would make the game-winning sales pitch and subsequently ensure the smooth transition to our outsourcing group, but first we needed to get in front of potential customers. Our team was too small and we had too little time to conduct broad-based sales prospecting activities, so instead we focused on the prospects we had determined would be the most likely to respond positively to our service.

We leveraged the fact that CoreCo had incredible geographic reach, with well-established operations, sales, and business development teams on every continent and in every region with a significant commercial airline presence. For the CFM to be effective I first secured the support of the regional vice presidents, who had operational control and oversight of the resources in their regions. Then my colleagues and I made sure the CoreCo sales and business development teams understood how to pitch the NewCo value proposition. Finally we completed a detailed customer analysis that narrowed down a potentially large sales pipeline to a small number of high-potential clients.

After being briefed, the CoreCo in-country sales and business development teams were tasked to open doors. To support their efforts we prepared a comprehensive ', a service description, and a Q&A document they used to gauge the interest of potential customers. The materials also prepared them to deal with questions and objections. We leveraged the CoreCo marketing CFM to create brochures and the CoreCo financial analysis and modelling CFM to build an outsourcing model that made financial sense for us and demonstrated value to our prospects. Once the doors were open we went in to close the deals and transition the customers' operations activities to NewCo.

Without the benefit of CoreCo's CFMs, our startup would have fallen flat. With them we had clout, credibility, and resources. Combined with the speed, agility, and creativity that were our in-house capabilities as a NewCo, we were able to secure our first two customers in a relatively short time. These customers helped us validate our business model, refine the offering, understand how to make money, and optimize the process of transitioning the customers' operations once they were outsourced. This early success led to more wins and more funding from CoreCo.

In my second example different CFMs were used, but the outcome was equally successful. I was the intrapreneur of a NewCo called CAE Healthcare. We started very lean – there were only four of us – and we were facing an unfamiliar market. Not knowing if the healthcare community had even the slightest interest in a new product from a player like CAE, which was our parent company, we opted for a soft launch, during which time we tested receptivity. The response was favorable, and this convinced CAE to make a much larger investment in us. It also considerably raised our confidence. We could see our launch on the horizon.

We were entering the world of simulation in healthcare, which was a fragmented market with many small players. Our parent company was a proven global leader in modeling, simulation, and training for the commercial aviation and defense sectors, and had an enviable reputation for innovation in all of its core businesses. Naturally, the first CFM we used was CAE's brand. It opened doors and got us heard. We found ourselves in the same room with key decision makers, engaging in conversations that players who had been in the market for some time were still waiting to have.

By harnessing the CFM of our parent's brand we were able to rapidly establish credibility with influential people. Remember, this was a new market for us. We never would have achieved such speedy acceptance as an independent startup. A bonus of CAE Healthcare landing in the market so suddenly and smoothly was that it created confusion in our competitors, who had underestimated our ability to leverage CAE's brand so effectively.

During the soft launch period we also conducted an exhaustive review of the simulation-based products and services already in the healthcare market with an eye to discovering the gaps in the existing solutions. We listened to innumerable users, recognized leaders, and key influencers who pointed out what needed improvement. Their feedback helped us create a list of product development and R&D activities and prioritize them.

It was time to leverage our second CFM: the technology and experts available within CoreCo. Having access to the most up-to-date simulation technology and some of the world's best experts allowed us to accelerate product development by years. We quickly advanced several prototypes and introduced beta versions of various solutions, which we tested and validated with early adopters. This new round of feedback helped us refine our products, polish our business model, and make good progress in executing the 37 marketing activities.

Now that we knew we could make a significant impact in our new market, it was clear that we required substantial funding to address the next phase of our product development needs. CoreCo's expectations were high, and we all recognized that a funding strategy was necessary if we were to meet its goals regarding our growth and financial materiality. Securing this funding was the final condition for getting the go-ahead to move to the formal launch.

This is when CAE's expertise in government relations and communications turned into a valuable CFM. By leveraging it, and at the same time leveraging our structured finance CFM, we secured a large government investment through an innovative partnership vehicle that allowed us to accelerate R&D and product development. CoreCo's backing and leadership brought us a level of funding that would have been unthinkable for an early-stage stand-alone startup.

A period of organic growth and intense learning followed, during which we had our official launch. By then we knew that meeting CoreCo's growth projections meant gaining access to niche technologies, specialized healthcare know-how, and new distribution channels. We short-listed companies that matched specific business plan criteria and tapped into a fourth CFM: our CoreCo mergers and acquisitions group. Leveraging this

CFM gave us access to contractual, legal, and negotiation expertise, which permitted us to move fast and avoid making costly acquisition mistakes.

I could give you many examples and they would each have a different CFM formula. This is because every corporate startup is unique and the CFMs available to them change from CoreCo to CoreCo. It is never an option to use someone else's CFM strategy in your particular NewCo environment. Even when several NewCos are being created within the same CoreCo, each NewCo will require its own CFM formula.

To add another twist, if a NewCo is being established as part of a joint venture between two companies, it will be even more challenging to formulate and carry out a CFM strategy. Admittedly, having two CoreCos means a broader range of CFMs for NewCo to choose from, but it also means having to navigate two corporate cultures, troubleshoot two immune systems, and win over a larger number of stakeholders.

Tailoring the CFM Strategy

Figure 10.2 introduces the corporate leveraging synthesizer, an invaluable tool for shaping NewCo's CFM strategy. It mimics a music synthesizer, which is used by artists and recording studios to invent new sounds and modify existing ones. The corporate leveraging synthesizer does the same for NewCo by helping the intrapreneur create, grow, or adapt corporate capabilities as required by NewCo as it focuses all its energies on growth.

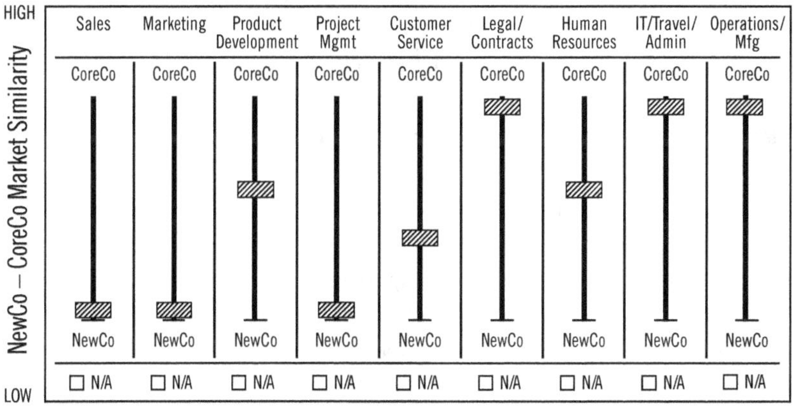

Figure 10.2 NewCo's Corporate Leveraging Synthesizer

The vertical control labeled NewCo-CoreCo Market Similarity provides a low-to-high setting. This represents the assessment of NewCo's market similarity in comparison to CoreCo's as covered in labor 8. Nine capabilities are listed across the synthesizer's top. These are not all-inclusive; rather, they show the types of capabilities CoreCo can offer. If a capability is not required, it is checked off as not applicable (N/A). Each capability bar shows NewCo at the bottom aligned with the low setting and CoreCo at the top aligned with the high setting.

The more market similarities, the greater the likelihood NewCo will benefit from leveraging CoreCo in a number of areas. The fewer the similarities, the greater the chance NewCo will have to establish its own capabilities. There are two main considerations. The first relates to how alike the two markets are, as discussed above. The second takes into account where NewCo is in its growth cycle. NewCo will require different levels of support as it grows from infancy to adolescence and adulthood, leading the intrapreneur to make changes that must be communicated clearly to all CoreCo functional leaders. Just because they are not part of the initial CFM strategy does not mean they will not be leveraged at a later date.

Mergers and acquisitions (M&A) provides a good example. Following a period of organic growth and after much learning has taken place, NewCo realizes it can accelerate its progress if it leverages CoreCo's expertise in M&A and corporate finance. To acquire comparable expertise in M&A negotiations, valuations, financial modeling, legal structures, contracts, and complex corporate financing options, an independent startup would need to hire a third party or find a venture capitalist or institutional investor, which takes time and comes with significant risk. This risk is nonexistent for the intrapreneur, who has every reason to trust CoreCo's CFMs. It is normal for the newborn startup to tick N/A under M&A on the corporate synthesizer, and keep it ticked in early adolescence. During later adolescence or adulthood there may come a day when M&A discussions surface and the marker is reset to high.

The corporate leveraging synthesizer does a good job of focusing the attention of the intrapreneur, sponsor, gatekeeper, NewCo's leadership team, and allied CoreCo functional leaders at brainstorming sessions. Brainstorming fosters a shared appreciation of the overall situation and leads to alignment on NewCo's CFM strategy, both of which are indispensible before delving into detailed planning. Other virtues of the synthesizer are that it helps the intrapreneur decide which corporate functions should be addressed first and is a convincing communication tool when presenting the CFM strategy at departmental meetings or to CoreCo's executives.

CoreCo's senior executives are a primary CFM. They have strong networks that can provide invaluable help with reach and access.

Detailing the CFM Strategy

Once you have set your NewCo leveraging synthesizer and reached alignment on how NewCo can leverage CoreCo's resources, you will need to move to the CFM planning phase, which is all about nailing down the details. The opposite of determining the particulars of your CFM strategy is to leverage your parent company on an ad hoc basis. The complications caused by an unplanned, ad hoc approach can include CoreCo's executives losing confidence when they conclude NewCo has little understanding of the best way to enter its new market, and confusion, annoyance, or even hostility on the part of CoreCo's functional leaders, who will find themselves in the awkward position of having no time to plan for a future NewCo need.

The three-step planning method I recommend is summarized in figure 10.3. It starts with four drivers that capture the major activities required to execute NewCo's strategy and how market penetration and subsequent growth can be accelerated. These drivers, in turn, point to the CFMs that can be leveraged to help NewCo progress quickly. The second box identifies the scope of the support the CFM strategy needs and gauges the availability of the resources to do the work and the willingness of the functional leader to carry it out and remain open to change. Having completed the analyses in the first two boxes, NewCo can now work with CoreCo to finalize how each CFM will be tapped.

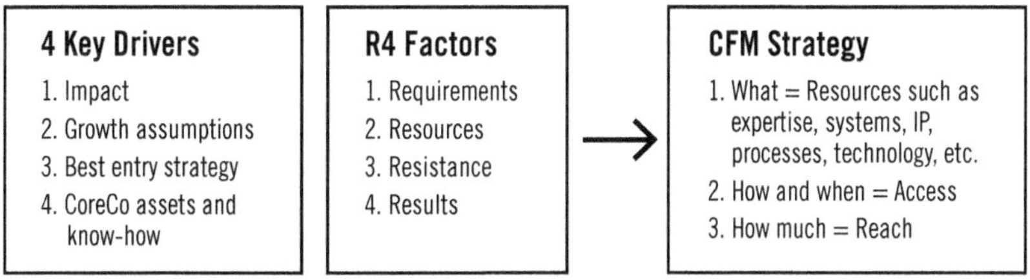
4 Key Drivers
1. Impact
2. Growth assumptions
3. Best entry strategy
4. CoreCo assets and know-how
R4 Factors
1. Requirements
2. Resources
3. Resistance
4. Results
CFM Strategy
1. What = Resources such as expertise, systems, IP, processes, technology, etc.
2. How and when = Access
3. How much = Reach

Figure 10.3 Establishing the CFM Strategy

4 Key Drivers

1. Impact

Make a list of what is required from NewCo to achieve its desired impact in the new market. This includes:

- Main strategic assumptions NewCo presented to CoreCo that were behind its decision to launch the startup and the basis for its conclusion that it would succeed
- Key assumptions made during the innovation and soft launch phases that validated why NewCo's product or service would fulfill an unmet need
- Major findings from the 37 marketing activities
- What executing the ABS model (see page 234) revealed about NewCo's mission, strategic intent, and business goals

2. Growth assumptions

NewCo must have a global understanding of its assumptions regarding growth in the first five years, with a more precise view of years one to three. Make a list that includes:

- Financial materiality projections and time expectations for NewCo's rate of growth
- Initial assumptions about an early adopters strategy
- Initial assumptions about a sales growth strategy
- Budgets allocated directly to NewCo in the current and next three fiscal years
- Preliminary budgets in CoreCo departments whose support will be needed

3. Best entry strategy

NewCo's leaders must possess validated ideas about how its new customer base will respond to NewCo's entry. This demands an analysis of:

- CoreCo's brand recognition (positive, negative, or neutral) as perceived by NewCo's target market, customers, and influencers
- NewCo's primary value proposition as a cost advantage: understand where NewCo will save its new customers money, how much, and why that matters to them

- NewCo's primary value proposition as a quality advantage: identify how NewCo will demonstrate that it can deliver on its claims and why that matters to potential customers
- NewCo's primary value proposition as a customer acquisition or retention advantage: identify how NewCo's target customers will be able to acquire new customers or keep the ones they have using the proposed solution, and why this matters to them
- CoreCo's existing market credibility vis-à-vis potential customers: know which CoreCo achievements give it credibility and how NewCo can translate these achievements into an asset

4. CoreCo assets and know-how

It is crucial for NewCo to have a firm grasp of all the knowledge and skills at CoreCo that can be leveraged. The next step is to determine which of these will help NewCo enter and grow in its market, how and when they can be used, and in what context. The list must be specific. Do not get preoccupied with whether or not they are available; you will assess availability in the following step. At a minimum review these categories:

- Technology, including intellectual property, prototypes, and products
- Product development and manufacturing capabilities
- Operational expertise and resources
- CoreCo brand and market reputation
- Customer relationships and links to NewCo's target customers
- Distribution channels
- Marketing expertise
- Customer support and services
- Geographic and market reach
- General business systems, processes, and best practices
- Other support functions such as finance, human resources, communications, legal, contracts, purchasing, IT support
- Government, regulatory, and environmental

A return to the example of the outsourcing service offered to aviation training centers will help you contextualize the application of the four drivers.

Driver 1. After segmenting our customer universe into relevant groupings and completing a competitive analysis, we concluded that no one else was serving this segment. Then we put together an offer that documented our value proposition. Rather than a set of vague, hopeful assumptions, it was a clear and compelling offer that we believed potential clients would find attractive. We outlined the cost to the airlines of doing the job we were proposing to do, the financial benefit of outsourcing the work to us, specified quality targets, and pertinent metrics of performance the customers could hold us accountable for such as defect rectification times and equipment availability and reliability. I captured our value proposition with the term "operational peace of mind" to reflect our commitment to flawless execution.

Driver 2. Using our SMART objectives as a starting point, my sponsor and I drew up a list of sales and marketing activities that would help us win our first clients. Then we considered how much time we would need. We agreed that NewCo's market was very similar to CoreCo's and negotiated for budgets and resources. The last step was to set the corporate leveraging synthesizer as follows: NewCo would establish its own functions in sales leadership, operational expertise, and marketing, and would leverage CoreCo's capabilities in sales, business development, marketing, and training center operations. My colleagues in CoreCo's business segments and support functions not only agreed to support our strategy, they understood that NewCo formed part of CoreCo's overall strategy and financial objectives. They felt engaged and decided to commit to the success of the new business venture.

Driver 3. We determined that our targets were airlines, owners of aircraft fleets, and operators of training centers. Our entry strategy was based primarily on cost savings with a secondary emphasis on improved quality and responsiveness. The challenge was to get access to the relevant decision makers, who were probably familiar with CAE but likely had a low understanding of the breadth and depth of its expertise in simulation center operations. Our goal was to communicate that expertise and our ability to leverage it to deliver attractive savings, and that this would result in impressive response times should their simulators be down.

Driver 4. Having defined in broad terms the NewCo resources that were required versus those we could tap CoreCo for, it was time to create a more exhaustive list of everything we could borrow or copy from our parent. A partial recap of the list includes engineers and technicians, finance, experts in regulatory accreditation, spares and logistics support, millions of dollars of spares inventory, IT systems, simulator maintenance and support processes, people in locations around the world, sales and legal functions, credibility with global federal regulatory bodies, and established client relationships. We then defined exactly what we needed and prioritized the list. We quickly realized that to reach out to potential international customers with our very small team, we would be traveling 365 days a year, which was unsustainable for both our bodies and budgets. In short order we brought the CFMs of sales, geographic reach, customer intimacy, and finance to the top of the list to acquire customers. To be ready to take over their operations once the deals were signed, we put operational resources, IT support, and spares and logistics lower down the list.

The R4 Factors

The second piece of the leveraging puzzle is best expressed by the question: Can CoreCo actually support NewCo in the manner it needs? Now that NewCo has established its list of CFMs, it is time to find out. R4 represents Requirements, Resources, Resistance, and Results. NewCo must assess these jointly with the sponsor, the gatekeeper, and the heads of the organizations whose resources and assets are being considered for leveraging.

R1. Requirements. Do the functional leaders NewCo will rely on recognize what is required to support NewCo? Do they genuinely commit to satisfying those requirements? This refers not just to the *what*, but also to the *when* and *how*. If you are the intrapreneur, be on the lookout for CoreCo leaders who express willingness, but on their own terms. Instead of making the effort to comprehend NewCo's actual needs, they plan to take the easier route of forcing existing processes, systems, and organizations onto NewCo. R1 is about making sure CoreCo's leaders disengage their immune system and approach your request with an open mind. They must have a true grasp of NewCo's needs before they bring you recommendations on how they will support the new enterprise.

R2. Resources. Having a commitment to help is not enough. A commitment must outline the resources to be delivered and show that the appointed employees will have time in their schedule to give the help required when it is required. It also includes the names of individuals who have enough clout to get things moving. I have seen qualified people assigned to support NewCo without their CoreCo workload being reduced.

The result was limited availability, slow progress, and incredible frustration and stress for everyone concerned. Some people might tell you not to worry, they will support you. They might even assign the right people for the work. But if they fail to free up their time, the commitment they offer is hollow.

Resources include more than just people. When evaluating how each CFM can contribute to NewCo's success, consider three broad areas: **1) resources**, which refers to expertise, people, products, services, assets, tools, systems, processes, operations, and facilities, **2) access**, which means the ability to connect with relevant people and organizations, and includes reputation, government and regulatory influence, customer relationships, sales channels, and business associations, and **3) reach**, which refers to moving your business beyond your local area to a broader geographic region where CoreCo operates or has influence.

R3. Resistance. You need to be on high alert for resistance. Ask yourself: Are CoreCo's functional leaders and their employees truly committed to supporting NewCo with the speed and flexibility it requires? Unfortunately, it can be difficult to detect resistance because most people will neglect to tell you they are resisting, especially if the CEO or president of their unit strongly endorsed NewCo and appealed for everyone's full cooperation. But you may find yourself negotiating with a functional leader who announced her support for NewCo only because she felt she had no other option. Leaders like that usually make it clear that their help will be provided on their terms.

When surveying CoreCo for resistance, stay objective and deal with reality as it is, not as you wish it to be. You will need to activate your emotional intelligence and corporate leadership skills. Do not hesitate to ask for input from the gatekeeper and sponsor, who are well placed to manage resistance. Whether passive or active, resistance can render a well-developed CFM strategy useless, so be thorough and pragmatic when evaluating R3.

R4. Results. Ask the CoreCo leader you are dealing with to guarantee the CFM's operational and budgetary results in writing. The operational results address what CoreCo will deliver and when. The budgetary results are the costs NewCo will be billed for the work CoreCo undertakes. CoreCo's budgetary commitments cannot be overlooked. Its managers are evaluated annually on their ability to work within allocated budgetary envelopes, and the last thing they want is for NewCo to be the source of missed performance objectives due to a misunderstanding.

If a CoreCo function cannot deliver the CFM support within the required budgetary envelope, then why bother leveraging it? This might be a case of the compounding cushion effect. Take the time to review the costs to ensure there are no false impressions regarding potential risks and that risk cushions are quantified and captured separately. If CoreCo is still unable to provide the support under a reasonable budgetary envelope, NewCo should consider setting up this capability on its own.

The methodology for funding CFMs must be in place prior to initiating the CFM discussions, and the leaders who will provide the services must agree to it. There are several approaches to funding, including transfer pricing, budget allocations, or pay-for-service methodologies. CoreCo will establish which formula makes sense for each CFM. For some functions the best way to support the new startup is to leave it alone. This is the case when NewCo has decided to create its own functions with its own processes and systems, and it does not want to be slowed down by meddling from the same functions at CoreCo.

Finalizing the CFM Strategy

The final stage when creating your CFM strategy is to list the CFMs you want to leverage along with their capabilities, at what point in NewCo's growth you will leverage them, the associated deliverables, and the budgetary envelopes. For example: CoreCo's HR function received a medium-high setting on the leveraging synthesizer. This indicates that several but not all its capabilities will be targeted. Facing tight deadlines and a different market from CoreCo's, the startup decides to handle wages, compensation, recruitment, and work environment on its own. It will tap into CoreCo's capabilities for manpower planning, employee onboarding, and labor and employment law compliance in the first three months, and in month 12 will leverage its annual performance process and workplace safety compliance program. To support its expansion plans, NewCo will take advantage of CoreCo's reach by accessing its HR partners in targeted locations in year 2. To complete the CFM strategy, CoreCo's HR leader and the intrapreneur will finalize the deliverables and negotiate and assign a budget.

With engineering and R&D, distribution channels, and finance and accounting as examples, table 10.1 identifies the resources that are available, what they give access to, and the benefits with respect to reach. Using the list on page 177, populate a CFM table that reflects your particular NewCo objectives and your specific CoreCo CFMs. Then, for each

CFM, document the support being retained, the expected deliverable, when it will be required, and the approved budget for CoreCo to do the work. These CFM details can be added to the table under new headings: retained capability, deliverables, timing, and budget.

Table 10.1 Leveraging CoreCo's CFMs

CORECO CFM	RESOURCES	ACCESS	REACH
Engineering and R&D	• Expertise in technology and the sciences • Subject matter experts • Employees to do the work • Reputation in innovation, thought leadership, and other areas	• Intellectual property • Labs and equipment • Products and technology • R&D programs and organizations • Ecosystem of technology partners • Technology forums and working groups	• International network of research centers and associations • Introduction to local partnerships
Distribution Channels	• Proven methods of selling in various regions or countries • Knowledge of distribution culture • Direct sales team provides boots on the ground	• Distributors, value-added resellers, retailers, Internet solutions, and other customer sales touchpoints • Potential customers within CoreCo's customer base • Established CoreCo clients of potential interest to NewCo	• In-country resources and influence prepares local market for NewCo's arrival • In-country resources conduct pre-sales and sales activities and accelerate market penetration

CORECO CFM	RESOURCES	ACCESS	REACH
Finance and Accounting	• Expertise in financial reporting and transactions, financing options, and accepted accounting principles • Experts in creating financial structures • Proven processes and systems • Employees to do the work	• Larger funding sources (backstopped by CoreCo) • Financing options at a lower cost of borrowing • Ecosystem of consultants and financial institutions • Infrastructure for reporting, billing, accounts payable and receivable, tax, and other finance and accounting business activities	• Regional/country/foreign finance and accounting expertise to accelerate entry • Helps secure in-country tax benefits, new business financial credits, and other incentives

NewCo's Customer Interface

There are certain functions NewCo must develop on its own during infancy and adolescence that will bring its team face to face with customers. They include direct sales, managing distributors and retailers, securing partnerships and alliances, product development, customer service, and project management. Interacting with customers and the various elements of the distribution channel is a critical aspect of the startup environment. It allows NewCo's team to learn about customer needs and expectations, verify a wide range of key assumptions, validate the MVP, understand its best options for promotion and distribution, and build customer intimacy.

The place for these functions is within NewCo's organizational structure, and NewCo must control them from start to finish, without any biases, filters, or interference from CoreCo. This does not mean that aspects of CoreCo's capabilities cannot be borrowed in a supporting capacity. Providing partial support is par for the course when corporate startups are launched. But it can be tricky. The CoreCo leaders giving the support must agree to defer to NewCo's intrapreneur, which may make them uncomfortable if they feel they are relinquishing control. The intrapreneur must be sensitive and well prepared when handling these kinds of negotiations with CoreCo's functional leaders.

Transitioning a CFM to NewCo

As the startup becomes successful it will demand more support from its parent, and a lot of time can be wasted trying to get the attention of part-time intermediaries from CoreCo who feel work overload or corporate bias against NewCo. Reluctant corporate employees typically prefer to force-fit CoreCo templates onto NewCo's customers. When this happens everyone's frustration soon mounts, not least of all the customers', and it becomes obvious that this approach is unworkable. Sooner or later some or all the CFMs will need to be transferred to NewCo's organizational structure.

In one NewCo I shepherded we eventually concluded that we had underestimated the contracting workload. We also realized that the contractual and financial terms that were right for our NewCo customers were very different from CoreCo's traditional terms. What was a manageable situation in the early days became highly problematic the more successful we became, and in due course we transferred the legal function into our structure. In a second NewCo, a similar situation developed with finance, where the workload associated with refining the business model, pricing, and financial reporting became so heavy that the CFM support was discontinued and we managed our own financial affairs. Corporate governance guidelines were established to address both situations, but the work was tailored to meet the needs of NewCo's customers and we carried it out.

Over the years I learned that HR can be one of the most challenging CFMs to leverage. This is because HR's functional leaders and NewCo's managers both tend to underestimate the difficulty of adapting corporate HR practices to a startup environment and a new market. The culprit might be overly ambitious assumptions that were used when creating the HR CFM strategy. What NewCo assumes will be an effective way of leveraging CoreCo for hiring, compensation, benefits, and employee onboarding proves to be the opposite.

I remember discovering that these activities, along with training and employee retention, are fundamental to a company's DNA. They evolve from the traditions and business culture of the marketplace the company operates in. HR requirements can differ enormously for employees being recruited from a NewCo market that is very different from its parent's. Trying to enforce corporate HR directives, practices, and benchmarks onto a NewCo can result in distressing hiring delays and grind progress to a halt, because without people the job does not get done.

The most difficult HR struggle I encountered was when we transitioned from an aviation and engineering culture with a strong manufacturing influence into the healthcare industry, which is mainly shaped by hospital healthcare professionals, the providers of medical equipment, and the pharmaceutical industry. Our corporate hiring and retention traditions had been established over years of hiring experts in aviation, aircraft simulation, and manufacturing such as pilots, software and aircraft systems engineers, and production technicians. Now we needed doctors, nurses, and subject matter experts from the medical equipment industry, and our sales force and business development leaders had to be recruited from the medical equipment and pharmaceutical talent pool.

Talk about a potential clash of HR cultures. After weeks of unsuccessfully using existing job descriptions, hiring scales, recruitment strategies, and compensation packages, we came to an agreement with the HR function that a dedicated HR business partner would take ownership of our people strategy and ensure that the approach reflected our new healthcare market realities.

We faced something similar when developing our marketing strategies. We had underestimated how very different, and market-specific, our marketing strategies and activities needed to be to have the intended impact on our new healthcare customers. We discovered it was futile to appeal to hospitals, medical schools, and medical regulatory bodies in the same way we had to airlines, flight schools, and aviation authorities. Many lessons were learned, which I shared in previous chapters, about the importance of objectively assessing NewCo's market similarity to CoreCo's core markets. Without these assessments you will not develop the insights you need to create a successful CFM strategy.

The CFM Charter

A useful tool for capturing your CFM strategy is the CFM charter. Its purpose is to identify NewCo's expectations, how they link with the successful implementation of NewCo's strategy, what is required from each CFM as detailed in table 10.1, and the timing of the delivery. It should also spell out the approved budgets and provide a list of potential risks CoreCo will run in providing the support. Creating the charter is a collaborative effort, and when the work is done it should be co-signed by the parties involved, namely, the intrapreneur, the sponsor, and the CFM functional leader. A separate charter must be written for each CoreCo function, and they must be updated as NewCo evolves.

Ultimately, leveraging CoreCo is the best road to success for a growth strategy founded on the launch of a new business. NewCo must take what it needs from CoreCo and leave the rest behind. This is not about pleasing everyone who wants to participate in NewCo. The intrapreneur and sponsor will have to turn away corporate functions that want to contribute but whose expertise is not required, or because the solution they propose is a poor fit for NewCo's needs. The gatekeeper is on standby to help the intrapreneur get this message across effectively.

COMING UP NEXT.....................

As NewCo's formal launch date approaches and CoreCo's management team becomes aware that some members will play a role in supporting NewCo (their involvement made real by the discussions surrounding the CFM strategy), the corporate immune system will be triggered.

The immune system is the flip side of the coin: on the one side, the emergence of NewCo, and on the other, CoreCo's protective response. In fact, the corporate immune system is a normal reaction that can be healthy for the corporation if properly managed. If left unchecked it can be a barrier to NewCo's progress and plague the startup for months or even years after the launch, which is not good for CoreCo either.

Avoiding the irreparable damage the corporate immune system can cause lies at the heart of the next labor.

The Apples of the Hesperides

King Eurystheus demanded two new labors of Hercules after deciding he had failed to follow the rules when he killed the Hydra and cleaned the Augean stables. For his eleventh labor Hercules was tasked with bringing back the golden apples of the Hesperides, nymphs who were the daughters of Atlas. The apples were given to Zeus by Hera as a wedding gift, and Eurystheus was sure she would never let Hercules take them. Furthermore, the garden was guarded by a hundred-headed dragon. Despite the obstacles Hercules set off to find the secret garden. As he traveled far and wide in search of it he fought and killed many challengers. Finally he came upon the sea god Nereus, who was revered for his knowledge, and after a long struggle he extracted the garden's location. Then he learned that Atlas should be asked to fetch the golden fruit in his place. Atlas agreed on the condition that Hercules hold the heavens on his shoulders while he was gone. Upon returning with the apples, Atlas told Hercules that he would take them to Eurystheus himself, wanting to be free of his eternal burden. Hercules tricked Atlas into reclaiming his duty and proceeded to carry the apples to Eurystheus as instructed.

LABOR 11

The Threat of the Corporate Immune System

On the face of it, the garden of the Hesperides sounds harmless, even blissful, and all Hercules had to do was pick some apples from its trees. In much the same way the intrapreneur might judge the labor of managing CoreCo's immune system as relatively straightforward. After all, how difficult can it be for NewCo to succeed when the CEO and executive sponsor have explained to the entire corporation that NewCo is essential to its strategic planning and must be supported by everyone? The intrapreneur is certain he saw most senior executives nod their heads in agreement.

But let's not forget the hundred-headed dragon or the many obstacles Hercules faced in his efforts to complete his eleventh labor. Just as the obstacles seemed to be endless and almost insurmountable, so the corporation's immune system activities will at times appear too numerous and powerful to overcome. Like the hundred-headed dragon, the immune system will attack on many fronts at the first sign of an intruder. In reality, the agreement the intrapreneur saw in each executive nod, while possibly genuine, was only part of the picture. Behind those supportive smiles some form of immune system reaction was beginning to take shape.

The creation of NewCo is essentially about making rapid progress and reaping the rewards of intrapreneurship, but even as its leadership team is working to address a mountain of business challenges, they will sustain repeated attacks from the corporate immune system. Some will be launched out in the open, while others will be subtle or even covert and difficult to recognize. The intrapreneur will need to do as Hercules did with Atlas: seek the assistance of influential CoreCo leaders to help him find and foil the obstacles that may trip him up on his way to turning NewCo into a success. He will need their help until NewCo achieves a level of maturity that allows it to stand on its own.

Identifying the Immune System

Gifford Pinchot wrote a research paper called "Innovation Through Intrapreneuring," in which he states that NewCo "triggers the corporate immune system, inviting resistance from people who see any change to the status quo as a threat." I mostly agree. In my experience immune system activity is often motivated by resistance to change, but not always. Sometimes its intent is positive. It can happen that CoreCo intervenes because a vice president observes that corporate expertise is needed, or a CoreCo leader who is convinced of the benefits of standardization may insist that NewCo stick to the company's business practices. In most cases, though, immune system activity is related to some kind of opposition.

Pinchot's insightful analogy between CoreCo's self-defense mechanism and the human immune system extends to the body's white blood cells, which are produced to fight infectious diseases and foreign substances. If too few white blood cells are produced, the body might succumb, but too many can also be a problem. An immune system can mistakenly send an onslaught of signals and the subsequent blitzing can do serious harm and in some cases be fatal. So it is with the corporate immune system, with its white blood cells in the form of systems, processes, practices, governance, metrics, and KPIs.

The corporation's immune system has been honed over many years or even decades and is part of CoreCo's DNA. Do not discount it as an interesting but abstract concept. It is always present and very strong, precisely because its activities are triggered and executed by the people who make your corporation successful. It is not a question of whether or not the immune system will intervene, but when. Like white blood cells confronting invaders, CoreCo's immune system is indiscriminate. It is predisposed to imposing CoreCo's business culture across all its divisions, organizations, and subsidiaries. Pinchot's analogy perfectly describes the delicate balance that must be struck between the right amount of CoreCo "defense," which will bolster NewCo's progress, and too much, which could eliminate it.

When properly managed the corporate immune system is a strength. As we all know, having a robust immune system is key to longevity. The same holds true in the business world. CoreCo's immune system keeps it out of trouble by helping it recover from economic downturns, fend off competitive attacks, identify and eliminate bad management practices, and detect fraudulent activity. But an immune system that blindly overreacts can kill a vital CoreCo organization, for example, by forcing it to adopt business practices that are unsuitable for its market or by pushing complex corporate practices onto a fledging startup that is too weak to support them.

NewCo's most important competitive advantage is its ability to leverage select CoreCo resources, systems, and processes. It sounds uncomplicated until we remember that the corporate immune system can put up roadblocks. The more similarity there is between NewCo's and CoreCo's customers, the more CFMs that are leveraged and the greater the likelihood there will be friction (immune system activity) between the parent company and its startup. What's more, the higher CoreCo's expectations are regarding NewCo's materiality and the bigger the gap between the two markets, the more vigilant the corporate immune system will be about possible threats. This is because both business assumption risk and corporate expectations risk will be significant.

Immune System Activity

Being able to spot corporate immune system activity is an important intrapreneurial skill. There are typically two lines of defense. The first includes nine behaviors that are hard to repel because they are embedded in the corporation's business practices, guidelines, and directives. They are: the subservient objectives, the metrics imposition, the standardization function, the forecasting fabrication, the business model rationalization, the meeting monopolization, the reporting inundation, the titles and promotions persuasion, and the PR proposition.

The second line of defense includes white blood cell activities that are subtle and sometimes furtive, but they can be just as devastating to NewCo's ability to make progress. They are: the organization design deflection, the loan shark, the compensation dissension, the work environment normalization, the best practice diversion, the technology transfer temptation, the HiPo defections, the recognition tensions, the quality combat, death by data, the defeatist mentality, and the blind do-gooders.

The First Line of Defense

1. The subservient objectives

Setting SMART objectives is central to ensuring that NewCo's employees focus on activities that will help the startup achieve its goals. Once the objectives are set, it is the responsibility of the intrapreneur to roll them out to the rest of the NewCo team. There should be no interference from anyone at CoreCo. Yet there often is. It can come in the form of a CoreCo manager trying to use objective setting as a way to retain or regain control of certain NewCo activities. The manager will introduce an annual performance objective that directs someone on NewCo's team to adapt, leverage, or deploy one or more CoreCo practices, even though they are not aligned with NewCo's objectives and CFM strategy. In fact, they are subservient to CoreCo's needs. Keep an eye out for the loan shark behavior listed under the second line of defense, because subservient objectives are sure to follow.

2. The metrics imposition

Performance metrics are used to drive behavior. Previously we looked at how establishing the right metrics leads to realistic expectations, and that CoreCo's forecasting process must be adapted to fit NewCo's learning environment. Similarly, NewCo's metrics must be tailored to its new business model and new market, as well as to its growth position. However, if a department head at CoreCo notices that NewCo is behaving in an unfamiliar way, she may worry that the startup is veering off course. Her response may be to try to impose "the corporate way," which could mean a set of metrics that are familiar to CoreCo but irrelevant to the startup. NewCo must block any attempts to impose metrics that do not reflect its business reality and maturity level.

3. The standardization function

Standardization is an important management tool that allows large organizations to achieve high levels of predictability and repeatability, which drive efficiencies and cost improvements. NewCo can expect some level of standardization, but its imposition can easily go too far. For example, after analyzing a NewCo request and finding that it requires the invention of a new process, CoreCo may decide instead to impose an existing standardized process with the goal of creating efficiencies, but the real goal may be to regain control of NewCo's activities in that area. Standardization should be limited to providing NewCo with a system of governance to ensure that the startup follows sound legal and ethical business practices and only runs business risks that are acceptable to the corporation.

4. The forecasting fabrication

Forecasting is a major area of immune system activity because it drives standardization and imposes metrics. CoreCo can effectively rein in NewCo by forcing it to adopt the corporation's forecasting standards and methodology. This can occur out in the open in the form of requests for mandatory weekly, monthly, or quarterly forecasting reports, or be hidden within two other immune system activities: the meeting monopolization and the reporting inundation (see below). Avoid this trap in the same way you will avoid the forecasting trap described in labor 7, by encouraging learning, knowledge sharing, and frequent validation, and by focusing on forecasting activities at both the macro and micro levels.

5. The business model rationalization

This is an attempt by CoreCo to bring NewCo's business model in line with the models of its core businesses. The perpetrators will be CoreCo leaders who fail to comprehend what NewCo is trying to achieve and are particularly confused about how it will make money and grow into a material business. We know that allowing NewCo to refine its own business model based on the feedback it receives from its market and customers and the validations it undertakes is fundamental to its success. The sponsor must step in immediately if CoreCo tries to impose a business model that has not been validated by NewCo.

6. The meeting monopolization

Another way for CoreCo to reel in NewCo is to require its leadership team to attend numerous CoreCo meetings. At first glance this request can seem reasonable. CoreCo may say that meetings are a good way for NewCo and CoreCo to maintain close links and share lessons learned, or that they provide a platform for NewCo to regularly brief CoreCo's functions. CoreCo may actually be attempting to slow down a NewCo function it perceives is driving too much change. A red flag to watch for is CoreCo's insistence at meetings that NewCo employees take on action items that suit CoreCo but do little for the startup.

Besides monopolizing the time of NewCo's busy team, meetings bring the startup back into the CoreCo fold, where it is susceptible to being persuaded to accept the corporate way of doing things. NewCo leaders who were transferred from CoreCo can be especially vulnerable to this tactic, either because of old loyalties or as a self-preservation measure given the possibility that one day they could be moved back to CoreCo. A healthy dose of hires from outside the corporation will ensure that NewCo has enough new blood to be less susceptible to old alliances, and it will be easier to spot ex-CoreCo employees who are blind to the meeting monopolization line of defense.

In a startup environment, where everyone's time is precious, the only CoreCo meetings NewCo should attend are those that help drive its agenda. As we saw in earlier chapters, meetings are an important forum for educating CoreCo's departments about the new business venture and engaging the support of functional leaders. They are also where NewCo and CoreCo work together to finalize and deploy the CFM strategy discussed in labor 10. In meetings, as in everything else, NewCo's needs come first.

7. The reporting inundation

This activity is similar to the meeting monopolization. Hoping to minimize the change being asked of it and ultimately wanting control, the corporation will try to impose a strict system of reporting governance and a level of reporting frequency that are ill-suited to a startup. Reporting can demand formats and information that are simply irrelevant, such as quality statistics and P&L reports. NewCo must refuse all attempts to impose reporting formats or frequencies that do not reflect its maturity level, business model, and new market. This is another area where the gatekeeper and sponsor may need to intervene.

8. The titles and promotions persuasion

CoreCo employees who transfer to NewCo leave a predictable environment for one where new job titles or sudden promotions reflect the needs of an environment where people wear multiple hats, and where quick decision making and having authority over broad areas is the norm. These may not be the norms at CoreCo and resentment can surface following the announcement of new job titles or promotions at NewCo. A typical response for CoreCo employees and even senior leaders is to question why someone at a similar level in NewCo is granted more decision-making authority or a larger span of control. Almost certainly these employees will not have taken the time to understand the new business environment.

NewCo employees hired from outside the corporation will face similar challenges. Most will have come from various locations in the market being entered, and will be used to different approaches to titles, responsibilities, spans of control, and compensation. But CoreCo may want to enforce existing corporate guidelines rather than create new ones. Or during the hiring process it might try to squeeze candidates into unsuitable systems, leading the candidates to question if they should accept a job in an organization that is unable to properly assess their skills and level of authority. I have lost many good people due to this immune system behavior. To avoid it, use benchmarks that match the new industry and NewCo's business needs, and call in the sponsor or gatekeeper to help HR get on board.

9. The PR proposition

Including NewCo in a PR campaign before it can deliver on the campaign's promises is like putting the proverbial cart before the horse. CoreCo might be tempted to send out a press release to show support for its innovative product and announce its drive towards a new market, but it is not a good idea, no matter how exciting NewCo's early successes. Press releases raise expectations among investors, who will shift their attention to NewCo, especially if CoreCo is showing poor results in its core businesses. NewCo will feel pressure to show financial progress ahead of plan, but by focusing on making short-term gains to keep up with CoreCo's PR agenda, the intrapreneur can easily take one or more wrong turns. Furthermore, if NewCo fails to deliver early on, CoreCo is left open to criticism. Another negative of creating expectations too soon is that it can prevent NewCo from pivoting its strategy, which would require its parent to issue a retraction, impacting branding and shaking investors' confidence in CoreCo's senior leadership.

Identifying corporate immune system activity is a crucial intrapreneurial skill.

The Second Line of Defense

1. The organization design deflection

We reviewed organization design in labor 10 when discussing the best way to establish NewCo as a stand-alone business. The corporate immune system will be triggered by any organization design that results in a loss of power and control at CoreCo. In response, some CoreCo leaders may claim duplication error and argue that CoreCo should retain particular functions. But what they are really doing is trying to deflect NewCo from its course. Their actions are based on subjective criteria rather than on what has been objectively determined is best for NewCo, which can be found in the CFM charter. The charter is a written commitment from the corporation's functional leaders that states precisely what is to be leveraged from CoreCo and how.

2. The loan shark

One of the more subtle ways CoreCo's functions can try to exert influence is through loaning employees to NewCo and having them retain a formal reporting line back to CoreCo. Startups are the most vulnerable to this type of white blood cell activity during their infancy because expectations and budgets are firmly in place and there is pressure to show results. This is when NewCo begins to feel desperate for qualified people to get the job done. The more politically savvy and control-driven leaders at CoreCo know this and will scan their resources to see who they can loan out. If their attempt to maintain control through establishing a formal reporting line fails, they will fight to retain the more informal dotted line under the guise of fostering collaboration, encouraging knowledge transfer, or ensuring NewCo's adherence to corporate governance.

Dual reporting – one line to the startup and one to the parent – is an effective immune system strategy because it dilutes the intrapreneur's authority, reduces his control over resources, and undermines his ability to use motivational tools such as annual objective setting, performance reviews and feedback, and reward and recognition mechanisms to make sure that everyone is aligned regarding NewCo's objectives. It can also lead to two sets of annual performance objectives and the needless duplication of meetings. In short, it limits the intrapreneur's ability to set and achieve goals focused on NewCo.

My take is that positions of influence at NewCo must be assigned exclusively to NewCo and report directly to the intrapreneur without any reporting back to CoreCo, whether formal or informal. The dual reporting structure is common in project-based organizations that need to address the complexities of working within matrix structures where some integration is required across projects. Nonetheless, dual reporting cannot find a home at NewCo. Nor does it need to. NewCo was launched to contribute to CoreCo's business results in the medium- to long-term, and the focus needs to stay on NewCo reaching its objectives. If one of CoreCo's functional leaders insists on a dual reporting structure, you may need to question his commitment to NewCo as an autonomous entity and review the qualifications of the NewCo transfer.

3. The compensation dissension

Despite what best practices tell us about how to establish compensation guidelines for corporate startups, most corporations fight tooth and nail to compensate NewCo's employees in line with CoreCo's. At the root of this tension is the practice of measuring job value with a corporate yardstick that uses budget P&L, budget approval levels and size, and total number of employees to assign titles and compensation. This bigger-is-better mentality blinds CoreCo to the need for a different yardstick to measure startups and capture other important factors such as job diversity and complexity, the multiple hats employees wear, the levels of market uncertainty, and the personal career risk individuals take when they jump to a startup. Compensation packages must especially recognize the high level of risk employees accept when they join NewCo. If corporate leaders fail to design and defend a compensation package that attracts and retains the right intrapreneur and the best risk takers, these people will find better offers elsewhere. In turn, this will fuel the people at CoreCo who say the corporation needs to retain control.

4. The work environment normalization

Employees recruited from the new market will enter NewCo expecting to find a work environment that reflects what is customary in their industry. I have a ready example from my experience with a manufacturing company that entered the software business via a NewCo. The CoreCo in this case had a manufacturing culture that depended on closed offices, lots of cubicles, limited common areas, large production lines, and a unionized workforce with scheduled break times. Last but not least, the employees bought their own coffee from a scattering of vending machines.

Over the years CoreCo developed software that optimized its internal manufacturing processes, supply chain, and workload management practices. Eventually it decided that its homegrown software package could be turned into an off-the-shelf product for third-party users and, over the long-term, worldwide distribution. After a soft launch to conduct further validation, NewCo proceeded to a formal launch and was given the right level of independence to achieve its goals. After some early successes it was ready to become a larger-scale operation, at which time it had to grow rapidly. It was now in the software business and had to recruit from a workplace environment where employees enjoyed open office spaces, common areas for informal exchanges, lots of natural light, meeting rooms equipped with brainstorming tools, and last but not least, free espresso and cappuccino.

Imagine the shock potential recruits experienced when they came for their interview and had a tour of their future work environment. How many declined to join NewCo because they perceived the business culture to be unattractive? But the corporate immune system will object to NewCo setting up a different work environment, especially a more pleasing one. Well, CoreCo will have to get ready for it because there is no way around it. This is not to say you need to build new office spaces while you are swamped with soft launch or even formal launch activities, or that you need to spend a lot of money. In my experience it takes very little to create an environment that conforms to your new industry, and the work can be done in the early period following the launch. In the meantime, show your team and future hires that NewCo is moving in the direction of an appropriate environment.

5. The best practice diversion

Sometimes a startup can feel pressure to transfer a newly established best practice back to CoreCo, such as an effective management idea it implemented or an approach it borrowed from its new industry or market. This can take place as early as a few months after the launch, when a corporate executive hears about the success and requests that a small team be assembled to make the transfer. Two or three of NewCo's key resources are assigned to the team and must now spend their valuable time helping bring the best practice to CoreCo.

Do not be persuaded by flattery or reasoning to participate. This is hard for me to say because of my background in operational efficiency and Six Sigma and my firm belief that best practices should be shared whenever possible. But this case is different because the startup is in learning mode and its core employees are running a lean organization that must be absolutely dedicated to the new venture. Pulling key people to help transfer best practices to CoreCo is a diversion and time sink that will slow down NewCo's progress.

The answer to this request is simple: NewCo was set up to establish a sustainable and profitable business that is material to CoreCo's results and until this objective is well on its way to being attained, nothing can distract it. NewCo was not set up to find and perfect best practices. If a secondary benefit of this type emerges, yes, it can eventually be leveraged, but not until 18 months after NewCo's launch, or better yet, 24 months.

6. The technology transfer temptation

In the course of launching new products or acquiring products through partnerships, mergers, or acquisitions, NewCo will find itself in possession of successful new technology. Eventually CoreCo may want access to it. If only it were as simple as tossing the technology over the corporate wall and having someone at CoreCo pick it up. Like the transfer of best practices, technology transfer is a great idea but comes with the same problems: the people at NewCo with the most technical knowledge – in other words, NewCo's top experts – will have to spend untold hours explaining the technology and modifying it to meet CoreCo's needs. NewCo cannot afford to allocate any hours at all to this very demanding exercise and must keep its technical staff focused on developing and improving its MVP, working on product roadmaps and releases, and interfacing with users.

7. The HiPo defections

As NewCo's successes mount and the intrapreneur celebrates the great work being done by his strongest performers, these employees gain exposure across the corporation. Corporate leaders are always on the lookout for high performers (HiPos) to help them drive results, and when they spot a few they are inclined to want to transfer them to CoreCo or attract them through promotions. Transferring strong employees can also be another way for CoreCo to access a best practice or a new technology. Some HiPos will be intrigued by the possibility of leaving NewCo, where there is no safety net, for a more senior position at the stable and successful parent company.

Losing key HiPo employees who have navigated NewCo's arduous learning curve and possess a mature understanding of its strategy and plans would be a major setback. They also support the startup through their vital relationships with customers, partners, and influencers in the new market. They must be retained. I suggest a three-year freeze on HiPo transfers, which the sponsor can include in a set of clear guidelines she puts together to stop this disemboweling from happening.

8. The recognition tensions

Every NewCo success demands a celebration of some kind. Marking achievements with an announcement or other event is an important change management activity that communicates progress to the parent company, garners its support, and boosts everyone's spirits. The message that the strategy is working should cause satisfaction, but this is not always the response. Contrary to what common sense tells us, celebrating successes can lead to tension or jealousy within the larger organization. The source is invariably people at CoreCo who never fully supported NewCo's status as a separate and independent business entity. They were detractors from the beginning and are more interested in exposing NewCo's shortcomings than enjoying its successes. Disgruntlement may also arise in people who feel their own good work has gone unrecognized. NewCo's countermeasure is to encourage its allies to be proactive and not allow their subordinate managers to minimize NewCo accomplishments. The intrapreneur would also be wise to be generous in his expressions of gratitude to CoreCo colleagues who have contributed in some way.

9. The quality combat

Most corporations have a quality program to verify that customers' expectations are being met. It can be found in ISO standards, Six Sigma programs, continuous improvement initiatives, software maturity models, quality standards, and product development and release specifications, to name a few. Having had ongoing success with this program, CoreCo might try to persuade the intrapreneur to adopt a CoreCo design methodology or delay releasing its MVP and subsequent early market-ready versions until they have passed the corporation's quality gate. But in so doing the startup will waste scarce money and time.

CoreCo's quality standards are not applicable when NewCo is still working with early adopters because not enough is known about customer needs to lock down the specifications. Aiming to achieve too high a level of quality too early will rush the startup's discovery and validation process, or it will force conclusions about specifications prematurely. NewCo must establish its own minimal quality guidelines and release program with the goal of getting as many iterations of its initial MVP prototype into the hands of early adopters as possible. Once enough validation has been accomplished, CoreCo's quality standards can be introduced in stages.

This does not mean allowing shoddy work and giving early adopters a poor product. Having quality standards that are too permissive during the early phases of development can lead to significant rework later on, as well as unexpected delays, serious cost overruns, and customer satisfaction issues. A better bet would be for NewCo to adopt CoreCo's quality program as part of its CFM strategy when it is more mature. In this case it would be a business decision that supports NewCo's market strategy and is anchored in solid customer feedback.

10. Death by data

This immune system activity goes hand in hand with two of the activities in the first line of defense: the metrics imposition and the reporting inundation. It stems from CoreCo's belief that more data will give it a better appreciation of the new business. Unfortunately, the less familiar CoreCo's functional leaders are with NewCo, the more likely they will be to ask for familiar data, meaning data the parent company uses to analyze its core businesses but is irrelevant to NewCo's business or level of maturity. NewCo must refuse to produce data that does nothing to help the team reach the product stability it needs to succeed.

Death by data can be useful to the intrapreneur as a way to gauge CoreCo's understanding of NewCo. The more data requested by CoreCo and the higher the frequency of its requests, the greater the likelihood that NewCo has been unsuccessful at explaining its business and clarifying how similar it is to CoreCo's, or how different. If this happens the intrapreneur must improve its communication with CoreCo. Another cause might be that the parent is concerned about the startup's progress. In this case the intrapreneur needs to work with the sponsor and gatekeeper to identify CoreCo's concerns and address them promptly.

11. The defeatist mentality

There will be times when people on NewCo's team feel self-doubt. This is a normal result of having to repeatedly fend off a very active corporate immune system. Self-doubt might start in one or two people who are frustrated by how little progress is being made due to interference from CoreCo, and it may express itself in comments like, "They won't let us do it anyway, so why bother"? They have buckled under pressure, and their defeatist attitude can spread like wildfire and bring down the morale of the entire group. The intrapreneur must be ever watchful for changes in morale. The reality is that the corporation will always be stronger than a handful of individuals inside NewCo, and the team needs the unwavering support of the sponsor, gatekeeper, and key executives. If you sense a defeatist undercurrent beginning to swirl within NewCo, get to its root as quickly as you can and put an action plan in place to remedy the situation.

12. The blind do-gooders

Blind do-gooders are CoreCo managers, department heads, or other leaders who genuinely want to help NewCo succeed. Nevertheless, they exert a negative influence because they go about helping in the wrong way. I call them blind because they have a poor grasp of the startup's needs, and consequently their actions are inappropriate for the market and in the end create extra work for NewCo's team. When these people are employed in a function being leveraged as part of NewCo's CFM strategy, the intrapreneur must sit down with them and clearly outline the help that is actually needed. If he succeeds, the blind do-gooders can become hard-working allies. If they are not part of the CFM strategy and are acting on their own, the intrapreneur will have to explain that their actions are counterproductive and that the best way to help NewCo is to cheer from the sidelines.

Risk as a Trigger

We saw in the previous chapter how NewCo's CFM strategy, with its plans to adapt existing CoreCo systems, processes, and resources or create new ones from scratch, brings the corporate immune system to life. In labor 9 we learned that the immune response springs into action when clear corporate objectives are set regarding NewCo's materiality and growth. Labor 8 explained why a startup's formal launch triggers the immune system, and how we can predict the level of immune system activity from where the initiative sits on the time versus materiality versus market similarity axes. It also looked at the importance to CoreCo of assessing the risks associated with the new venture. With the help of figure 11.1 we can see how CoreCo's risk assessment directly influences its immune system response.

	Current Products or Services	New Products or Services
New Markets	Entering a new market using an existing CoreCo solution being sold in an existing CoreCo market	Entering a new market with an innovation that will satisfy the unmet needs of new customers
Current Markets	Entering a market already served by CoreCo using an existing CoreCo solution being sold in a different CoreCo market	Entering a market already served by CoreCo with an innovation that will satisfy the unmet needs of existing CoreCo customers

Figure 11.1 Risk and Immune Response as a Function of Product and Market

Figure 11.1 captures in broad terms the concept of business assumption risk and how it relates to technology and the market (covered in labor 8). We know that companies grow by bringing innovations or existing or modified products to a known market or a new one. The more innovation required to develop a solution to an unmet need and the more dissimilar the new market is to CoreCo's core market, the more unknowns exist and the higher the business risk. Conversely, when the market being entered is familiar and the product being introduced is similar to or the same as an existing product, the lower the risk. The least risky approach is captured in the lower left quadrant of figure 11.1, where we see an existing product from an existing CoreCo market being launched into one of CoreCo's other markets. The upper right quadrant shows that launching a new product into a new market carries the most risk. Figure 11.1 also demonstrates that the immune system's level of reaction directly correlates to the level of risk CoreCo perceives.

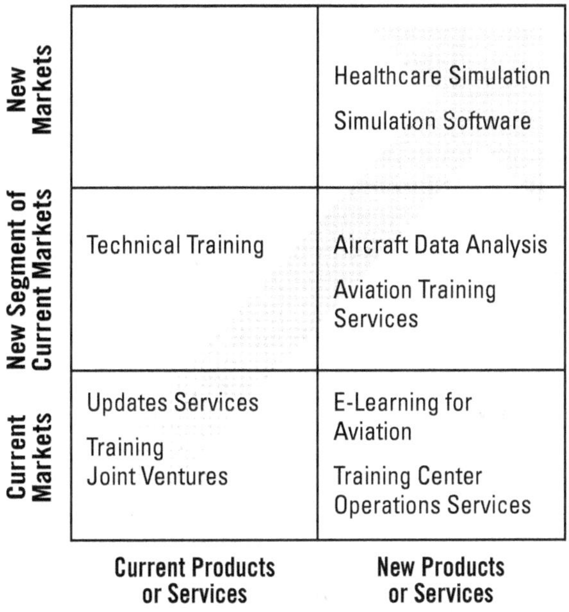
New Markets
Healthcare Simulation
Simulation Software
New Segment of Current Markets
Technical Training
Aircraft Data Analysis
Aviation Training Services
Current Markets
Updates Services
Training Joint Ventures
E-Learning for Aviation
Training Center Operations Services
Current Products or Services
New Products or Services

Figure 11.2 Risk Profiles of NewCos

Determining the risk profile of your new business idea will tell you a great deal about the level of immune system response you can expect when the idea is launched as a NewCo. This will allow you to prepare yourself to meet the resulting threatening activity head on. Figure 11.2

considers examples of nine NewCos I was involved with and shows my assessment of their risk level vis-à-vis the corporation. In the bottom left quadrant existing services were launched into a market the corporation knew extensively, and the risk was low. The level of risk and accompanying immune system activity increases in the middle right quadrant, which holds a new product and new service that were offered in an unknown segment of our existing market. The upper right quadrant has NewCos that were created to launch new products into markets CoreCo was largely unfamiliar with. This quadrant carries the highest level of risk and with it the most intense immune system reaction.

Figure 11.3 illustrates the risk and corporate immune system response related to NewCo's materiality to CoreCo versus CoreCo's market similarity. It reflects what we already know about business risk: the more material NewCo is projected to be to CoreCo's financial results and the more unfamiliar NewCo's market is compared to CoreCo's, the higher the perceived risk. The higher the risk, the more vigorous the corporate immune system response.

	Low Market Differences	High Market Differences
High Materiality	Entering a market similar to CoreCo's/ expected financial contribution is high	Entering a market dissimilar to CoreCo's/expected financial contribution is high
Low Materiality	Entering a market very similar to CoreCo's/expected financial contribution is low	Entering a market dissimilar to CoreCo's/expected financial contribution is low

Figure 11.3 Risk and Immune Response as a Function of Materiality and Market

Perception Is Reality

CoreCo's systems and processes are managed by people in leadership positions. They have the authority to decide which are to be enforced in their current form and which can be changed to suit a different need. When choosing between the status quo and change, most leaders base their decision on two factors. The first is the perceived impact the change will have on their work. In labor 5 we saw that resistance to change is a function of people's perception that change will result in more work or the loss of control or both. The second is the perceived risk the change will have on the corporation. If the risk is high the change will be viewed as a threat. How aggressively CoreCo reacts to the threat will correlate with how dangerous the threat is perceived to be. The key factor guiding CoreCo's assessment is its perception of change, and this can often trump NewCo's needs or long-term strategy.

An intrapreneur who comprehends how the perception phenomenon works is better prepared to deal with immune system activity. As chain reactions go, it is quite simple. It begins when NewCo makes a request of CoreCo, either formally or informally. The request is analyzed by someone at CoreCo who categorizes it as a demand that is familiar or new. The person doing the categorizing is predisposed to fit the demand into an existing work category and match it to corresponding systems and processes. This is because the human brain is programmed to use pattern recognition when evaluating external stimuli and deciding on how to react. It can happen that the category is more of a force-fit than an actual fit, but choosing the status quo reduces the workload of CoreCo's employees, helps them retain control of the activity, and reassures everyone that the request can be treated as business as usual. The status "business as usual" communicates that the risk is low to none. The immune system has done its job and CoreCo is happy.

CoreCo is less happy if it is compelled to recognize that the request does not fit into existing business practices. Fulfilling the request now means an unknown volume of extra work that is unfamiliar. One unknown plus one area of unfamiliarity equals a lot more risk and a high level of immune system activity. NewCo's team must keep in mind that CoreCo's leaders and employees are categorizing demands and responding with immune system activity at all times, consciously and subconsciously. This is standard protective behavior that enables corporations to maintain a stable and predictable work environment.

A demand-perception gap can occur when NewCo demands something of its parent and neglects to communicate the reason behind the demand or its scope or substance, and the parent is left on its own to interpret it. When this occurs CoreCo will categorize the demand solely according to how much change it will impose on its regular way of operating. This can lead to one of three corporate immune system reaction levels:

- Low to no reaction when NewCo's demands do not differ, or differ very little, from CoreCo's existing business practices
- Medium reaction when NewCo's demands require CoreCo to adjust its regular business practices to some degree
- Strong reaction when NewCo's demands require major changes to CoreCo's way of doing business or the invention of something new

There are two routes to significantly narrowing the demand-perception gap. The first is to be proactive when communicating with CoreCo. By educating CoreCo's functional leaders about the nature of the demand and the reasons behind it, they will no longer feel compelled to fill in the blanks with imaginary worst-case scenarios. While mystery and misperception lead to confusion and suspicion, clarity leads to shared understanding and teamwork, and ultimately lowers immune system activity. Should the first approach fail, remember to enlist the help of the gatekeeper, whose role includes addressing unjustified immune system reactions and blocking the access of uncooperative CoreCo leaders.

Managing the Immune System

It is impossible to totally avoid corporate white blood cell activity. In fact, an inactive corporate immune system is unhealthy. The intrapreneur's challenge is to preempt overly intrusive activity, at the root of which is ignorance and fear. The good news is that ignorance can be addressed through communication and education, which the intrapreneur can control with the help of the sponsor, the gatekeeper, and NewCo's leadership team and allies. Everyone who believes in NewCo must be proactive in keeping their colleagues supplied with enough information to transform their ignorance into knowledge, which will calm their fear.

Keep in mind that some of the most successful people at CoreCo achieved their power and influence through effectively using the corporate immune system. I am referring to leaders of major functions who were promoted, at least in part, because of the role they played in developing the immune system and their expertise in managing it. This is the nature of corporate politics. Leaders in this category will likely be resistant to new ways of conducting business, and it may take the intervention of the sponsor or gatekeeper to bring them onside.

Mitigating misunderstandings and concerns that arise in CoreCo starts with the change management strategy described in labor 5. Besides communication and education, it includes aligning NewCo objectives with CoreCo incentives, having NewCo write CoreCo's report card regarding the quality of its support, and appointing a strong gatekeeper. To ensure that all sides appreciate the expectations, NewCo's education strategy must be founded on a solid CFM strategy, a well-communicated CFM plan, and the CFM charter, as well as ongoing monitoring to validate that the CFMs are being deployed as intended. The education strategy must be supported by communication activities that are fresh, frequent, and written for everyone concerned, and are constantly shored up by an elevator speech that stays relevant at all times.

COMING UP NEXT........................

Completing the first 11 labors is already a testament to the sponsor's and intrapreneur's commitment and to CoreCo's desire to see NewCo succeed. Yet there remains one very dangerous obstacle that on its own can bring down the enterprise.

Labor 12 looks at the controlled descent into failure, which can result from having a business environment that is not primed to assimilate information learned from the market or pivot as the evolving circumstances require.

Cerberus

For his twelfth and final labor Hercules was commanded by King Eurystheus to bring him Cerberus, the three-headed monster that guarded the entrance to the underworld. This was the most difficult of all his challenges. Not only was Cerberus savage and cruel, no mortal had ever returned alive from the land of the dead. Hercules sought the help of a priest, who taught him sacred rituals that would safeguard his journey. He also asked Athena and Hermes to protect him during his entry and exit from Hades' kingdom. Once inside he overcame many trials. Finally he was granted an audience with Hades, who consented to his request on two conditions, that he capture Cerberus without using weapons and that he return the hellhound when the labor was done. Hercules threw himself on Cerberus, choked him into submission, and began the long journey home. When Eurystheus beheld his latest prize, he was so terrified that he promised to release Hercules from his labors if he took the monster away.

LABOR 12

How to Prevent a Controlled Descent into Failure

No intrapreneur wants to fail. Given the years-long task of making NewCo a success, he will face every challenge with determination and imagination, as Hercules did, and will venture into unknown territory with the help of advisors and allies, where he will battle resistors and possibly even slay a few dragons. As the intrapreneur executes his labors he will acquire tremendous knowledge and enjoy early success, but this success will turn against him if he misinterprets the signals. When this happens he might experience what I call a controlled descent into failure™, or CDIF. This is a one-way ticket to the underworld of unsuccessful NewCos.

At the heart of CDIF is the tendency for NewCo leaders to lose their objectivity over time and begin to interpret their data from the viewpoint of CoreCo. They do this when CoreCo sees NewCo's early successes and imagines it has the winning formula for growth, and impatiently pushes NewCo to scale its operations prematurely. It is understandable that NewCo's leaders may be persuaded to comply. But we have seen that NewCo, especially in its early stages, is strikingly different from CoreCo, and the intrapreneur and his team must stay consistent in interpreting data from the perspective of a startup. This means remaining objective when considering the causes of early successes, taking into account the multiple unknowns, remembering to be flexible and responsive, and knowing that a change in strategy may be around the corner.

For the intrapreneur, seeing data as it actually is and not as he wants to see it becomes harder if he takes on the corporation's bias towards making rapid progress and big gains. Wanting to satisfy CoreCo, which feels safer than finding out from the data that some of his original assumptions are wrong, he might stubbornly stick to the original assumptions. Staying the course will lead him to draw false conclusions, for example, about his customers' needs, and just like that the downward spiral begins. The better choice would have been to dig deep to get to the root of the unexpected indicators. By constantly questioning NewCo's sources of information and being open to what they say, the intrapreneur will discover the key drivers that will create success.

The term CDIF refers to choosing to continue on a predetermined path despite having market indicators that show change is necessary. This will likely end in failure, while heeding the messages that point to change will result in a new trajectory that will significantly increase the probability of growth and success. The CDIF concept was inspired by a phenomenon in the aviation industry called controlled flight into terrain, or CFIT. This describes a situation where a perfectly fine aircraft, under the control of a highly capable pilot, flies straight into a mountainside, cliff, or building. You might ask yourself, how can this happen?

Aircraft cockpits are filled with instruments that provide pilots with all the information they need to avoid a terrain collision. Yet some planes still crash (fewer now than before, but we will get to that later). Similarly, workplaces are humming with people gathering data and carrying out business processes with the one goal of helping their leaders make well-informed decisions that will create success. Yet some companies still fail. This phenomenon occurs the world over. Leaders disregard vital information and instead focus on details that are less meaningful, intent on seeing what they want to see, with the result being that they steer their business into a controlled descent into failure, just as pilots unintentionally take their planes into a controlled flight into terrain.

The idea of CFIT was introduced during a period in the aviation industry when airplanes were crashing into geographic terrain or other visible objects at an alarming rate. The industry was perplexed. Reviews of the information stored in black boxes and other recorders recovered from the crash site, including pilot instructions, aircraft performance data, and conversations among the crew, indicated no mechanical problems. It was often concluded that the pilot and co-pilot should have visually spotted the danger or deduced from their instruments that they were on a collision course. In some cases there was a single malfunctioning instrument that painted a safe picture while several others provided data on the looming object, and apparently the pilots chose to base their decisions on that one instrument, with catastrophic results.

Further investigation into CFIT revealed that aircraft accidents were usually the outcome of a series of noncritical mishaps that together led to disaster. Aircrew fatigue and bad weather sometimes came into play.

One recurring contributing factor was poor situational awareness. This describes a scenario in which pilots incorrectly assess their aircraft's orientation with respect to the earth's surface and anything else in the vicinity. They do not properly evaluate the information they are given and the consequence is a crash that was probably preventable.

Maintaining good situational awareness becomes more difficult the higher the stress level and the more complex the external environment. The risk increases again in situations where there is little room for error, for example, when flying in a war context at low altitudes and high speeds with other aircraft nearby while dodging enemy fire. Feeling overwhelmed might lead pilots to focus on the wrong information or disregard critical information altogether. These challenges are quite different from those of a commercial airline pilot flying in less stressful conditions on cruise control at a high altitude under clear weather conditions.

To prevent CFIT, terrain awareness and warning systems were developed and installed in every cockpit. A further innovation of a different kind was named crew resource management, or CRM. This is a set of procedures and interpersonal communication and leadership skills aimed at eliminating hierarchical bias and encouraging open communication, all with a view to maximizing the exchange of information. The goal is to create an environment where anyone who thinks they see something wrong can speak up and be heard, whether a co-pilot, flight attendant, air traffic controller, or member of the ground crew.

The need to augment terrain awareness and warning systems with crew resource management came about as a result of studies that showed that people involved in flight operations that ended badly often had information the pilot could have used to avoid making the mistake. They were reluctant to share it for fear of reprisal or ridicule, or because there were no communication channels available to them. These findings confirmed the importance of open and clear communication in avoiding accidents.

The Market Awareness Warning System

The aviation industry was able to dramatically improve its safety record by developing complementary measures to counter CFIT. By adapting these measures to the corporate world, we can similarly increase the success rate of NewCos, which are under the gun to process large quantities of information while trying to grow in a stressful, fast-evolving environment. The equivalent of aviation's terrain awareness and warning system is what I like to call MAWS, for market awareness and warning system™.

MAWS is comprised of the various sources of data that help business leaders understand how their markets are trending, what the competition is doing, how their customers' behavior changes over time, and if and how their products, services, or business assumptions must be adapted to keep pace with their markets. These data sources, which include reports, spreadsheets, dashboards, and key performance indicators (KPIs) that sift through information and summarize key findings, should be reviewed on a biweekly or monthly basis for an unstable startup like NewCo, and annually or semi-annually for a mature business like CoreCo.

As in the aviation world, where sophisticated instruments and avionic systems alone are not sufficient to prevent accidents, corporate startups need more than a well-established market awareness and warning system to be successful. NewCo's MAWS must be augmented with a system of collaborative information receptivity management™, otherwise known as CIRM (pronounced see-rum). CIRM recognizes that NewCo's employees are invaluable sources of MVP feedback and market news. During interactions with customers, partners, investors, key opinion leaders, and even competitors, they can capture important information that is beyond MAWS and bring it to the intrapreneur.

A healthy CIRM thrives in a workplace that is without hierarchical bias where communication, information sharing, and receptivity are the norms. It encourages the participation of diverse employees such as business development leaders and members of the sales team, who are particularly useful in the early days given their constant interaction with potential clients and their work testing NewCo's value proposition and gathering feedback from early adopters. Other employees who interface with customers include the people responsible for product development, customer service, and project management. CIRM should also take into account distributors and retailers. The broader the circle of CIRM contributors, the more effective the system will be.

But there is an inherent difficulty during NewCo's infancy and early adolescence: the startup has neither the time nor manpower to establish a reliable set of data sources to feed its market awareness and warning system. The solution is to supplement its unsophisticated MAWS with a CIRM culture that does such a good job of motivating its leaders and employees to capture and share information that NewCo can benefit from good market situational awareness despite its weak MAWS.

Another way for NewCo to stack the odds in its favor is to make MAWS and CIRM part of every business model review. Information will be easily shared among team members and there will be a constant flow of data to feed the model's validation activities. Finally, the secret to a highly successful CIRM is an intrapreneur who is receptive to *all* incoming information, even items that suggest his initial business assumptions were wrong or contradict what is being reported via MAWS. I will go one step further and say that if a startup has leaders who have never been wrong about their assumptions regarding strategy or the business model, it is probably heading for a controlled descent into failure.

The consequence of all this CIRM and MAWS activity, which we know relies on emerging and inaccurate data, plus the frequent reviewing of the business model to make certain it remains relevant to the desired outcome, is that as NewCo moves forward it will need to make several minor and some major corrections to its strategy. Whether minor or major, CoreCo would never tolerate this volume of corrections from its established core businesses, which it expects to be stable and predictable, but this is precisely what will save NewCo from a controlled descent into failure.

CoreCo has been in business for a long time and many lessons have been learned and absorbed. It has a clear picture of its core markets thanks to tested and honed data sources that provide excellent information about key market drivers, customer buying behaviors, and business metrics. Its MAWS is supported by the tribal knowledge of leaders in customer-facing positions such as sales, marketing, product development, business development, and strategic planning, who contribute essential insights into buying patterns and market shifts. These well-validated sources of information form the foundation of a CoreCo CIRM that is extremely reliable. The upshot is highly accurate market projections.

NewCo has nothing like CoreCo's deep market intimacy. It might be operating in a new segment within CoreCo's existing markets, meaning some market information can be shared, or maybe its market is unknown to everyone and CoreCo has no insights to offer. Unlike CoreCo's army of employees practiced in managing validated data sources and business processes, NewCo's few eager new hires are wearing multiple hats and using unproven methods. NewCo may have access to consultants or subject matter experts who comprehend the new market, but their combined abilities do not remotely resemble CoreCo's corporate know-how. NewCo's MAWS and CIRM are unstable and undependable. This is why the intrapreneur has to make much more frequent and sometimes abrupt course corrections than CoreCo is normally comfortable with.

A pilot can have state-of-the-art instruments that provide the most relevant information, but it is the pilot's ability to take the right action at the right time that will lead the plane to a safe landing. The same goes for the intrapreneur. In addition to establishing and maintaining NewCo's MAWS and CIRM to create situational awareness in relation to the market, the intrapreneur must have the authority to modify the start-up's strategic direction as necessary. This authority comes from CoreCo through the sponsor, and it must be total. The danger of CoreCo pressuring NewCo to resist making changes is that NewCo's pilot and crew might feel compelled to withhold information that questions the status quo. Instead they will focus on data that provides information the parent wants to see. To avoid CDIF, they need to stay open to sources that point to an urgent need to modify the trajectory.

It is standard behavior for startups, whether independent or corporate, to have to adapt to a new business reality and modify their assumptions and strategy several times before getting it right. Adapting and modifying are essential ingredients for success. Intrapreneurs and entrepreneurs who stubbornly hang on to what they believe should happen end up initiating a descent into failure. Those who are held to their initial assumptions by the sponsor or CoreCo's senior leaders often suffer the same fate.

NewCo must use its MAWS and CIRM, however rudimentary, to arrive at a best educated guess regarding its starting line. As we saw in labor 7, it is perfectly acceptable to launch with a best educated guess. Accuracy in market data and business assumptions is not the point at this stage. The point is to be able to adapt and modify as required. NewCo's learning cycle, as it takes in and responds to new market data, is identical to the iterative learning cycle illustrated on page 123: making an educated guess, forecasting, testing, validating, and refining.

Data Quality, Not Quantity

Failure to receive, categorize, and act on the right data will distort NewCo's market situational awareness and prolong its journey down the road to failure. In my experience the warning signs are always there to see. Downplaying their relevance or disregarding them out of hand happens more readily in the corporate environment because of CoreCo's powerful presence. In its enthusiasm for a potentially lucrative innovation, it can mistake the original business model for a blueprint for success. It can happen that NewCo's leaders, wanting or being pressured to hold to the original, send their team on a "fact-finding" mission, hoping for data that will cancel out the data that points to the need for change.

When gathering data, a rule of thumb is to focus on the few data points that are vital rather than on the many that appear to be useful. The answers almost always lie in a handful of KPIs, not more. This is not to say that NewCo's team should refrain from seeking a variety of information sources. On the contrary, more sources will augment their learning and teach them to separate primary sources from secondary ones. Because the possibilities are innumerable and can end in analysis paralysis, the intrapreneur should make sure there is never so much data gathered that the team becomes overwhelmed.

Peter Senge offers sage advice in *The Fifth Discipline, The Art & Practice of the Learning Organization:* "The increasing complexity of today's world leads many managers to assume that they lack information needed to act effectively. I would suggest that the fundamental 'information problem' faced by managers is not too little information but too much information. What we most need are ways to know what is important and what is not important, what variables to focus on and which to pay less attention to – and we need ways to do this which can help groups or teams develop shared understandings." This statement is more valid today than when it was originally made nearly 25 years ago.

Focus on the few data points that are vital, not on the many that are useful.

Developing Market Intimacy

Data acquired from research firms is useful, but it tends to provide generic guidance rather than specific information about the market and how NewCo's customers feel about the new product or service. To get the granularity that leads to good decision making, NewCo's leaders need to complement generic data with feedback gathered during encounters with customers, partners, market influencers, and important players in the industry such as competitors, suppliers, and regulatory bodies. It is through these interactions that subtle insights are gained and customer intimacy is developed.

The best intrapreneurs lead by example. They are conscious of continuously building on their market and customer knowledge, and to that end they regularly and frequently meet with customers to hear first-hand what they like and dislike about NewCo's solutions. They also make themselves available to witness MVP validation in person.

Avoiding CDIF in 7 Steps

1. Have a validated growth strategy that is clearly articulated in the strategic plan (described in the book's final chapter on page 232).
2. Set up clear lines of communication between the intrapreneur and the sponsor, gatekeeper, and NewCo's leadership team.
3. Establish the initial data sources that over time will grow into a reliable market awareness and warning system. Update MAWS frequently to stay abreast of marketplace trends and evolving customer needs.
4. Make sure NewCo's stakeholders buy in to your collaborative information receptivity management system, keeping in mind that in the early days CIRM is more important than MAWS.
5. Stay focused on data that is particular to NewCo. Neither the pull of conformity nor the supposed benefits of standardization are reasons to spend even one minute on data that mimics CoreCo's.
6. Regularly review the information generated via MAWS and CIRM in an environment that is open and nonthreatening. This promotes learning and situational awareness and lays the groundwork for NewCo's business culture.
7. Compare new data and lessons learned to your original assumptions and modify accordingly. The frequency of this activity should keep pace with NewCo's rapidly evolving environment.

The Pivot

By nurturing productive CIRM and MAWS and being open to change, the intrapreneur has positioned NewCo to avoid CDIF. The next part of the challenge is what makes this the most difficult of the 12 labors: deciding that the time has come to modify NewCo's initial business assumptions. While this can be a difficult decision, it should never be made with reluctance. Success includes embracing the fact that modifying the startup's basic strategic hypotheses and business model assumptions is a crucial aspect of the early growth cycle. This is the whole point of the learn-iterate-learn activities that feed the business model.

Albert Einstein has a definition of insanity that I have often shared with my teams: "Doing the same thing over and over again and expecting a different result." If NewCo finds that it identifies with this definition, it must pause and revisit its original assumptions. It is at a crossroads, and the best way forward is to adapt and modify. Proponents of the lean startup methodology such as Eric Ries and Steve Blank use the term "pivot," which refers to the basketball pivot, when a player shifts the direction of play while keeping one foot on the floor. Similarly, a business pivot makes a calculated and structured change to the business model or strategic plan based on customer feedback while keeping one foot anchored in the lessons learned from the marketplace. The online *Financial Times Lexicon* has this definition: "When used in relation to entrepreneurship, pivot (which generally refers to a shift in strategy) describes the tortured path that most startups go through to find the right customer, value proposition, and positioning." Every corporate startup will face the decision of whether to change direction or stay the course at least once and possibly more than once.

I have faced this challenge many times. It is a defining moment for an intrapreneur, and often a tough one. Do we keep going or do we adapt to the reality of the external environment by modifying our strategy? If you are a CoreCo executive or NewCo's sponsor, allow pivots to take place when necessary and resist the temptation to judge the act of pivoting as a mistake or a failure or a sign of poor management. Quite the opposite is true. Pivoting demonstrates sound business acumen, courage, and strong leadership. If your CoreCo culture concludes that pivots spell disaster, then you are dooming your intrapreneur to stand, as if frozen, at a critical crossroads that demands action. If no corrective action is taken, NewCo will languish, eventually lose ground, and very likely head into a controlled descent into failure.

The sponsor needs to be on the lookout for signs of struggle. At some point NewCo might travel down a road that eventually stops delivering the expected results. Despite putting everything it has into clearing the road and achieving results, NewCo will begin to stagnate. Working harder will bring no relief and implementing improvements to the product or service will generate little interest from early adopters. The NewCo team is stuck and something appears to be wrong with the learning metrics. They fail to show that the team is no closer to finalizing the business model on which the new product or service was founded. If this happens the sponsor must step in and help the intrapreneur analyze the situation. A pivot may be necessary.

Pivoting is not an all-or-nothing game. If the NewCo team is stagnating it is probably because an original strategic hypothesis needs to be refined, and not because the overall vision behind NewCo and its business model is wrong (though this is a possibility). Minor refinements or adjustments are exactly what they sound like, minor. They do not require changing the business model. Major pivots are a different story. They are the outcome of major shifts in NewCo's strategy or important changes that are made to key hypotheses underpinning the business model.

10 Types of Pivots

Pivots can be necessary for any number of reasons. In *The Lean Startup: How Today's Entrepreneurs Use Continuous Innovation to Create Radically Successful Businesses*, Eric Ries identifies 10 types. Four relate to the assumptions that were made about the startup's product or technology, two are concerned with customer needs, and the last four focus on the way the business will make money.

1. **Zoom-in**: turning a single feature in the original product into a new product
2. **Zoom-out**: creating a new larger product, of which the initial product represents a single or small portion
3. **Platform**: changing from an application to a platform or vice versa
4. **Technology**: replacing the original technology with one that has a better chance of achieving the vision
5. **Customer segment**: targeting a more suitable customer segment
6. **Customer need**: identifying a more important customer problem to be solved
7. **Business architecture**: redefining the basic assumptions about the business model, for example, from high margins-low volume to low margins-high volume
8. **Value capture**: making modifications to the revenue model
9. **Engine of growth**: rethinking the way the company will drive growth and become sustainable
10. **Channel**: changing how the company plans to achieve sales

Several years ago, as an intrapreneur launching a software solution in the aviation industry, I realized we needed to execute a zoom-out pivot. The solution was an IT tool we had developed for our network of training centers that was now packaged as a series of integrated modules. We planned to sell the series to the operators of training centers, believing they would value having help managing their simulators with respect to scheduling, preventive and corrective maintenance, spare parts, and logistics. After getting all sorts of constructive feedback from early customers, I realized that the value proposition was not compelling enough. My next decision was to pivot.

We made the product the centerpiece of a much larger outsourcing service and anchored our new value proposition in the fact that not only would customers have access to our comprehensive maintenance and logistics solution, their training center would be integrated into our global network. They would gain real-time visibility into the key performance metrics of their training equipment, be provided with automated reports to meet regulatory requirements, and benefit from swift access to a global pool of technicians and spare parts when facing a critical situation.

On another occasion I had to execute a customer segment pivot. Our initial targets for an operations outsourcing initiative were the world's largest airlines. They had huge training centers, and the bigger the centers, the bigger the operations and the greater the efficiencies and savings we could offer. Our business model assumptions were quite accurate and the cost savings we could commit to were very attractive, plus we promised operational improvements and a high level of customer service. It was a compelling value proposition, but success was elusive.

I decided to ask potential customers who had turned us down why they refused our offer. The bottom line was that for very large airlines, the savings we guaranteed, though significant in percentage terms, were insubstantial in terms of absolute dollars. Furthermore, outsourcing simulator maintenance activities would have forced some of them to open labor agreements and cause considerable strain to their organization.

It was time to pivot to a new customer segment composed of startup airlines and noncommercial airline customers. In their world, labor agreements were not an issue and the savings we proposed were substantial, in some cases freeing up valuable cash that could be reassigned to other areas of their operations or to training activities. Establishing this win-win scenario led to early victories. In time, with numerous successes under our belt, we returned to several of the larger airlines, demonstrated the benefits of our service, and enjoyed some successes there as well.

My most difficult experience with pivoting involved two types: engine of growth and channel. This was a complex situation because the NewCo had made several acquisitions that gave it a broad portfolio of simulation software tools that were unique to the industry. After hiring an external firm to carry out an extensive customer review, I went on the road to meet with our top customers to find out what we were doing right and what needed improvement. Then our team spent weeks analyzing the data from different angles. We looked at customer profiles, growth, and retention, software renewal patterns and requests for features, and pricing, attrition metrics, the competitive landscape, and many other factors.

It turned out that the company had been successful with early adopters who continued to drive our product roadmaps with very detailed requirements and features. However, the needs of the broader customer base had evolved dramatically. They wanted to use our products to deliver increasingly complex and cost-competitive projects of their own, and were looking for solutions that were easy and cheap. While we had made inroads into many of the world's largest aerospace and defense organizations, they were actually more like small beachheads. The stark truth was that our products were far from being adopted across our customers' broader organizations.

We realized we had to adapt to this reality and modify our strategy accordingly, and at the same time separate ourselves from the early adopter market. The subsequent pivot involved the overhaul of our product roadmaps, namely, replacing thousands of product features in our development plans with measures that addressed product ease-of-use and interoperability. Other major changes were instituted across the organization, including redefining our sales channel strategy and positioning ourselves to be more vertically integrated within our customers' ecosystem of partners.

I am also familiar with the business architecture pivot, which I executed during the growth of our healthcare simulation business. The initial business model was based on selling simulation equipment to organizations to help them train healthcare professionals more efficiently. We had reviewed the competitive landscape and concluded that the majority of the existing equipment providers did nothing more than provide equipment, so our plan was to offer solutions that were more comprehensive while also being cost-effective.

After the launch we began to receive mixed messages from the user community. While most of the equipment on the market at the time was in need of improvement, the feedback told us again and again that this was not the burning issue. Medical and nursing schools, hospitals, and healthcare simulation centers were able to work around equipment problems, but they seemed unable to incorporate our solutions into their educational curriculum. I encouraged my team to find out why our potential customers could not figure this out. Aviation had been embedding simulation in training for decades. I understood simulation-based training very well and had access to the world leader in this field for aviation and defense. What were we missing?

It was time to go on the road again. After speaking with key opinion leaders from around the globe, it dawned on me that one of our major assumptions was flawed. We were looking at the problem from the perspective of an industry that had developed expertise over decades. The people responsible for training pilots and aircraft technicians knew how to leverage simulation to meet their training needs. The healthcare domain had nowhere near the same experience or industry know-how. Our mistake lay in taking a while to realize this. Now that I understood that the healthcare industry was ill equipped to integrate new simulators into their training infrastructures, I modified our strategy. Instead of simply providing simulation equipment, we aimed at providing integrated educational solutions that facilitated our customers' ability to introduce simulation-based training. Our business model assumptions had to be changed to reflect a new mix of higher-margin products and lower-margin educational and services solutions.

NewCo's team must make sure that a pivot is based on data that unambiguously demonstrates that change is necessary. The team can know this only if it objectively validates the information on which the decision to pivot is based. When in doubt, talk to as many customers as possible in person and measure their feedback if possible. The number-one rule for encouraging quality learning and continuous improvement when forecasting customer and market responses is to go back to your customers to test, validate, and refine assumptions.

The validation process equally applies to feedback from CoreCo. The intrapreneur has access to capable corporate experts who will not hesitate to volunteer their opinions on how NewCo should adapt to the market. CoreCo's own product development, sales and marketing, or engineering teams may have ideas about why certain NewCo activities are not progressing as well as planned. Remember that the information they are basing their opinions on may be anecdotal or secondhand, and though their position makes them credible and influential, what they have to say may not be as solid as it sounds. Do not ignore their views, but before reacting, validate them with your market and customers. The sponsor and gatekeeper can step in if well-intentioned senior stakeholders push for an approach that has not been validated.

If you are the intrapreneur in charge, spend a lot of time with your customers. Let them define the important problem they are trying to solve and for which they are willing to spend money, and listen to what they think of your proposed solution. There is nothing more helpful. When confronted with the decision of whether to stay the course or pivot, return to the information gathered from your MAWS and CIRM and review it with care, but know that above all you can rely on the feedback you have heard directly from your customers.

The ability to transfer learning into an eventual pivot is a crucial skill. If your ability to adapt and modify is not nurtured, and instead you are concerned only with CoreCo's or your own expectations of sticking to the original plan, your new enterprise might end in CDIF. These guidelines will help you chart a more successful path:

1. Develop keen market awareness by seeking user feedback early and frequently and by validating your business model often.
2. Resist the parent's demands for NewCo to prematurely return to the fold. CoreCo's mature businesses are measured by how well they maintain their strategy and stick to approved operational plans. NewCo's needs are profoundly different.
3. Be at the ready to adapt to new business realities and modify NewCo's original business model. If this leads to a pivot, embrace it.

Achieving Buy-In for the Pivot

A successful pivot requires ongoing communication and education to ensure that CoreCo recognizes the need for it and offers full support. Pivoting is not something established corporations do often. If not handled properly, a NewCo pivot can shake people's confidence in the new business and decrease the level of commitment from internal and external stakeholders.

A successful pivot begins at the time of NewCo's launch when the intrapreneur clearly communicates the underlying assumptions on which the business model is based. It is achieved by sharing what is learned along the way and how that learning is being transformed into a sharper appreciation of the customers' needs. By being transparent with the sponsor, the gatekeeper, the primary allies, and NewCo's employees during the early phases of NewCo, the intrapreneur can prepare key stakeholders for an eventual pivot.

COMING UP NEXT.........................

Working to avoid CDIF encapsulates many of the concepts discussed in the first 11 labors. Labor 12 also reinforces the message that anyone taking on intrapreneurship must do so with a thorough understanding of the challenges to come.

I have reiterated the importance of establishing a set of assumptions on which NewCo's success is premised. The final step is to create a solid strategic plan. In fact, to successfully complete any of the 12 labors, you will need to start with a plan. CoreCo should demand it. It will not be perfect at the outset, but it will form the basis for future learning and decision making, for leveraging corporate functions and keeping the immune system in check, and one day for pivoting.

Developing a well-articulated strategic plan is a critical tool and why I dedicate the final chapter to it.

Creating the Right Strategic Roadmap

By now you have a comprehensive understanding of the obstacles associated with intrapreneurship that will be set in motion within the corporation, and you have been exposed to the strategies and tools that will help you tackle these obstacles and mitigate their impact. You understand the need for a committed sponsor and for a senior executive with clout to take on the role of gatekeeper. You definitely recognize the importance of selecting a qualified intrapreneur to lead the new business initiative.

Let's say your company is far enough along in the process to have assigned the intrapreneur, who has reviewed the 12 labors with an eye to how they apply to the company's specific culture and goals. Perhaps he has begun to lay the groundwork for NewCo's soft or formal launch. But is he fully prepared to tackle the labors to come? Just as Hercules went forward well-armed with weapons, plans, allies, and advice, the intrapreneur needs to map out a clear trajectory as soon as possible after agreeing to lead the startup. A map will make certain that he heads in the right direction and it will indicate the tools that will be helpful along the way. This intrapreneurial adventure calls for two kinds of tools: navigational and success.

Navigational Tools

The corporate world has developed an impressive catalog of best practices in the domain of business leadership and management. As an intrapreneur or sponsor, do not make the mistake of thinking they are not applicable to startups. In fact, this body of knowledge includes many proven tools that are extremely useful when adapted to the intrapreneurial environment.

Over my 25-year career in leadership positions, managing complex operations, running corporate businesses, and launching corporate startups, I have identified my favorites and gathered them into a toolkit I call the Achieving Business Success™ model, or ABS. Tested and honed in the real world of intrapreneurship, it will help you create the map, compass, and ruler you need to succeed.

Business lore would have us believe that successful startups are launched on the back of a napkin, but nothing could be further from the truth. Your idea can start on the back of a napkin, but corporate executives are ill disposed to even listen to ideas that are represented in hasty sketches, and they certainly will not invest money in them. To achieve the success you seek, your innovation must be articulated in a well-documented strategic plan.

The strategic plan is different from the business model discussed previously. It lays out the broader vision. By outlining your startup's long-term financial goals, how you plan to achieve them, and what will differentiate you from the competition, it establishes what your business is trying to achieve. The business model, on the other hand, provides the details of how you will create value for your clients and your company. It documents the best way to produce what you have to sell and the most effective way of selling it.

The ABS model in figure 13.1 will help you develop your strategic plan. It has six steps: in one and two a map and compass are established, in three and four important milestones are identified as well as the activities that will help you reach them, in five the criteria for measuring success are defined, and in six the process that will ensure frequent validation is created. This last step is critical. NewCo needs to constantly confirm that it is on track and moving closer to its destination, and that as it moves it recalibrates its trajectory whenever necessary. At the end of the ABS process you will have a solid strategic plan. It is an essential navigation tool whatever the size of your business.

The information you gather while carrying out these steps will be instrumental when you are working through several of the 12 labors, and it will form the cornerstone of your argument to convince CoreCo's executives to support the soft launch and say yes to proceeding to the formal launch. It will also be central to your CFM strategy because it will provide CoreCo with insights into where NewCo is heading, how it will get there, and where and when it will make sense to leverage the parent company.

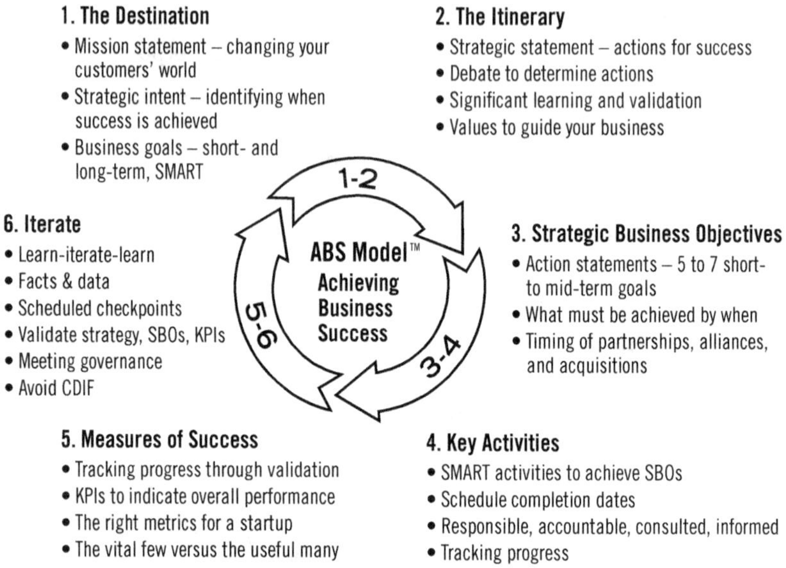

1. The Destination
• Mission statement – changing your customers' world
• Strategic intent – identifying when success is achieved
• Business goals – short- and long-term, SMART
2. The Itinerary
• Strategic statement – actions for success
• Debate to determine actions
• Significant learning and validation
• Values to guide your business
1-2
ABS Model™
Achieving Business Success
3-4
5-6
3. Strategic Business Objectives
• Action statements – 5 to 7 short- to mid-term goals
• What must be achieved by when
• Timing of partnerships, alliances, and acquisitions
4. Key Activities
• SMART activities to achieve SBOs
• Schedule completion dates
• Responsible, accountable, consulted, informed
• Tracking progress
5. Measures of Success
• Tracking progress through validation
• KPIs to indicate overall performance
• The right metrics for a startup
• The vital few versus the useful many
6. Iterate
• Learn-iterate-learn
• Facts & data
• Scheduled checkpoints
• Validate strategy, SBOs, KPIs
• Meeting governance
• Avoid CDIF

Figure 13.1 The ABS Model

A properly documented and communicated strategic plan is an integral element in change management activities and very useful during organization design discussions, and it sets the starting point for the internal communications strategy. It gives the intrapreneur and his team a sound framework for validating NewCo's business model and ensuring it is frequently iterated, which will reassure CoreCo that it is right to trust the intrapreneur's decisions. It also gives the sponsor and other CoreCo executives the substantiation they require to support eventual pivots. Finally, it provides crucial input into NewCo's market awareness and warning system (MAWS), whose purpose is to help the intrapreneur and sponsor avoid the dreaded controlled descent into failure (CDIF).

In the process of executing the ABS model you will:

Step 1: Specify NewCo's mission, intent, and goals, through which you will gain a firm grasp of how NewCo will change its customers' world

Step 2: Determine the strategy that will most effectively achieve NewCo's mission, intent, and goals

Step 3: Select the strategic business objectives (SBOs) that will help you execute the strategy

Step 4: Establish the key activities you must undertake to achieve your SBOs

Step 5: Identify the key performance indicators (KPIs) that will track the progress of the SBOs and activities in steps 3 and 4, as well as NewCo's overall performance

Step 6: Iterate the business model frequently, thus validating your strategy, SBOs, KPIs, and accountability structure, and avoiding CDIF

Step 1: The Destination

This activity captures in writing how NewCo's solutions will improve the world of its targeted customers by addressing an unmet need. It involves three distinct components: the mission statement, the strategic intent, and business goals. Together, these three components map out NewCo's destination.

Create an explicit mission statement

Writing a mission statement can be confusing. This is because people wrongly believe it should tell every notable detail about their organization. Simplify by separating the mission statement from the strategic intent. NewCo's mission should explain, using only a few words, how it will make the world of its customers a better place. Its purpose is to create a new vision the customers can believe in and ultimately empower change.

A helpful exercise is to ask yourself: In what ways will our customers be better off because of our innovation? Or imagine their reality without it. Reflect on what NewCo will provide that is new, improved, stronger, faster, or dare I say, revolutionary or disruptive. A good mission statement is a bold one. NewCo's reason for being is to make a real difference in people's lives, not just now, but in the long-term.

Another trick is to create your mission statement from your customers' perspective, not from CoreCo's or yours. If your customers are asked five years from now to describe NewCo, what will they say? Did NewCo transform how things are done in its market? Did it drive cost improvements? Quality improvements? Efficiency or availability? Time to market? Is NewCo's offering safer to use, or easier or simpler? Does it result in more effective decision making? Despite all these questions, remember that your mission statement should be succinct. It might look something like the statements on the next page.

NewCo will revolutionize the robotic surgery industry by bringing dramatic advances in accuracy and safety resulting in significant improvements in patient outcomes.

NewCo will greatly improve the ability of corporations to make better and faster decisions about corporate Internet security, allowing them to offer more appropriate and affordable software service solutions to their clients.

Set the strategic intent

The strategic intent identifies what CoreCo and NewCo will gain from their efforts once the mission is achieved. The intent differs from the mission in that it is stated from NewCo's perspective and not the customers'. The question to ask is: What does NewCo intend by entering its new market? This sounds like a question about goals when it is actually about pinpointing the position NewCo wants to find itself in down the line. Perhaps we can say that it is about the ultimate goal. Does NewCo want to become the industry leader in the delivery of its product within a certain segment? Does it want to be the partner of choice for businesses engaged in a complementary project? Whatever it is, the strategic intent must support NewCo's mission and describe a powerful future that will inspire NewCo's leaders to stretch. These two examples are straightforward, as all strategic intents should be.

To be the industry's most innovative player.

To be the preferred supplier of end-to-end solutions.

Establish clear business goals

We know that business goals must be SMART – Specific, Measurable, Achievable, Realistic, and Time-bound. They must also be phrased in two parts: a short-term goal aimed at demonstrating financial progress that connects to a long-term goal that expresses NewCo's eventual relationship with CoreCo in terms of materiality and summarizes the strategic intent. Both need to be well articulated so that NewCo's leadership team and employees know what to aim for and what to measure their progress against.

Corporate stakeholders can choose where to invest their funds and management time to achieve the desired return on investment. If they invest in NewCo, it is because they expect it will grow into a material and sustainable business. The intrapreneur had better know what NewCo's market potential is, the percentage of market share NewCo will capture over time, and how much money CoreCo will make from investing in NewCo.

When considering the two examples below of part one, remember that the short-term goal will be reset with bigger numbers once the old numbers have been achieved. Resetting will continue as NewCo matures and advances towards its final objective, which is expressed in the second part of the goal.

> Part one: NewCo will achieve $35 million in sales by year 5, generating 15% profit margins, ...
>
> Part one: NewCo will reach $25 million in revenues by year 6, generating 17% margins and becoming self-funded, ...

The second part of goal setting establishes the point at which NewCo reaches the expected materiality in relation to CoreCo. In essence, it shows what NewCo has to ramp up to and situates the startup as a sustainable business rather than a short-term success. It must also embody the strategic intent, setting NewCo apart as, for example, the industry leader or the highest-quality provider, or the company with the most innovative product or whatever it is that NewCo is going for.

> Part two: ... and will be positioned to grow and represent 12% of CoreCo's total revenues and 15% of CoreCo's margins contribution by year 10, with an EPS contribution of $1.25.
>
> Part two: ... and will have created distribution channels and a sales pipeline of opportunities that outline the path to $70 million in annual revenues by year 10.

Here are the two examples in full:

> NewCo will achieve $35 million in sales by year 5, generating 15% profit margins, and will be positioned to grow and represent 12% of CoreCo's total revenues and 15% of CoreCo's margins contribution by year 10, with an EPS contribution of $1.25, having established itself as the industry's most innovative player.
>
> NewCo will reach $25 million in revenues by year 6, generating 17% margins and becoming self-funded, and will have created distribution channels and a sales pipeline of opportunities that outline the path to $70 million in annual revenues by year 10, having established itself as the preferred supplier of end-to-end solutions.

The combination of mission statement, strategic intent, and business goals constitutes the first part of your map: the destination. Having NewCo's destination set down succinctly and simply in one place is a powerful tool that can be useful in a variety of ways: persuading CoreCo to lend its support, motivating employees to work hard, attracting candidates to join the startup, and engaging the participation of customers, partners, and suppliers. As we saw in labor 1, it forms the core of the elevator speech.

The intrapreneur will lead the ABS process, but he must work closely with the sponsor to see to it that the various strategic options are considered and evaluated. To accurately pinpoint NewCo's mission, intent, and goals, they must both reach out to major CoreCo stakeholders, potential CoreCo allies, and the members of NewCo's leadership team. Despite pressures to keep moving, the intrapreneur must resist executing the work in a rush. Getting these components right is of crucial importance.

Step 2: Set the Itinerary

The purpose of this step is to determine the itinerary NewCo will follow to arrive at its destination. The itinerary is expressed in a strategic statement that is operational in nature and captures NewCo's specific actions. I want to stress that the statement must be documented in writing. In my experience, transforming ideas and intentions into written language makes them real. The process includes a number of questions that will lead to considerable debate. The answers you eventually arrive at will constitute the best possible strategy.

1. How does NewCo's product or service differ from what already exists?
2. How will the product or service be validated to ensure that it fulfills the mission, intent, and goals?
3. What initial business model will lead to NewCo making money and what growth trajectory will lead to NewCo being profitable and sustainable?
4. How will NewCo enter the market?
5. How will NewCo gain credibility in its market?
6. What approach will be followed to secure early adopters?
7. What partnerships will supply the strategic links that will help NewCo penetrate its market?

8. What CoreCo CFMs will NewCo leverage?
9. What skill sets will NewCo require to execute its strategic plan, where will they come from, and when will they be required?
10. How will NewCo be funded?

The following is an example of a strategic statement:

> NewCo will enter the surgical robotics market with a product line based on CoreCo's robotics arm technology that will be adapted to meet the needs of NewCo's customers. We have validated the need for better robotics arm solutions to achieve new levels of patient safety and surgical accuracy, which current surgical robotics arm suppliers are unable to get from existing designs. To make certain that we focus on the most pressing challenges, we will validate our prototypes with the help of influential surgeons and robotics surgery research institutions that we will select with the purpose of working together to determine the best solution.
>
> The chief users of surgical robotics are in the United States, followed by Germany and France. We will start by creating alliances with four key influencers in the US, two in Germany, and one in France. We will leverage CoreCo's brand as the leader in use of robotics in space applications with a proven track record for safety and reliability via innovation and partnerships. We will also leverage CoreCo's expertise in haptics technology, and we will open doors as needed by leveraging CoreCo's government and corporate reach in the US and Europe.
>
> The surgical market has many distributors. Some have quality and client satisfaction standards that fall short of what is expected of CoreCo's brand, one of our primary CFMs. For this reason we will target one of three distributors in the US, one in Germany, and one in France that possess a reputation for quality, service, and influence within the main regions they serve: Distributors Alpha, Bravo, and Charlie in the United States, Das Distributor in Germany, and A la Carte Distributor in France.
>
> Our approach is to gain credibility through signing technology development and research partnership agreements with the three prominent teaching hospitals in the US and three in Europe. We will complement this with an aggressive speaking tour that hits significant robotics surgery conferences with the goal of

educating our new market about what is innovative in NewCo's robotics arm solutions and how we will solve their safety and accuracy needs.

Establishing NewCo's strategy will kick off a massive learning and validation period. Because many changes will arise from all that learning and validation, do not consider NewCo's strategy to be set in stone. As we discovered in labor 12, forcing NewCo to hang on to its strategy, despite the fact that new market data points decisively to a reset, will end in CDIF. As NewCo investigates its new market and becomes familiar with its early adopters, it will probably need to modify aspects of the strategy. A long time ago when I was an officer in the military I learned a critical lesson: Start with a strategy to reach your objective, map it out as best you can with as much intelligence as you can muster, and be ready to adapt and modify when the bullets start flying.

The overarching objective of NewCo is to deliver on its mission, strategic intent, and goals. It will face any number of predictable and unpredictable obstacles along the way and will need to remain nimble and open to change. NewCo is starting out as a Zodiac and will grow into a navy corvette. Despite the exciting speed and power of a corvette, it is a far cry from a battleship. While NewCo is growing the intrapreneur and his team must watch for threats, learn from feedback, and plot a new course when the data points in that direction.

The last part of finalizing the strategy is to spell out the work ethic the people at NewCo will be expected to adhere to. Make this as powerful a statement as you can, underlining the attitudes and behaviors that are vital to NewCo's success. No one should automatically assume that NewCo will adopt CoreCo's value set. It is understandable that similarities will emerge, but they should not form the starting point. Instead, NewCo's values should be conceived from the perspective of its future clients and market.

I have found that each market has a unique set of values that governs the people working in it. If NewCo wants to do business in that market, its employees need to absorb and live by those values. It can happen that the customers in a particular market are dissatisfied with how business has historically been conducted and desire the entry of new players who bring fresh values, attitudes, and behaviors. If you can identify what they are and incorporate them into NewCo, you will have cleverly established a competitive advantage. With one of my NewCos operating in the health-care market, I realized that trustworthiness, as measured by the ability to deliver on commitments, was a decisive factor. I immediately made being trustworthy central to our operations and was vigilant about demonstrating this value at all times.

In another venture, after having been hugely successful in the pilot training market, we shifted our attention to aircraft engineering and maintenance training and realized that the values important to aircraft technicians differed from those of the pilot community. The former placed significant value on authenticity and teamwork, so we made sure to incorporate both into our offering.

Other values a corporate startup will want its team members to embrace include entrepreneurial ones such as risk taking and collaboration. Cooperation and transparency should also be high on the list considering the importance of leveraging CoreCo, as should adaptability and quick decision making, which will come in handy in NewCo's rapidly changing market. Compassion is essential if your organization is aimed at people with disabilities. If your focus is innovation, your business culture needs to nurture creativity and knowledge sharing. If there are problems with trust between customers and suppliers, add trustworthiness to your values.

Values must be worked out in advance because they go to the heart of how the startup will be run and how its employees will be expected to act and react when executing the strategy, dealing with each other, and interfacing with customers. Whichever values are chosen, the sponsor, the intrapreneur, and everyone in NewCo must behave in a manner that reinforces them, all the time and in everything they do. NewCo's customers should know what they are, as should suppliers and partners, so they can hold NewCo accountable to its own standards.

Values must be authentic. In their book *Built to Last: Successful Habits of Visionary Companies*, Jim Collins and Jerry Porras tell us that values come from within, referring to NewCo's leaders and the core ideology they personify. It is not enough for NewCo's intrapreneur to borrow values from somewhere and pretend to live them. His words and actions must be so genuine as to make the values concrete. For example, if trust is central to the success of NewCo, a trustworthy leader must be selected. In turn, he must surround himself with people who demonstrate the same value. As the old saying goes, you have to talk the talk and walk the walk.

Step 3: Establish strategic business objectives

Now that NewCo has a map that shows its destination and summarizes the route, a compass is needed to guide it on its journey. The purpose of the compass is to represent the strategic statement in the form of strategic business objectives that will act as milestones. SBOs are proven tools that enable the startup's team to execute its strategy in a deliberate manner. I have translated strategy into SBOs many times and have usually arrived at between five and seven. When developing your own, keep in mind the rule of the vital few versus the useful many.

SBOs are action-oriented statements that capture the short- to mid-term goals that need to be achieved to support the overall long-term goal. Every company has its own definition of short-, mid-, and long-term. As a startup, your SBO time horizon should be closer to near term than that of an established business. Use 18 to 24 months for the short-term horizon and three to five years for the mid- to long-term. If your organization tends to adopt time horizons longer than five years to achieve its SBOs, establish five-year intervals to make the route more tangible. At this point do not worry about the many activities that must be undertaken to complete each SBO. They will be defined in step 4.

A startup's first 12 to 24 months constitute its infancy. This is the foundational period when the intrapreneur needs to concentrate on securing early adopters, validating the MVP, refining the value proposition, understanding the market, building up capabilities, refining the strategy, and creating sales channels and partnerships. During the last few months of this period NewCo will grow into adolescence, which roughly spans years three to five and is marked by more meaningful growth. During the first two of these years NewCo will focus on moving beyond its early adopters towards a broader customer base. It will scale its operations and distribution channels, increase its global presence, launch new products, and take more market share.

The following six SBOs represent the strategic statement on page 239:

SBO 1 Validate the MVP for the robotic arm and haptic touch prototypes and convert them into products ready to be launched in months 18 and 21 respectively.

SBO 2 Sign three partnership agreements with research centers or teaching hospitals in the US in the first nine months and four more by month 24: one in the US, two in Germany, and one in France.

SBO 3 Sign a leading distributor in the US in the first nine months, one in Europe by month 12 and another one by month 18.

SBO 4 Complete five major speaking engagements and 10 workshops by month 24.

SBO 5 Build a three-year capabilities roadmap by month 3 that identifies the capabilities required to achieve the SBOs.

SBO 6 Validate the business model and create a sales channel and business infrastructure that will generate $35 million in sales by year 5.

These SBOs were set from the viewpoint of a startup and are concerned with establishing a business foundation. They will be reviewed and modified annually as the startup grows, and by year 6 will no longer revolve around foundational objectives. By then NewCo will resemble a more mature business and its objectives will follow suit, emphasizing continued growth, geographic expansion, branching out with new products and services, signing strategic partnerships, and introducing mergers and acquisitions activities.

Step 4: Determine the Key Activities

You are now ready to identify the key activities that must be accomplished to achieve each of the SBOs. Here, the focus is on what must be completed by when. Getting the time element right for each activity will ensure those that rely on each other for completion are properly scheduled. When making your list, remember that the activities must be SMART. Even though you will eventually change some of them in response to new business realities as you learn about your market and customers, it is necessary to set them up properly from the outset. I have provided some examples.

SBO 1. Validate the MVP for the robotic arm and haptic touch prototypes and convert them to products ready to be launched in month 18 and 21 respectively.

Key activities:

1.1 Finalize the robotic arm prototype by month 6.

1.2 Validate the robotic arm prototype with three US partner hospitals by month 12.

1.3 Turn the robotic arm prototype into a product in time for its launch in month 18.

1.4 Finalize the haptic touch prototype by month 9.

1.5 Validate the haptic touch prototype with three partner hospitals by month 15.

1.6 Turn the haptic touch prototype into a product in time for its launch in month 21.

1.7 To support the deployment of the robotic arm and haptic touch products, establish systems to handle these areas: project management, customer support, shipping, installation, and warranty.

SBO 2. Sign three partnership agreements with research or teaching hospitals in the US in the first nine months and four more by month 24: one in the US, two in Germany, and one in France.

Key activities:

2.1 Finalize a list of preferred partners in the United States, Germany, and France by month 1.

2.2 Sign one US partner by month 3, one by month 6, one by month 8, and one by month 24.

2.3 Sign one European partner by month 12, one by month 18, and one by month 21.

2.4 Make sure the partnerships are set up to support the prototype work in SBO 1.

SBO 3. Sign a leading distributor in the US in the first nine months and one in Europe by month 12 and a second one by month 18.

Key activities:

3.1 Finalize a list of top three preferred distributors in both the US and Europe by month 3.

3.2 Initiate discussions with the three preferred distributors in the US by month 4.

3.3 Identify the US distributor that best aligns with NewCo's strategy by month 6.

3.4 Sign one US distributor by month 12.

3.5 Initiate discussions with the three preferred distributors in Europe by month 6.

3.6 Identify the European distributor that best aligns with NewCo's strategy by month 9.

3.7 Sign one European distributor by month 12 and a second one by month 18.

SBO 4. Complete five major speaking engagements and 10 workshops by month 24.

Key activities:

4.1 In years 1 and 2, secure a speaking engagement at the International Surgical Robotics Conference.

4.2 In year 2, secure a speaking engagement at the Annual US Robotics Surgery Symposium.

4.3 In year 2, secure a speaking engagement at the European Conference on Robotics-Assisted Surgery and the European Surgeon's Conference.

4.4 Conduct two workshops at each of the above events to attract potential customers.

SBO 5. Build a three-year capabilities roadmap by month 3 that identifies the capabilities required to achieve the SBOs.

Key activities:

5.1 In the first 90 days complete a 36-month capabilities roadmap that includes the roles and capabilities NewCo will require to support its growth and when they will be required. Dates should be approximated to the week for resources needed in months 1 to 18, and to the quarter for resources needed in months 19 to 36.

5.2 Define the resources to be acquired from CoreCo and those that will be recruited externally in support of activity 5.1 and receive budgetary approvals by month 4.

5.3 Create a communications strategy to educate CoreCo's line and functional leaders about the resource plan and to secure buy-in and support by month 3 and initiate communication activities by month 4.

5.4 Align the capabilities plan with SBO 1 to ensure that products 1 and 2 will be supported once deployed.

SBO 6. Validate the business model and create a sales channel and business infrastructure that will generate $35 million in sales by year 5.

Key activities:

6.1 Validate the business model in conjunction with the MVP and product launch activities in SBO 1.

6.2 Establish a marketing plan for review within six months and be ready to launch by month 9.

6.3 Establish a preliminary sales strategy for final review and approval within nine months and be ready to initiate sales activities by month 15.

6.4 Create infrastructure in line with activity 6.1 that will manage sales delivery and provide after-sales support. Make sure it aligns with SBO 5.

6.5 Make three sales of the robotic arm product by month 21 and three sales of the haptic touch product by month 24.

Responsibility and Accountability

You have identified the activities following the what-by-when approach. Now you need to add the final element: the who. It is critical that everyone is clear about who is responsible for making sure that each activity is completed as planned. A useful tool that helps with this exercise is called the RACI model. RACI stands for Responsible, Accountable, Consulted, and Informed. It summarizes the roles people will play.

One person, and only one, should be assigned the responsibility of getting the job done. She can enlist the help of others, but the responsibility is hers alone. The person who is accountable also acts alone. His duties include making sure the job is done on time, on budget, and within the agreed parameters, and he is the one who decides when the person responsible should be approached for guidance. In some instances the same person is both responsible and accountable. For "consulted" there can be more than one person whose opinion or expertise is required, and the same is true of "informed." Sometimes several people need to be informed because the outcome will somehow impact their area.

The following two examples actualize activities 1.1 and 5.1 using the RACI model.

Activity 1.1 Finalize the robotic arm prototype by month 6.

Responsible: Head of engineering

Accountable: Head of product development

Consulted: Heads of marketing and R&D

Informed: Head of sales, CoreCo head of engineering and R&D

Activity 5.1 In the first 90 days complete a 36-month capabilities roadmap that includes the roles and capabilities NewCo will require to support its growth and when they will be required. Dates should be approximated to the week for resources needed in months 1 to 18, and to the quarter for resources needed in months 19 to 36.

Responsible: NewCo's HR business partner

Accountable: Intrapreneur

Consulted: Heads of engineering, operations, product development, marketing, sales, and customer service

Informed: CoreCo HR, sponsor

Step 5: Define the Measures of Success

The next tool in your toolkit is a ruler that tells you everything you need to know about your progress as it unfolds. Called the measures of success (MOS), it tracks progress by validating that the key activities leading to the SBOs are completed. MOS is also valuable for showing NewCo's leaders how the business is doing.

In the workplace it may seem obvious when an activity is done, but "done" can mean different things to different people. An MOS has the kind of specificity that makes the completion of an activity meaningful. Take this example: *Complete a competitive analysis within 60 days for segment A of the market.* When the activity is done, many people might label it with the following MOS: *Market analysis for segment A of the market was completed by day 60.* Can you tell why this is an incomplete MOS? It is commendable that the analysis was finished, but it will be ineffective if it sits on a shelf until someone asks for it. An MOS always communicates closure: *Market analysis for segment A of the market was completed by day 60, and a Word document summarizing the findings was distributed to NewCo's leadership team, with a meeting scheduled for within one week of the report summary distribution to review its findings.*

This MOS was created for activity 1.1 of SBO 1:

> Finalize the robotic arm prototype by month 6.
>
> **Responsible:** Head of engineering
>
> **Accountable:** Head of product development
>
> **Consulted:** Heads of marketing and R&D
>
> **Informed:** Head of sales
>
> **MOS:** Prototype 1 ready and scheduled for partner validation by month 6 in accordance with the prototype specifications

Measures of success that track the progress of business activities should not be confused with key performance indicators (KPIs), also called metrics of performance. While MOS indicates when business activities have been successfully completed, KPIs are used to measure the overall health of the business. You could think of them as business-level MOS. In mature businesses they refer to indicators such as sales, revenues, margins, cost of goods sold, cycle times, market share, earnings per share, customer retention, on-time deliveries, return on capital, and a slew of other activities that are charted and monitored at regular intervals.

The corporate startup needs KPIs to make sure that the new company is progressing in the right direction. There is a saying in the corporate world that you can only move what you can measure. In other words, unless you track the KPIs that matter most to your business, it will be hard to know how well it is doing and if the actions you are taking to improve the KPIs are having the desired impact. When choosing KPIs for a startup you must start from scratch, meaning they must be customized to your business model and market. As discussed in previous chapters, do not make the mistake of copying CoreCo's KPIs. Using metrics that are unsuitable for a startup will lead to CDIF.

I have seen the following scenario repeated many times: NewCo is launched and soon CoreCo decides to impose revenue and profitability targets that mimic what is expected of its core businesses. As a new startup with no credibility or proven track record in its market, NewCo struggles to make its first sales. Under sudden pressure from CoreCo, it switches gears to focus on accelerating revenue gains. This conflicts with the expectations of its early adopters, who had agreed to work with NewCo, despite the risk, in exchange for free or heavily discounted access to the innovation. Unable to bend on sales and profit margins, NewCo makes no progress with its early adopters and consequently suffers from a lack of critical feedback. Without feedback NewCo has no idea how well its new solution solves the actual problem. Validation is not possible, sales are delayed, and things get worse from there. Focusing on profitability too early is a bad idea.

Table 13.1 shows how metrics can be used as KPIs in the different stages of NewCo's growth. As your business venture matures you must be sure to reset the metrics accordingly. It is key to match them to the business cycle. Be on the lookout for people working very hard to excel at what they have failed to grasp is a wrong metric. Their efforts will drive wrong behaviors and deliver wrong results.

During NewCo's early phase financial KPIs typically look at whether or not budgets are being used effectively to achieve the stated goals. As the new business progresses to early adolescence, the KPIs begin to reflect the need to track the product's success in the market through increased sales. They also track how well NewCo is succeeding at growing its distribution channels and partnerships. KPIs that look at product cost reductions and business profitability are introduced at around this time. Finally, as NewCo enters early adulthood, its KPIs will increasingly resemble those of CoreCo's established businesses, where the emphasis is on standard financial performance metrics.

Table 13.1 Adapting KPIs to NewCo's Growth Stages

INFANCY	EARLY ADOLESCENCE	LATE ADOLESCENCE/ EARLY ADULTHOOD
Validate the MVP	Refine and standardize the product or service	Continually improve the product or service
Place the new product or service with early adopters	Create growth in customer interest, track customer retention and dropouts, improve sales growth	Institute customer satisfaction and retention programs, continue shifting to the broader market, increase sales growth and market share
Use budgets effectively	Improve budgeting and forecasting accuracy	Maintain forecasting accuracy, track COS and COGS
Build NewCo's business infrastructure	Demonstrate progress towards profitability	Meet profitability and margins targets
Verify the CFM strategy's effectiveness	Ensure the success of the CFM strategy	Scale the business
Develop distribution channels, secure strategic partnerships	Add distribution channels, use strategic partnerships effectively	Ensure the distribution channels keep pace with business scaling
Frequently validate the business model and strategy	Demonstrate progress towards materiality	Track ROCE, RONA, ROE
Learn, be ready to pivot	Learn, be ready to pivot	Learn, be ready to pivot

Early-phase metrics mostly focus on two questions: 1) Is NewCo's team properly validating that its solution is something customers need and will pay for? and 2) Have the assumptions behind the business model been validated and will they position the company for profitable and sustainable growth? The answers these KPIs deliver will help the intrapreneur firm up NewCo's strategy and validate it.

Step 6: Iterate Frequently

The final step is to iterate the ABS model over and over again. It will help if you schedule regular checkpoints at which you will take stock of how NewCo is doing, review the KPIs, and track the team's progress in completing the key activities. Frequent validation will depend on the information generated by your awareness and warning system (MAWS) and collaborative information receptivity management (CIRM). As we learned in labor 12, the infant startup will need a strong CIRM during the months it is developing a more reliable MAWS. This is when the information the intrapreneur uses to validate NewCo's initial assumptions will come from employees and customers.

Do not leave the iteration of the strategic plan to chance. By establishing regular checkpoints you will know exactly when they will take place. Once a month is appropriate, whereas for the business model, certainly during NewCo's early phase, once a week is necessary. As the business model stabilizes over time it can be iterated biweekly or monthly. The same holds true for the strategic plan. As NewCo matures and it becomes evident that the business model is solidly established and that NewCo's economic engine for making money is understood and scalable in line with its financial goals, iteration of the strategic plan can shift to quarterly.

At the heart of iterative reviews is the information gathered by NewCo's team during interactions with customers, partners, suppliers, distributors, and competitors. NewCo's weekly, monthly, and quarterly meetings should overflow with facts, opinions, and comments discovered externally. This information is not meant to provoke sudden changes on the fly; rather, its purpose is to educate, bring stability to the original business assumptions, help NewCo's leaders identify what is necessary to succeed, and confirm that NewCo is on the right track.

3 Types of Meetings

- **A weekly market update and operational status meeting** where what is being learned in the market is shared. This information is used to track progress, identify and remove roadblocks, and ensure movement towards upcoming milestones. Typically, the meeting starts with sales and business development people presenting data, following which a product development leader working on prototype validation might contribute significant insights, or the heads of the main groups might communicate substantial accomplishments and findings. These meetings offer the perfect forum for NewCo's leadership team to develop its management and communication styles.
- **A monthly SBO update meeting** to evaluate how progress in the marketplace and with customers is impacting the SBOs and strategic plan. As with the weekly meetings, the first part is devoted to sharing findings from customer interactions and feedback. The second part consists of reviewing the progress being made on the key activities, with short updates presented by the people responsible for making sure each activity is successfully completed.
- **A quarterly strategy, SBO, and KPI meeting** that starts with a review of the business KPIs, with the aim of grounding everyone in the objective data. Longer than the others, its purpose is to monitor the progress being made on the SBOs and strategic plan and to make certain that the group is aware of the latest developments (or lack thereof). It is an excellent forum for questioning assumptions and understanding what is working and what is not. A portion of the meeting should be spent evaluating how well NewCo's operations are ramping up and if its capabilities are developing as planned. How is the hiring going? Are transfers from CoreCo on schedule? Are the CFMs being leveraged in a timely way? Are the product development activities on course?

  The meeting should end with a review of the strategic plan and SBOs in relation to what has been learned from the customers, with the purpose of identifying any adjustments that should be made. At the end of the meeting the intrapreneur should ask his team: Are we following the right strategy to achieve our goals? Are our SBOs still the right ones to lead us to success? Are we overlooking a major finding that points to a need to pivot our strategy or business model?

Wasting time at meetings can be avoided with an agenda that lists the topics to be covered and how much time each topic will be allotted. This will keep everyone around the table focused. The agenda, which will have been delivered prior to the meeting, will outline how the attendees need to prepare. At the start of the meeting appoint someone to each of the following roles: a timekeeper to make sure speakers stay on topic and within their allotted time, a scribe to write down the main conclusions and action items (what is to be done, by when, and by who), and a referee to point out when the rules of the meeting are being broken. The rules are basically acceptable behaviors that are set out before the meeting gets under way. They instruct everyone in the room on how to share and listen to ideas, decide and follow up on issues, and generally behave with each other. Rules reflect the values NewCo has chosen and play a big part in setting the tone that will govern the new business.

Remember to invite the sponsor and gatekeeper to some meetings and copy them on all meeting agendas, whether they are invited or not. Key allies should also be invited from time to time. If you want their continued support and commitment, fan the flames of their engagement by keeping them up to date with NewCo's learning and any changes to the strategy and business model. They only need to attend the parts of the meetings dedicated to sharing lessons learned from the market and feedback from partners and customers. Both are essential when trying to comprehend the nature of the new startup.

Success Tools

Having executed the ABS model, the intrapreneur and his team are now equipped with the necessary navigational tools and can turn their attention to the success tools. These come in the form of two pivotal management insights I refer to as the first and second laws of business success. I believe in these laws because I have used them when launching new businesses and achieved the desired results. The intrapreneur and sponsor need to believe in them too. As Larry Bossidy, the former CEO of Allied Signals and a best-selling business author, states so well, "Execution is the ability to mesh strategy with reality, align people with goals, and achieve the promised results."

The First Law: Success

The engineer in me likes to come up with equations:

First Law of Business Success: S = f (Q, A, R, I) + FE, where

S = Success	f = Function of
Q = Quality strategic plan	A = Acceptance
R = Resources	I = Iteration
FE = Flawless execution	

According to this law, success is a function (f) of having a quality strategic plan (Q), getting acceptance (A) of the plan, making sure the resources (R) are available in a timely manner to execute the plan, and seeing to the plan's regular review and iteration (I) so it can adapt to its external and internal environments. Once in place, the quality plan – with its acceptance, proper resourcing, and regular iteration – will have only a limited impact unless NewCo's team and CoreCo's CFM providers flawlessly execute it (FE).

Quality

The quality of your strategic plan is directly related to the quality of your assumptions. Do your best to base them on reliable data. I am not suggesting that you fall into an analysis paralysis situation, far from it. NewCo will not have access to the same quality of data or level of market insight and intimacy that CoreCo is used to, and early on will be driven to make broad assumptions and educated guesses. All I am saying is that whenever possible, assumptions should be backed up by facts that reflect what you have learned about your business from your customers.

Acceptance

A new business that is launched within a larger corporation does not exist in a vacuum. This is a reality of the corporate world. Recall the earlier discussion on separate and distinct versus isolated. NewCo risks isolation if it fails to secure the right level of acceptance from its parent. Isolation will lead to a poorly executed CFM strategy and a lessening of CoreCo's interest in supporting NewCo.

This is where the intrapreneur's change management skills come in, which does not mean expending piles of energy trying to convince every last CoreCo employee to accept NewCo's plan. What it means is working hard to get CoreCo's key stakeholders and influencers behind it, as well as a majority of the company's formal and informal leaders, particularly those who control the CFMs NewCo intends to leverage. The bottom line: NewCo can only achieve success if CoreCo accepts its strategic plan. It goes without saying that acceptance is not limited to the realm of CoreCo. Acceptance of the strategic plan by NewCo's employees is vital if they are to properly execute it.

Pause, reflect, and learn, and have the courage to pivot as necessary.

Resources

The execution of a plan requires resources such as R&D facilities, product development labs, IT, manufacturing capabilities, and several others the intrapreneur will have painstakingly identified and measured when putting together the CFM strategy. Above all else, NewCo needs people. What speeds progress is having the right people with the right talents on board at the opportune time. It is not strategies, SBOs, and KPIs that get the job done and build companies. It is people who are qualified, engaged, talented, and willing to work hard together under the leadership of an A-type intrapreneur.

On the subject of human resources, I have often found that resource planning is the weakest part of a new business plan. A large organization that is implementing major change has the advantage of a critical mass of employees who will carry a project until new resources are acquired. This is not the case at a startup, where few people wearing multiple hats are working to carry out an aggressive agenda while facing an unbelievably steep learning curve.

When leading a corporate startup that to some degree will rely on the transfer or loan of talent, the intrapreneur needs to develop a resource strategy that is reflected in one of the SBOs, and then he needs to be maniacal about having the objective executed as planned. The skills that are required, and the moment in the growth cycle they are required, must be carefully specified. Knowing these requirements allows CoreCo's organizations to assess their resources and prepare to backfill their transferred employees. It also holds the HR leader accountable for finding the people you need, when you need them.

Iteration

The need for frequent iteration based on facts and data applies to many of the activities that go into making NewCo a success, and the first law of business success is no exception. Iterating often is an indispensible component of getting your strategic plan right. As we saw in earlier chapters when discussing the business model, iteration is the generator of the mountain of learning your team will have to absorb, which is what fuels the validation process that will refine and confirm your major business assumptions. It is the "I" that leads to improved accuracy and predictability.

The strategic plan works the same way. It is through frequent iterations that NewCo will find out if it is viable or if a timely pivot is next on the agenda. Regular reviews make frequent validation and assumption refinement a sure thing, so include an iteration philosophy in your meeting governance. Mature corporations review their strategic plans annually or semi-annually, but NewCos should do so quarterly.

Flawless Execution

Even though all the elements of the first law are in place, there is still a risk that NewCo's team will deviate from its stated SBOs, for example, by succumbing to pressure from CoreCo to deliver in the short-term. Or some employees might decide to go rogue, thinking they have found a better route to success. Flawless execution means no one strays from the plan unless agreed to as part of a strategic shift. It also means you do not tolerate mediocre work from anyone on the team. Flawless execution is partly a function of measuring progress against clearly articulated objectives. More importantly, it flows from strong leadership and from the example of everyone on the team being accountable for delivering on their commitments.

A startup remains small in size for some time, and the smaller the team, the more devastating mediocre work and mistakes can be. Mistakes are inevitable due to the uncertain nature of startups, but they should lead to learning and improvements. For this reason it is wise to encourage and reward transparency, even when information that is shared is not news you want to hear. But repeating the same mistakes, frequently missing deadlines, hiding information, not respecting commitments to the team, clients, or partners, or deviating from the strategy without approval are behaviors that cannot be tolerated. Ultimately these lead to missing KPIs and falling behind on SBOs, which in turn hurt the team's ability to execute the strategic plan.

There is a danger that comes with flawless execution. The intrapreneur must be careful not to turn the pursuit of it into stubborn adherence to an objective that actually requires adjustment. He must watch for people who overcommit to flawless execution to the point of limiting their ability to correctly interpret market feedback. Blind spots will result in missed opportunities to pivot and possibly lead to CDIF. Flawless execution is about having the discipline to follow through on your commitments, the tenacity to overcome obstacles, and the passion to inspire people to get the job done. It means taking the time to pause, reflect, and learn, and having the courage to pivot as necessary to achieve the stated mission. At all times NewCo's intrapreneur must demonstrate the behavior he expects of others, a simple concept that for some people is hard to put into practice.

The Second Law: Organizational Alignment

Over the years I have witnessed many leaders underestimate the power of organizational alignment. This is not a one-time event that is accomplished by standing in front of your team at the launch of your initiative and delivering a brilliant motivational speech. Achieving organizational alignment requires the hard work of repeatedly checking that your people understand how each major component of the business works together in pursuit of the ultimate goal.

My methodology for reaching organizational alignment is shown in figure 13.2. I call it the Integrated Clarity (IC) Model™, in which each lens is aligned to provide clarity throughout the organization. The lens metaphor reinforces the concept of transparency, which is essential when dealing with CoreCo and when providing everyone at NewCo, regardless of their position on the organizational chart, with a clear view of NewCo's strategy and how they will contribute to the startup's success.

A major component of the IC model is to achieve organizational alignment by design rather than circumstance. Alignment starts with the sponsor, gatekeeper, and intrapreneur. Because they are the dominant voices inside CoreCo and NewCo, they must use the communication tools at their disposal to achieve and maintain alignment at all times. Next comes alignment between the intrapreneur and NewCo's leadership team. Formal communication tools are less important during the early phase because NewCo's small team will experience numerous casual points of contact on a daily basis, allowing them to discuss, clarify, and align activities. This setting, which can be maintained up to about 25 employees, encourages the CIRM that is so critical prior to and following the launch.

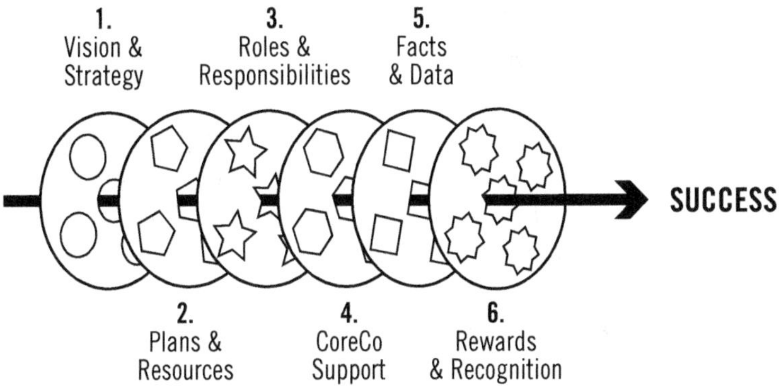

Figure 13.2 Integrated Clarity Model™

As more employees are added and more demands are made on the team's time, the number of impromptu gatherings will diminish drastically and the intrapreneur will recognize the need to establish a meeting and information-sharing strategy as discussed earlier in the chapter. In addition, he must see to it that all new hires are briefed on the startup's strategy and SBOs. The best approach is to add new-employee meetings to your agenda as monthly events and never move them. I also believe in quarterly all-hands meetings where the intrapreneur and leadership team reinforce the strategy, inform the troops of any modifications that were made, congratulate everyone on milestones reached, and answer any and all questions.

A minimum of six lenses must be aligned if your team wishes to follow the path of least resistance when executing NewCo's strategy.

Lens #1: Vision and strategy

Executing steps 1 and 2 of the ABS model constitutes half the work of developing your vision and strategy. The other half is to share the outcome of your work with NewCo's stakeholders, who need to know where NewCo is heading, why it is heading there, and how it plans to reach its destination. Use the information generated during the ABS process to create a presentation that includes the mission statement, strategic intent, and business goals, as well as a summary of the strategic intent and list of the SBOs. Share it quarterly with everyone who is part of making NewCo's success happen. This may sound too frequent, but you want the key points about NewCo to be deeply lodged in the mind of every stakeholder. Keep the presentation fresh and relevant by updating it with what is being learned.

Lens #2: Plans and resources

A consequence of identifying the key activities that will achieve the SBOs is that each member of NewCo's team will have clarity regarding the actions they need to take and the resources they require to take them. One approach I use to establish alignment is to require my direct reports to create action plans that link to the SBOs and the strategic plan, and I recommend the intrapreneur do the same. By requiring subordinate leaders to show how their organization will achieve the SBOs, the intrapreneur can validate that his leaders have grasped the strategy and their role in executing it. If you are the intrapreneur and you notice that people on your team are working on an activity unrelated to an SBO, ask why they are wasting limited time and resources instead of helping NewCo deliver on its strategy.

Lens #3: Roles and responsibilities

Identifying who is responsible for what in a mature organization where roles and areas of accountability are relatively stable and well understood is challenging enough, so imagine how complicated this can be in a startup environment, where most employees wear multiple hats. As the old navy saying goes, you are chief cook and bottle washer at the same time. The purpose of properly validating roles and responsibilities is to avoid the duplication of effort and conflict among team members. Roles and responsibilities evolve rapidly as a startup grows, so the intrapreneur needs to pay close and constant attention to this lens to ensure there is no confusion.

Lens #4: CoreCo support

We have discussed the CFM strategy at length. Making 100 percent sure that both CoreCo and NewCo understand what is being leveraged, why, and when is critical to minimizing immune system interference and ensuring that the right support is available as needed. A natural outcome of growing a new business is that the CFM strategy will be modified to adapt to what is being learned about the market. When these modifications show they will impact one or more CoreCo leaders, the intrapreneur must tell them in advance so they can prepare. Constant communication – presenting new information and lessons learned, making requests ahead of time, creating forums to answer questions – will keep CoreCo aligned with NewCo's strategy and needs as they evolve.

Lens #5: Facts and data

Managing by facts and data is central to the success of any business. This is particularly true of new startups because facts and data are at the heart of MAWS, which feeds the iteration process that leads to a winning business model, the completion of the ABS model, and achieving forecasting accuracy. The use of facts and data includes measuring the progress of SBO activities and the startup's overall health through KPIs and metrics. Finally, they are at the center of every learning activity and constantly add to NewCo's body of knowledge about the new market. The beauty of objective knowledge is that it grounds everyone in what matters most and over time equips the team with the insights they need to make NewCo a success.

Lens #6: Rewards and recognition

Recognizing certain types of effort and aligning them with rewards can have a long-term positive influence on the behavior of employees: it demonstrates what is important to NewCo's leaders and reinforces NewCo's values. But not all reward systems are good. Be on the lookout for systems that pop up in your organization that neither reinforce the chosen values nor align with the key activities that must be successfully completed to achieve the SBOs. When you find some, give your leaders an alignment check. With that taken care of, remember to celebrate often and to ensure that CoreCo allies are part of the celebrations.

Transparency's Evil Twin

A discussion of alignment would not be complete without looking at the flip side of transparency, which is exposure to judgment and criticism. The transparent leader is a courageous one. Being transparent about your business strategy, objectives, and values opens the door for others to observe the organization's progress and gauge whether it points to success or failure. It creates more opportunities for naysayers, resistors, and saboteurs to do their best to poke holes in the business and discredit its leaders. But in my experience transparency is the best way to lead because it lays the groundwork for alignment.

The leader of a startup is even more exposed to subversive behaviors. The huge amount of learning that occurs during infancy and early adolescence, which leads to changes to the key assumptions, SBOs, and possibly the strategy itself, can result in raised eyebrows, at the least. We know that changes of this type are to be expected, but many people in the corporate world fail to appreciate the startup environment and will judge change as a function of poor management or lack of planning. The sponsor, the gatekeeper, and NewCo's allies need to squash such judgments as soon as they come across them. Otherwise, the transparent intrapreneur will become less transparent, which increases the likelihood of misalignment with CoreCo. Misalignment will lead to poor execution and poor execution will lead to failure.

Alignment Is Everyone's Business

The task of aligning the different lenses of the IC model does not rest on the intrapreneur's shoulders alone. His direct reports must equally stay alert to the issue of alignment and make corrections as necessary. Because the world is not perfect, occasional misalignment will occur due to organizational and strategic wear and tear. As NewCo evolves it will accumulate new business mileage similar to the road mileage accumulated by a car. It will hit several startup bumps on the road, face strong early-phase headwinds, and maybe have an occasional strategic fender bender, all of which will take their toll on the alignment of NewCo's lenses.

Realignment is a necessary strategic and operational maintenance activity that ensures everyone stays on course. I have used the IC model both at large CoreCo organizations and young NewCos, and not surprisingly I have found the need for alignment is far less urgent at CoreCos, with their mature business models and growth based on incremental changes, than at NewCos, where unfamiliar environments and constant learning demand repeated adjustments. A startup provides an action-packed and exciting environment, which is a satisfying place to be when you are equipped with the right knowledge and tools. Now that you have both, you can feel confident that you are in possession of the strategic plan you need to succeed.

Conclusion: The Winning Intrapreneur

You have completed a comprehensive review of the 12 labors that constitute intrapreneurship and you understand the ways each labor must be tackled so that a CoreCo innovation can successfully be transitioned from under-the-radar development activities to the high-stakes world of post-launch NewCo. The sponsor and CoreCo's executive team are aware of the risks and rewards of the intrapreneurial journey and are ready to back the new business with a strong commitment to funding, making CFMs available when required, and approving necessary pivots. The intrapreneur is armed with new knowledge and the navigational and success tools that are essential to transform NewCo into a profitable and sustainable business. Perhaps most importantly, everyone recognizes the need to watch for corporate immune system activity so it can be averted before irreversible damage is done.

I have purposely focused this book on the corporate-driven obstacles that will begin to surface the day NewCo is announced. This is not to minimize the challenges that will come from the external environment. The new market and customers, the economy, the competition, the regulatory environment, and many other variables will introduce surprises and difficulties that at one point or another will demand everyone's utmost efforts. NewCo will need to have the right people, systems, and practices in place to track these influences and manage them, but it will have little or no control over them.

Where NewCo and CoreCo can have a real impact is on how the startup is positioned to increase its probability of success, how well equipped it is to reach its goals, and whether or not it is genuinely encouraged to learn from its external environment and pivot when the indicators point in a new direction. Accomplishing the above will require a qualified intrapreneur who is capable of managing CoreCo's demands and deflating its corporate immune system while remaining focused on the startup's customers and business objectives. These are the internally driven factors that are underestimated or overlooked by corporations worldwide. All too easily they will lead to NewCo's demise.

Whether you are a senior executive within CoreCo or one of its leaders, or NewCo's assigned sponsor or gatekeeper, you must not tolerate behavior from either the parent company or startup that will jeopardize NewCo's success. This is especially critical in the early years, when the fledgling business will be at its most vulnerable to internal interference and corporate distractions. What a waste it would be if well-meaning meddling from the corporation or resistance fueled by ignorance drained NewCo's energy to the point of collapse. Instead, every bit of energy should be focused on identifying the needs of NewCo's customers and market, testing and validating the proposed solution, iterating the business model, and growing stronger week by week.

If you are a CEO, president, general manager, or COO who seeks to create an intrapreneurial culture, remember the five gears described in the book's introduction. The members of your leadership team must become knowledgeable about all five, but they may need your encouragement to accept the fifth gear because it is the least familiar and can be uncomfortable due to its focus on internally generated obstacles. By taking the time to understand these 12 labors, you will be ready to spot corporate immune system activities and address them. Then you can help your team do the same.

But everything starts with the first gear: managing the innovation process. The quality of your handling of these early activities will directly influence the quality of the innovations that will be selected to move to a formal launch. Once they are launched, the most effective way to deploy them in the marketplace will be by leveraging your company's resources. At the same time, intrapreneurship requires the corporation to adapt its control mechanisms for the benefit of the startup and to allow the startup to create controls of its own. Both will demand skillful change management.

A well-run innovation process backed by a corporation that is prepared to be leveraged and is comfortable with change management and the need for pivots is a good start, but it will not be sufficient if a strong and highly capable intrapreneur is not appointed to NewCo. Appointing the right leader will go a long way to ensuring flawless execution. The venture capitalists discussed in labor 2 were wise to bet on great people first and great ideas second.

If you are the intrapreneur or a member of NewCo's leadership team, keep in mind that CoreCo's leaders and managers are putting all their mental and physical energy into ensuring that CoreCo's day-to-day activities are executed properly with the goal of meeting the corporation's objectives. Be aware that educating your CoreCo colleagues and helping them deal with the changes NewCo will bring will be an uphill battle, as will convincing them to give you access to their organization so you can leverage their CFMs.

Remember to include your CoreCo allies and supporters in your celebrations, because without them you cannot succeed.

The Evolution of Intrapreneurship

In 2013, I traveled to the Galápagos Islands and visited the Charles Darwin Research Center on Santa Cruz Island. I went there almost every morning before embarking on whatever excursion the day held. On my last visit I spent considerable time at the empty enclosure of Lonesome George, who had passed away about a year earlier, on June 24, 2012. Lonesome George was a Pinta giant tortoise that was discovered in 1971. According to the wooden plaque overlooking his enclosure, he was the last of his species.

That morning dawned clear and cool. When I arrived at the enclosure it was still early and I discovered I was the sole visitor. My only company was the quick activity of Darwin finches and other exotic birds. In the distance several marine iguanas were making their way to the ocean to feed. The Galápagos giant tortoises living in nearby enclosures were going about their morning routine, and I watched them as I reflected on the story of Lonesome George. What compelled my attention was that many attempts had been made over the decades to ensure the survival of his species by mating him with others of his kind. They all proved unsuccessful. It struck me that despite the extensive and heartfelt efforts of some of the world's best experts, the Pinta giant tortoise was now extinct. I could see it in the empty enclosure. It felt very real.

You may be familiar with the following statement, which is often used to summarize Darwin's work on evolution: "It is not the strongest species that survive, nor the most intelligent, but the ones most responsive to change." As I contemplated the end of the Pinta giant tortoise my thoughts turned to intrapreneurship, and eventually I was inspired to write *Winning at Intrapreneurship*. I will close with the statement that opens this book.

It is not the new business backed by the strongest corporation that succeeds, nor the one with the most compelling business model. Rather, it is the corporate startup led by a qualified and engaged intrapreneur who is able to effectively leverage the corporate parent, fend off its immune system, learn from the marketplace, adapt and modify as necessary, and execute flawlessly.

Acknowledgments

From the moment I decided to put pen to paper or, more precisely, fingers to keyboard, I received incredible support from many people. I wish to begin by thanking my family, starting with my wife and steadfast companion, Carol-Lynn. She supported me wholeheartedly, like she has always done. Writing a book is a solitary project and she gave me all the space and time I needed, which was a lot. Our sons, Nicolas and Alexandre, were great cheerleaders who also knew when to tiptoe around Dad because quiet and solitude were what I required to focus.

I could not have published this book without several people who helped me on my journey. I was fortunate to have a formidable team to call on when I needed a fresh pair of eyes, the viewpoint of a business executive, or a critical look at the manuscript's structure and grammar. I want to especially acknowledge Susan Kim Hervé, who dedicated considerable time and energy to reviewing my first manuscript, energy she had in scant supply because she did this work while recovering from breast cancer surgery and treatment. Her feedback was pivotal in bringing the book to where it is today.

Winning at Intrapreneurship grew out of the encouragement I received from fellow business executives and others who convinced me that I had something important to share. My ideas about intrapreneurship had been germinating for a while, but it was their encouragement that grew the seed into a manuscript. Here I want to thank my brothers, Xavier-Henri and Hugues, and my very good friends Ben Minicucci, Tom Paterson, and Dany Belanger. My sincere thanks also go to Daniel Mongeau, a well-read and incisive critic who reviewed the manuscript and provided valuable observations, and to Claudine O'Donnell of Pearson Canada, who so generously gave of her time to share her experiences in publishing. Her positive reaction to my manuscript and her enthusiasm convinced me that this book had to be published.

The fear of being a first-time author can make writing a book seem daunting. I was lucky to have people connect me with authors who were open about their experiences of writing their first book. They also introduced me to other authors who were instrumental in getting me to the finish line. These include Mario Patenaude *(The Performance Equation)*, Carolyne Van Der Meer *(Motherlode: A Mosaic of Dutch Wartime Experience)*, Dr. Christopher Ragan *(Economics, 14th Canadian Edition)*, Keith Matthews *(The Empowered Investor)*, Etienne Garbugli *(Lean B2B: Build Products Businesses Want)*, Steve Harvey (dean of Concordia University's John Molson School of Business), and Mike and Kim Simpson of The Business Box, who made several of the above connections possible. Finally, to those business leaders I contacted to test out the book's title, I am eternally grateful. Your invaluable comments led to a book-title pivot.

Like a conductor who turns talented musicians into an orchestra that delivers a great performance, I discovered that the right editor is like a maestro of the written word, turning chapters, paragraphs, and sentences into an easy-to-follow structure in which ideas flow from one to the next. Jane Pavanel of Knockout Communications was this book's maestro. She instantly put herself at the service of the book, taking ownership of its success and teaching me how important it is to protect the reader at all times. She did this while respecting my ideas, style, and vision, and I am very grateful.

The next step was to bring the manuscript to life in paper and electronic form, with its own personality and unique look. This is what Sara Morley of Design Postimage did so brilliantly. Her creativity and design insights immediately reassured me that it was possible to come up with a cover and design that would distinguish this book from the many other business books on the market. My thanks to her and her team.

During my career I have been supported by outstanding professionals who provided me with innumerable opportunities to learn and grow. To the business leaders who entrusted me with leadership positions that I always felt privileged to hold, I thank each of you for your confidence. To anyone I have had the honor of leading, I hope I stayed true and transparent. To colleagues who helped me along the way, thank you. One never succeeds alone. Like so much in my work and life, writing *Winning at Intrapreneurship* was truly a team effort.

Glossary

ABS model Refer to Achieving Business Success

Achieving Business Success™ (ABS) model An iterative process for creating successful strategies and ensuring they remain relevant. Includes six steps: Destination, Itinerary, Strategic Business Objectives, Key Activities, Measures of Success, and Iterate.

Business assumption risk Associated with the number of disruptions a new product or service will rely on to succeed. Three business activities lead to disruption: introducing new technology, entering a new market, and leveraging new distribution channels.

CDIF Refer to Controlled descent into failure

CFM charter A document that captures how the selected CoreCo functions will be leveraged. It describes NewCo's expectations, how they link to the implementation of the strategic plan, what is required of each corporate force multiplier and when, and associated risks. It also includes approved budgets. The charter must be signed by the intrapreneur, the sponsor, and the CFM functional leader.

Change management model A systematic process for introducing major change in organizations. Among the several models available, this book refers to the eight steps developed by Dr. John Kotter: create a sense of urgency, build a guiding coalition, form the strategic vision and supporting initiatives, enlist a volunteer army, enable action by removing barriers, generate short-term wins, sustain acceleration, and institute change.

CIRM Refer to Collaborative information receptivity management

CFMs Refer to Corporate force multipliers

Collaborative information receptivity management™ (CIRM) Describes an environment that eliminates hierarchical bias through promoting communication, information sharing, and receptivity. A healthy CIRM culture ensures that important information from sources external to NewCo's MAWS is provided to the intrapreneur. CIRM was inspired by the aviation industry's crew resource management.

Compounding cushion effect The over-inflation that occurs when a work estimate seeks approval at every level of the CoreCo organization. As it moves up the chain each level adds a risk mitigation correction, which is the norm when predicting the unknown.

Controlled descent into failure™ (CDIF) The consequence of business leaders choosing to continue on a predetermined path despite having market indicators that show change is necessary if success is to be achieved. CDIF was inspired by the aviation industry's controlled flight into terrain.

CoreCo An existing corporation or a division, business unit, or organization within a corporation.

Corporate expectations risk Relates to NewCo's contribution to CoreCo's overall business strategy and financial results. The more dependent CoreCo is on NewCo executing its strategy successfully and achieving the expected financial contributions, the higher the level of corporate expectations risk.

Corporate force multipliers™ (CFMs) The strengths, attributes, relationships, and proven capabilities that exist within a corporation and can be leveraged by smaller organizations within it. CFMs provide capabilities that are well beyond what can be expected of an independent business similar in size. They include people, organizations, materials, know-how, solutions, systems, processes, assets, and technology.

Corporate immune system A term coined by Gifford Pinchot that describes the resistance exhibited by people in an organization when they perceive change as a threat. Resistance often takes the form of forcing NewCo to adopt CoreCo's systems, processes, practices, governance, metrics, or KPIs. In some cases immune system activity is triggered by a misplaced desire to help.

First law of business success Business success is a function (f) of having a quality strategic plan (Q), getting acceptance (A) of the plan, making sure the resources (R) are available in a timely manner to execute the plan, and seeing to the plan's regular review and iteration (I). To achieve maximum impact the plan must be flawlessly executed (FE).

Formal expectations Also called objectives, they constitute what NewCo is expected to deliver to its parent company and are the reason NewCo was given the go-ahead in the first place. They must be SMART: Specific, Measurable, Attainable, Relevant, and Time-bound.

Formal launch The activity of establishing a startup business (NewCo) that will enter a new market or a new segment of an existing market and will be distinct from and independent of CoreCo's other businesses. A formal launch requires a corporate strategic commitment and an official declaration.

Gatekeeper A senior corporate executive whose ideas and opinions carry real weight and whose primary task is to support NewCo by controlling access to it and barring access if necessary.

IC Model Refer to Integrated Clarity (IC) Model

Informal expectations Expectations that develop in the minds of CoreCo's senior management team that feel very real to them, though they are undocumented and inaccurate.

Integrated Clarity (IC) Model™ A methodology for reaching organizational alignment. The goal is to create and maintain transparency within NewCo and in its relationship with CoreCo so that everyone in both organizations understands the strategic plan and what their individual contribution is to the startup's success.

Intrapreneur An employee within a corporation who combines entrepreneurial skills and concepts with leadership and change management skills and a strong understanding of how to leverage the corporation to position innovations in the marketplace as viable businesses that drive new sources of profit.

Intrapreneurship Organizing and executing the activities that are necessary to monetize an innovation and turn it into a profitable and sustainable business within a corporate environment.

Key performance indicators (KPIs) Measures of performance that track the progress of important business activities and metrics.

KPIs Refer to Key performance indicators

Iterative learning cycle A five-step cycle that includes making an educated guess, forecasting, testing, validating, and refining. It is used in several NewCo activities such as improving forecasting accuracy and validating and refining the business model.

NewCo A new line of business that springs from CoreCo and is aimed at generating an original source of revenues and profits. NewCos are often very different from their parents' other lines of business.

Materiality The threshold that defines when a financial event such as an investment, transaction, or level of debt becomes material to a company's performance and health. Companies use materiality to measure whether or not an activity is making a positive or negative contribution.

Market awareness and warning system™ (MAWS) The many sources of data used by business leaders to learn about their markets, the competition, customer behaviors, and how their products, services, and business assumptions must be adapted to be successful. MAWS was inspired by the aviation industry's terrain awareness and warning systems.

Marketing activities The 37 micro-level activities that must be completed before the launch of a new product or service. They fall into seven broad categories: market, focus, business, planning, programs, readiness, and support.

MAWS Refer to Market awareness and warning system

Measures of success (MOS) Measures used at all levels of an organization or activity to track progress. At the micro level they validate that the activities necessary to achieving the strategic business objectives have been completed properly. At the macro level they help leaders evaluate how NewCo's business is progressing.

Minimally viable product (MVP) A term made popular by the lean startup movement that describes a preliminary version of an innovation (prototype, alpha, or beta version) used by early adopters who are willing to contribute money and/or time to improve it.

MOS Refer to Measures of success

MVP Refer to Minimally viable product

Perception expectations Expectations held by people working at levels below senior management that take shape around NewCo's launch and are typically communicated to team members despite being nothing more than false assumptions. Because of the large number of CoreCo employees, there are many more perception expectations than formal or informal ones.

Pivot Refers to changing the assumptions behind a startup's product or service, technology, customers, market, business model, go-to-market strategy, financial model, or overall strategic plan. Minor pivots constitute slight modifications that do not affect the strategic plan. Major pivots involve changes to key hypotheses in the business model that lead to profound shifts in the strategic plan.

Rule of 2 A rule associated with venture capital (VC) firms: for a startup to be successful it will require twice the investment it thinks it needs, take two times longer to reach its investment goals, and achieve half the projected revenue. After applying the Rule of 2 to an entrepreneur's business case, the VC evaluates if the business is worth investing in.

Second law of business success This law is concerned with organizational alignment and is essential for creating and maintaining transparency within NewCo and in its relationship with CoreCo. It is represented in the six lenses of the Integrated Clarity model: vision and strategy, plans and resources, roles and responsibilities, CoreCo support, facts and data, and rewards and recognition

Sensitivity analyses The "what if" scenarios created by CoreCo so it can understand the level of risk in a business case and decide whether or not to support it. They hypothesize various cost projections and take into account a range of optimistic to pessimistic views of revenue growth.

Soft launch The phase preceding the formal launch that mimics the early stages of an independent startup, when activities are focused on validation and efficiency. The soft launch gives NewCo time to complete these activities before facing the challenges related to moving onto CoreCo's radar and rapidly scaling its operations.

SMART objectives Objectives that are formulated to be Specific, Measurable, Attainable, Relevant, and Time-bound.

Sponsor The senior executive at CoreCo who is accountable for the startup's success and responsible for selecting the intrapreneur, setting the business objectives, and approving the budgets. This position is self-appointed or appointed by another senior executive within the company.

WIIFM Stands for "What's in it for me?" and describes the thinking of someone who is focused on how an activity or change will directly affect him or her.

Illustrations

Index

About the Author

Guillaume Hervé is an international senior business executive and corporate intrapreneur with over 25 years of leadership and management experience. A strategic thinker with an extensive innovation and operational background, Guillaume has launched several new business ventures in the form of corporate startups, subsidiaries, joint ventures, and strategic partnerships, and has worked extensively in North and South America, Europe, Asia, and the Middle East. His broad experience spans several sectors, including aviation, defense and security, software, healthcare, and government. He has worked with leading aircraft manufacturers, some of the world's most recognized airlines, top modeling, simulation, security, and defense companies, and healthcare and governmental organizations.

As a former Canadian Air Force officer who served in Canada and the United States, Guillaume was awarded the Canadian Forces' Decoration. He is a graduate in mechanical engineering from the Royal Military College of Canada (RMC), and holds a master of science degree in business administration from the State University of New York (SUNY) and a post-graduate degree in equipment acquisition and program management from the Canadian Forces School of Aerospace Studies. He is the president of G3point0 Consulting, a company he founded to help business leaders succeed with growth strategies and intrapreneurship, also called corporate entrepreneurship. He volunteers his time to mentor entrepreneurs launching technology startups and is a frequent blogger on leadership and intrapreneurial issues. To learn more about Guillaume, please visit his website at **www.g3point0consulting.com**.

www.ingramcontent.com/pod-product-compliance
Lightning Source LLC
Chambersburg PA
CBHW061140220326
41599CB00025B/4302